A New Decade of Language Testing Research

A New Decade of Language Testing Research: Selected Papers From the 1990 Language Testing Research Colloquium

Dedicated in Memory of Michael Canale

Dan Douglas and Carol Chapelle

Editors

Teachers of English to Speakers of Other Languages, Inc.

Typeset in Times Roman by
World Composition Services, Inc., Sterling, Virginia

TESOL gratefully acknowledges permission to reprint the following:

Bachman, L., Davidson, F., & Foulkes, J. (1990). A comparison of the abilities measured by the Cambridge and Educational Testing Service EFL Test Batteries. *Issues in Applied Linguistics*, *1*, 30–55.

Helen Kornblum *Director of Communication and Marketing*
Marilyn Kupetz *Senior Editor*
Ellen Garshick *Copy Editor*

Teachers of English to Speakers of Other Languages, Inc.
1600 Cameron Street, Suite 300
Alexandria, Virginia 22314 USA
Tel 703-836-0774 • Fax 703-836-7864

ISBN 0-939791-43-9
Library of Congress Catalog No. 92-62190

Table of Contents

Preface   **vii**

1. Foundations and Directions for a New Decade of Language Testing
   Carol Chapelle and Dan Douglas   **1**

PART I PRODUCING VALIDITY EVIDENCE FOR LANGUAGE TESTS   24

2. A Comparison of the Abilities Measured by the Cambridge and Educational Testing Service EFL Test Batteries
   Lyle F. Bachman, Fred Davidson, and John Foulkes   **25**

3. Judgments in Language Testing
   J. Charles Alderson   **46**

4. Testing the Specificity of ESP Reading Skills
   Thom Hudson   **58**

5. A Comparison of Indices for the Identification of Misfitting Items
   Kyle Perkins and Sheila Brutten   **83**

6. The Effect of Prompt in Essay Examinations
   Mary Spaan   **98**

7. Computer-Assisted Testing of Reading Comprehension: Comparisons Among Multiple-Choice and Open-Ended Scoring Methods
   Grant Henning, Michael Anbar, Carl E. Helm, and Sen J. D'Arcy   **123**

8. The Role of Instructions in Testing Summarizing Ability
   Andrew Cohen   **132**

PART II DEVELOPING NEW TESTS OF COMMUNICATIVE LANGUAGE ABILITY   162

9. A Comprehensive Criterion-Referenced Language Testing Project
   James Dean Brown   **163**

10. A Collaborative/Diagnostic Feedback Model for Testing Foreign Languages
   Elana Shohamy   **185**

11. The Relationship Between Grammar and Reading in an English for Academic Purposes Test Battery
   J. Charles Alderson   **203**

12. Assessing Speaking Proficiency in the International English Language Testing System
   D. E. Ingram and Elaine Wylie   **220**

13. Performance on a General Versus a Field-Specific Test of Speaking Proficiency by International Teaching Assistants
   Dan Douglas and Larry Selinker   **235**

14. Is ESP Testing Justified?
   Caroline Clapham   **257**

EPILOGUE   **274**

   Dedication   **275**
   The Wandering Mistrial
   Ted Rodgers   **276**

   Works by Michael Canale   **285**

Preface

The 12th annual Language Testing Research Colloquium (LTRC), held in San Francisco in March 1990, was dedicated as a memorial to Michael Canale, an applied linguist whose work has influenced language teaching and testing research. The theme of the colloquium, "a new decade of language testing research: collaboration and cooperation," suggested the title for this volume, which includes many of the papers presented in San Francisco. The papers reflect the diversity of research approaches and topics addressed at the colloquium and project a fascinating decade of language testing research.

The first paper in this volume, Foundations and Directions for a New Decade of Language Testing Research, explains how Canale's theoretical work on communicative competence and its measurement laid a foundation for much of the current research in language testing and introduces the two parts of the volume: Producing Validity Evidence for Language Tests and Developing New Tests of Communicative Language Ability.

Part I includes studies that explore a variety of approaches to producing validity evidence for language tests. Lyle F. Bachman, Fred Davidson, and John Foulkes report on a large-scale study investigating the comparability of two widely used tests, the Test of English as a Foreign Language and the Cambridge First Certificate in English. J. Charles Alderson addresses problems of content analysis for test validity. Thom Hudson, and Kyle Perkins and Sheila Brutten, examine validity issues of reading tests at the item level. The three final papers in Part I report on research in which validity is studied by manipulating facets of tests of writing (Mary Spaan), summarizing (Andrew Cohen), and reading (Grant Henning, Michael Anbar, Carl E. Helm, and Sen J. D'Arcy).

The papers in Part II report research on attempts to develop new tests of communicative language ability. In the first two, James Dean Brown and Elana Shohamy respectively describe the interdependence of testing and teaching programs. J. Charles Alderson, and D. E. Ingram and Elaine Wylie, report new developments in the British testing service examinations. The final two papers describe research and development in English for specific purposes testing in reading (Caroline Clapham) and speaking (Dan Douglas and Larry Selinker).

The Epilogue consists of two pieces in memory of Michael Canale. The first is the script from a musical comedy written by Ted Rodgers and performed

by LTRC participants in San Francisco; the second, a bibliography of Michael
Canale's writings, which continue to contribute to language testing research.

We appreciate the resources made available for this project by Iowa State
University and the University of Hawai'i at Manoa and are grateful for the
cooperation of the authors as well as for assistance from Frances Butler, Claire
Trepanier, and Liz Hamp-Lyons.

1

Foundations and Directions for a New Decade of Language Testing

Carol Chapelle and Dan Douglas
Iowa State University

The 12th annual Language Testing Research Colloquium, "A New Decade of Language Testing: Collaboration and Cooperation," was dedicated as a memorial to Michael Canale, who devoted much of his professional career to issues fundamental to language testing. One such issue is the question of what it means to know a second language. This question is important for language testing researchers, who attempt to construct tests that can be shown to indicate accurately how well students know their second language. To demonstrate that a given test reflects learners' communicative competence, language testers require a definition of communicative competence. Canale's work not only contributed to forming such a definition but also explored its implications for language testing and underscored the need to refine our incomplete picture of communication in the hope of improving testing.[1]

Beyond the technical concerns of defining and measuring communicative competence, Canale also emphasized the human dimension of language testing—an event he portrayed as having social origins and consequences. Test development and test use, he asserted, carry with them social responsibilities so important that the name for the current "tradition" (Spolsky, 1978) of language testing, *naturalistic-ethical* (Canale, 1988), should reflect the social responsibility (ethical) aspect of testing along with concerns for naturalistic language use in tests.

Because it was instrumental in shaping hypotheses about communicative competence and raising academic consciousness regarding the sociological aspects of testing, Canale's work continues to affect research in language testing, as evidenced by the papers in this volume. To clarify the impact of Canale's work as it pertains to language testing research, we review its two dimensions: Canale and Swain's framework for communicative competence, which has been used as a foundation for some language testing research, and elements of Canale's vision of a naturalistic-ethical tradition in language testing. We outline the evolution of the definition of communicative competence and describe the implications of Canale's naturalistic-ethical tradition as they pertain to the fundamental questions of language testing: what to test, how to test, and why to test.

1

Communicative Competence

Specifying what it means to know a language is a difficult but essential task for language testers. Testing researchers require such a definition because they attempt to demonstrate that their tests are indicators of the degree to which learners have attained aspects of communicative competence. To do the empirical research and formulate the logical rationales required as evidence of valid test use, testing researchers need an explicit statement of what communicative competence means. As a consequence, testing research will for some time be influenced by the theoretical framework of communicative competence articulated by Canale and Swain in their 1980 paper in *Applied Linguistics*. According to their theory, effective communication relies on three types of competencies:

- *grammatical competence*: elements of language code (e.g., vocabulary, syntax, linguistic semantics)
- *sociolinguistic competence*: sociolinguistic appropriateness and coherence and cohesion in text
- *strategic competence*: a means of enhancing the effectiveness of communication.

Canale and Swain identified these three components by reviewing theory and research in linguistics and other relevant areas such as psycholinguistics and sociolinguistics. Although the 1980 theory did not precisely define communicative competence, it laid the necessary foundation on which some theoretical and empirical work has built (e.g., Savignon, 1983; Bachman, 1990).

From the beginning, Canale and Swain's work was useful to language testing researchers. At the 1979 Language Testing Research Colloquium, English as a second language (ESL) teachers and testers raised questions concerning the construct validity of tests of oral proficiency: To what extent could learners' scores on oral proficiency tests be considered to reflect the construct of communicative competence? In the introduction to the volume of papers from that colloquium (Palmer, Groot, & Trosper, 1981), Palmer and Groot defined *construct validation* as the process by which "one validates a test not against a criterion or another test, but against a theory" (p. 4). In other words, they distinguished *criterion-related* evidence—indicating that a test measures the same thing as another test—from *construct* evidence—indicating that a test measures a theoretically defined construct (in this case, communicative competence). To obtain the latter type of evidence from empirical research, of course, the researcher must specify the definition of the construct the test is supposed to measure. Recognizing the need for a construct definition but the absence of a definitive theory, Palmer and Groot suggested adopting the three elements of Canale and Swain's framework "as components constituting a provisional definition of communicative competence" (p. 5).[2] The framework thus served as a background to that adopted by Bachman and Palmer (1982), who sought construct evidence for the validity of several language tests. In doing so, they produced empirical results that contributed to an evolving definition of communicative competence.

While these empirical researchers benefited from Canale and Swain's work, Canale himself reexamined it in light of other perspectives on language proficiency (Canale, 1983a) and applied it to specific testing problems (Canale, 1984). As a result of his continued theoretical work, Canale distinguished between sociolinguistic and discourse components of the communicative competence framework. He reasoned that speakers' competence in the correct sociolinguistic use of language could be independent of their competence in discourse rules. The former refers to "the extent to which utterances are understood appropriately in different sociolinguistic contexts" (Canale, 1983b, p. 7), and the latter "concerns mastery of how to combine grammatical forms and meanings to achieve [through coherence and cohesion in meaning] a unified spoken or written text in different genres" (Canale, 1983b, p. 9).

The resulting four-component framework—composed of grammatical, sociolinguistic, discourse, and strategic components—remains evident in the field's evolving understanding of communicative competence as represented by Bachman (1990). He continued the evolution by placing each component within a hierarchical model on the basis of empirical results and additional theoretical considerations (see Bachman, 1990, pp. 81–110). The resulting model of communicative language ability reflects hypothesized relationships among components and postulates how the components might work within a context of language use. In 1988, Canale cited Bachman's model as representing our current understanding of communicative competence: "This framework was developed on the basis of the extensive second-language teaching of its proponents, reviews of theories of communicative competence, and state-of-the-art empirical and measurement techniques" (Canale, 1988, p. 68). These developments represent the current state of evolution of this view of communicative language ability, which will continue to guide language testing research because of its role in the naturalistic-ethical tradition in language testing.

The Naturalistic-Ethical Tradition

Demonstrating the role of communicative competence theory in testing practice, Canale throughout the 1980s formulated elements of what he later named the "naturalistic-ethical" tradition in language testing (Canale, 1988). He suggested the term for a fourth trend in language testing, following what Spolsky (1978) had defined as the "pre-scientific," the "psychometric-structuralist," and the "integrative-sociolinguistic" traditions. The term *naturalistic* reflected to Canale the belief that language tests should measure students' competence in using what theory defines as natural (i.e., authentic) language and assess competence by observing students as they perform natural language tasks. *Naturalistic* also implies the need for substantial evidence concerning the meaning of scores on test tasks, which in reality deviate from contexts of natural language use (e.g., Spolsky, 1985). *Ethical* reflects the responsibility of test users to ensure that language tests are valuable experiences and yield positive consequences for all involved. In Canale's words, the focus of the naturalistic-ethical trend is "what to test, how to test, and why to test, thus reflecting the view that language testing is very much an ethical issue" (Canale, 1988, p. 77). Below we review Canale's perspectives on each question and their implications for language testing research.

What to Test?

In addressing the question of what to test, Canale emphasized the role of a theory of communicative competence: writing language tests requires a definition of what language is. In 1988, he noted both the important progress that had been made toward understanding communicative competence (Bachman, 1990) and toward placing communicative competence within broader theories of linguistic and nonlinguistic abilities (e.g., Bialystok & Ryan, 1985; Cummins, 1983). At the same time, Canale identified additional challenges for understanding the process of authentic communication, an understanding testers need in order to produce naturalistic tests of learners' communicative language ability.

One challenge Canale (1988) noted was the need to characterize stages in the development of communicative competence. Despite the work that has resulted in proficiency-level descriptions (American Council on the Teaching of Foreign Languages, 1986), little empirically or theoretically based consensus exists as to the characterizations of global "levels" (Bachman & Savignon, 1986). Questions also have arisen concerning the dimensions needed to describe such levels (Pienemann, Johnson, & Brindley, 1988). It is essential to characterize stages of the various aspects of communicative ability in order to construct criterion-referenced tests, which measure students' ability against a known criterion level of performance rather than against the performance of other test takers (Brown, this volume, chap. 9). Criterion-referenced language tests based on levels of development are valuable in educational contexts (Cziko, 1981, 1982) and second language acquisition research (e.g., Gass, 1987), both of which attempt to document the progression of language abilities learners attain as they develop. Therefore, second language acquisition researchers and language testers (e.g., Douglas, 1988) pursue the objective of characterizing levels of language development.

A second challenge Canale saw was the need to understand better the process of communication as a situation requiring problem solving. He described communication as composed of simultaneous cognitive, interactive, affective, and linguistic problems (Canale, 1985). The work on strategies in language performance throughout the 1980s (e.g., Faerch & Kasper, 1983; Bialystok, 1990; Oxford, 1990) began to identify and classify some observable communication strategies. However, it remains unclear to what extent one can define or measure what Erickson (1986) terms "emergent communicative knowledge, . . . the capacity to create sense in addition to following rules, to go beyond what is culturally learned and, in the midst of the fortuitous contingency of the moment, to play interaction by ear" (p. 296). Erickson emphasized that such knowledge is essential in communication, noting that in its absence a listener's and speaker's attention and reaction to each other's communication would proceed in a robotlike manner. The communication-specific nature of such a capacity may preclude its study under the rubric of cognitive strategies; moreover, emergent communicative knowledge may not be generalizable from one situation to another, as a view of a stable "strategic competence" would suggest. Thus understanding the nature and role of this ability, which appears to be crucial in real-time communication, remains a challenge for research in the 1990s.

A third challenge identified by Canale results from the cultural dimension of communication. Erickson (1986) defined two capacities that allow for success in speech situations: "emergent" (defined above) and "institutionalized," culturally learned "general systems of rules or operating principles for the conduct of talk" (p. 297). Because rules of conversation are culturally based, communicating in a second language requires adopting an unfamiliar and perhaps uncomfortable set of institutional rules. In some respects, the use of these rules can evidence sociolinguistic competence, but from the perspective of language testing it is not clear how sociolinguistically competent one can expect a second language learner to act when competence requires working within a different set of institutionalized norms. In fact, as Connor-Linton (1991) asserted, participants in cross-cultural communication often intentionally maintain their own institutionalized rule systems to manipulate a conversation and gain what they perceive to be a higher status. In light of such a suggestion, language testers need to consider further the impact of "cross-cultural pragmatics" (Olshtain & Blum-Kulka, 1985, p. 29) on measurement.

In the 1980s Canale interpreted the necessary cross-disciplinary sources to frame a view of language that speaks to the question of what to test. In doing so he demonstrated that language testers must consider it their responsibility to construct and refine a definition of communicative competence that they can use to address this question. Definitions of language have, of course, been implicit in language tests throughout history, as Canale emphasized. But he placed on the research agenda of language testers the additional responsibility of improving their understanding of communication; only with a clear view of what to test, he argued, can language testers address the question of how to test.

How to Test?

With reference to the question of how to test, *naturalistic* means that testers should use authentic tasks to elicit samples of learners' performance. With this in mind, Canale attempted to describe tasks that could yield evaluative information while maintaining authenticity (Canale, 1984). Use of less-than-authentic tasks (arguably, all language tests), then, must be justified on the basis of evidence concerning the meaning of their scores. In other words, what does a score on a language test task indicate about a student's ability to use the language effectively in a real situation? Canale argued that tests were likely to tell us more if they reflected the natural characteristics of language. Here we review what Canale saw as the naturalistic potentials for language tests and summarize methods for accruing evidence concerning the meaning of scores on unauthentic tasks— potentials and methods that will be reflected in the next decade of language testing research.

Naturalistic Potentials for Language Tests

Despite our incomplete understanding of communication, Canale identified several known properties of authentic language use and asserted the need for language test tasks to reflect those properties. He argued that language tests should ideally reflect the properties of communication: contextuality, productivity, process orientation, interactivity, and adaptivity; others have worked to put these principles into practice. As researchers have attempted authenticity, however, they have met practical, statistical, and theoretical dilemmas that challenge the language testing research of the 1990s and beyond.

Contextuality. Canale argued that, because language occurs within social and linguistic contexts (Berns, 1990; Halliday, 1978; Hymes, 1972) and is used in psychologically motivated situations, language tests should be composed of context-dependent language tasks that are inherently interesting to test takers. He proposed that a test constructed on the basis of a thematic organization, such as a day in the life of a university student (Canale, 1984, p. 354), might reflect the contextual nature of language. The principle of context dependency supports tests of language for specific purposes, which engage test takers with authentic language in academic and professional areas of importance to them (e.g., Smith, 1989; Alderson, this volume, chap. 11; Clapham, this volume, chap. 14; Douglas & Selinker, this volume, chap. 13). The notion underlying this work—that communicative competence is tied to particular contexts—poses practical, empirical, and theoretical challenges to language testing research.

From a practical perspective, language tests that incorporate specific content require testers to collaborate with subject specialists to produce and rate tests in different special fields. As Douglas and Selinker report in chapter 13 of this volume, those specialists may have their own ideas about the content of the test— ideas that must be honored if collaboration is to be successful. Moreover, in a test setting, students' subject areas must be identified correctly and an appropriate test must be available for all examinees. In chapters 11 and 14 of this volume, Alderson and Clapham respectively describe their solution to this problem in a setting with a large number of diverse students.

A remaining question in such situations is whether subject-specific tests are sufficiently marked by appropriate topical material to engage examinees' specific-purpose language competence. This question is underscored by the mixed results obtained by research comparing performance on general and specific-purpose tests (e.g., Douglas & Selinker, this volume, chap. 13) as well as performance by specialists and nonspecialists on specific purpose tests (e.g., Alderson & Urquhart, 1985; Clapham, this volume, chap. 14). Research is needed, then, to clarify what makes a subject-specific test subject specific for a given student. There may be more to context dependency and psychological motivation than is guaranteed by constructing a test around a particular theme. Based on the work of Erickson and Shultz (1981) and Gumperz (1976), Douglas (1989) hypothesized that selecting a particular topic for test materials may be insufficient to produce a test of specific-purpose competence. Instead, a cumulative threshold level of "contextualization cues" (Gumperz, 1976) may be necessary to engage learners' specific-purpose competence in a testing situation. As Wesche (1987) pointed out, research is needed to discover and operationalize "those contextual features that theory and experience suggest may have an important influence on language test performance" (p. 31).

This suggestion calls for research in the area of schema theory (Rumelhart, 1980), which Widdowson (1983) discusses under the headings "frames of reference" (cf. Goffman, 1974, and van Dijk, 1977, on "frame") and "rhetorical routines" (cf. Schank and Abelson, 1977, on "scripts" and "plans"). The former refers to procedures for relating specific propositions to existing knowledge structures as a way of making sense of incoming information; the latter denotes procedures for interpreting illocutionary acts and speech events. Because of the individual nature of frames of reference and rhetorical routines, research that seeks to identify contextual features that comprise authentic, interesting language tasks for learners challenges typical large-sample approaches to testing research. Recognizing that individuals vary in their knowledge and interests, researchers will have to investigate contextualization cues individually.

The view of content-dependent language ability also affects a theoretical definition of communicative competence because it blurs the distinction between linguistic and subject area knowledge. Are the linguistic abilities required for various tasks so different that communicative competence must be defined as it relates to specific purposes? Must scores on tests of communicative competence be interpreted as an examinee's competence with language in a specific area? Is the construct of general "communicative competence" too abstract to be useful on a practical level? The theoretical and practical implications of the fusion between language and subject-specific schema promise to be part of the research agenda for the 1990s.

Productivity and process orientation. Because language is productive and process oriented, language tests should allow test takers to produce language that yields information about comprehension and production processes. Canale saw that tests requiring students to produce language rather than selecting alternatives might make language testing more consistent with language teaching. Moreover, when students are required to produce language on a test, the sample of language performance obtained may allow for inferences concerning students' productive processes. As a consequence, such tests may elicit more informative data on examinees' language abilities, thereby enabling meaningful feedback to examinees and score users. In fact, many efforts have been made over the past decade to develop and refine tests of productive language ability, including tests of oral communicative proficiency (Bachman & Palmer, 1982; Educational Testing Service, 1990; Douglas & Selinker, this volume, chap. 13; Ingram & Wylie, this volume, chap. 12), writing ability (Stansfield & Ross, 1988; Spaan, this volume, chap. 6), and other language abilities (e.g., Cohen, this volume, chap. 8; Alderson, this volume, chap. 11). As this work continues, researchers recognize that tests requiring students to construct linguistic responses offer new challenges for principled test development and response analysis.

Research on test development attempts to characterize features of items that affect students' performance so that we can better assess content representativeness and relevance as well as produce tests with known characteristics (Embretson, 1985; Carroll, 1989). Some work in this area tries to identify item method characteristics that can be associated with levels of difficulty (Bennett, Ward, Rock, & LaHart, 1990). For example, the characteristic multiple choice might predict an easier item than an equivalent item requiring a constructed response. The potential complexity of some constructed-response items (e.g., essay prompts) complicates the question of all the factors affecting performance (e.g., Spaan, this volume, chap. 6). Even on simpler item types, Alderson (this volume, chap. 3) found a less than desirable degree of agreement among experts concerning what items measure and how difficult they are. Understanding item content is an important challenge for language testing research, and it is a difficult one when associated with constructed-response items.

Constructed responses also challenge testing researchers who devise methods of response analysis to obtain the maximum information about students' language processes. Constructed responses consisting of students' language contain a wealth of specific information about linguistic abilities. However, testers can realize the feedback potential for constructed-response tests only to the extent that their scoring methods yield more information than those for selected-response items. Continued research is needed to explore methods of scoring constructed-response tests that maximize the quality of information gained by evaluating students' language. The challenge lies not only in defining scoring criteria adequately but also in training raters sufficiently to evaluate constructed responses reliably. The papers by Bachman, Davidson, and Foulkes (chap. 2); Spaan (chap. 6); and Cohen (chap. 8) in this volume illustrate how this challenge has been addressed. Future research is needed to improve methods of making human raters more consistent and to explore computational linguistic analysis for scoring some types of constructed responses.

Interactivity and adaptivity.   Because language functions interactively and adaptively, Canale believed language tests could be most effective if they, too, were interactive and adaptive. Canale envisioned language tests that would be individually unique and appropriate to the level of each student, precluding the frustration or boredom associated with testing experiences for many students and supplying precise information to score users. Tests such as the ILR oral interview (Lowe, 1982), in which examinees engage in a multistage conversation with a human, have already demonstrated these features. The examiner adapts the test as the examinee's level is estimated through their interaction in the target language. Canale extended these principles to suggest adaptive, interactive tests administered by computers. Citing existing instructional programs in mathematics as examples (Burton & Brown, 1982), he projected language tests that would allow learners to use the target language in dynamic, interesting tasks. To interact effectively with students, such programs would probably have to be constructed based on a model describing how students solve a communicative problem. This type of computer-adaptive test, based on substantive models of problem solving, challenges language testing researchers.

The challenge lies in specifying a model sufficiently detailed to serve as the basis for writing an interactive program. A description would include explicit definitions of the competencies (e.g., aspects of grammatical and strategic competence) necessary to solve the problem successfully. For the program to respond adequately to students and to infer accurately about aspects of their competence, the model would also have to hypothesize the types of competencies indicated by the variety of ways one might fail to solve the problem. Canale's vision of a substantive model (i.e., based on elements of communicative competence) contrasts with the current practice of constructing computer-adaptive tests on the basis of statistical properties of items similar to those on paper-and-pencil tests. Canale (1986, p. 34) argued that the assumptions associated with a statistical approach to computer-adaptive testing are problematic if a single ability must be considered responsible for solving communicative problems.[3] Moreover, the information gained from such tests is not a single score on a unidimensional scale; instead, information on multiple competencies would be reported and used diagnostically as needed.

Language testing research of the 1990s has much groundwork to lay if Canale's vision of computer-based interactive, adaptive language tests is to become a reality. First, we need to identify computer-based activities that are computationally feasible, interesting to students, and informative to score users. Computer-assisted language learning (CALL) researchers (e.g., Ahmad, Corbett, Rogers, and Sussex, 1985) have developed some activities that meet the first two criteria; however, the third criterion—yielding informative data—has not been a priority in these activities. Obtaining informative data will require language testers to work with programs for linguistic analysis in addition to statistical software. Development of the former is the work of computational linguists, some of whose work has been applied to CALL activities (e.g., Sanders & Sanders, 1989). However, because of the project-specific nature of such work, language testers are unlikely to find existing linguistic analysis software that is completely usable for their purposes. Finally, researchers need to perform the analysis necessary to hypothesize the relevant linguistic and strategic data that can be obtained from computer-based activities. Despite Canale's general proposal, we still do not know within what domains researchers might use computer-student interaction to create practical tests of communicative problem-solving activities.

Our ability to obtain detailed data reflecting learners' processes from content-based, constructed-response, adaptive tests is likely to affect our conception of communicative competence. Much of the current empirically based understanding of language ability has been gained from multiple-choice tests, which may inaccurately flatten many of the variable contours of students' productive language processes. Test methods that allow students to demonstrate, and that adequately record, more of the complexity of communicative performance are more likely to contribute empirical data that do justice to the intricacies of a theory of communicative ability. The research challenge of the 1990s, then, is not only to produce language tests demonstrating natural properties of language but also to score those tests in a way that will reveal the complexity of students' abilities, and to use that data to support the evolution of a theory of communicative ability.

Canale speculated on how to design test activities that encompass the authentic properties of contextuality, productivity, process orientation, interactivity, and adaptivity. However, as Spolsky (1985) has pointed out, in the end a language test is a language test:

> The criterion of authenticity raises important pragmatic and ethical questions in language testing. Lack of authenticity in the material used in a test raises issues about the generalizability of results. Any language test is by its very nature unauthentic, abnormal language behavior, for the test taker is being asked not to answer a question giving information but to display knowledge or skill. (p. 39)

As a consequence, the primary focus of language testing research is to produce evidence concerning the meaning of test scores so that they may be interpreted and used appropriately.

Evidence Concerning the Meaning of Test Scores

Because test situations differ from authentic contexts, students' performance on a test probably offers a distorted picture of the ability they would demonstrate in authentic contexts. For tests to be used appropriately, test developers must demonstrate, and test users must consider, evidence concerning the meaning of test scores. Throughout the 1980s, Canale was among the foremost advocates for recognizing these responsibilities, which have affected current views of the nature and scope of *validity*. The current conception of validity has evolved significantly from the definition of construct validity cited over a decade ago (Palmer & Groot, 1981), and this evolution promises to affect future language testing research.

Construct validity is no longer viewed as one form of validity alongside content-related and criterion-related validities. Messick (1989) recently defined validity as a unitary concept that "refers to the degree to which empirical evidence and theoretical rationales support the adequacy and appropriateness of interpretations and actions based on test scores" (p. 13). Thus, according to Messick, validity encompasses both the justifications for testing and the outcomes of testing. Within the broad domain of validity, construct validity is one justification for the outcomes of test interpretation and test use.[4] Content-related and criterion-related considerations are subordinate to construct validity; each is considered among the admissible types of evidence for construct validity. This view of validity emphasizes that the "varieties of evidence [e.g., criterion-related evidence] are not alternatives but rather supplements to one another" (p. 16) and that validation is a process of scientific inquiry. In that process, evidence concerning the meaning of test scores is accrued from a variety of sources and applied to questions about the appropriate use and interpretation of tests. Messick names the following as sources of evidence to use in developing an argument for the validity of test interpretation and use:

> We can look at the content of the test in relation to the content of the domain of reference. We can probe the ways in which individuals respond to the items or tasks. We can examine relationships among responses to the tasks, items, or parts of the test, that is, the internal structure of test responses. We can survey relationships of test scores with other measures and background variables, that is, the test's external structure. We can investigate *differences* in these test processes and structures over time, across groups and settings, and in response to experimental interventions—such as instructional or therapeutic treatment and manipulation of content, task requirements, or motivational conditions. Finally, we can trace the social consequences of interpreting and using the test scores in particular ways, scrutinizing not only the intended outcomes but also unintended side effects. (p. 16)

The research of the 1990s, including many of the papers in this volume, will provide such evidence on the meaning of test scores—evidence that partly justifies test score interpretation and use. Below we explain each type of validity evidence, noting language testing research that exemplifies the variety of approaches to validity evidence, and suggest directions for language testing research in the near future.

Content evidence. Content evidence demonstrates that the content of a test is both relevant to and representative of the domain the test measures. Along with test material, content denotes the types of behaviors test takers exhibit and the processes they engage in while taking the test. Language testing researchers have investigated problems in establishing content evidence. For example, Spaan (this volume, chap. 6) studied her writing tests from a content perspective by attempting to define salient aspects of her essay examination prompts. Bachman, Davidson, and Foulkes (this volume, chap. 2) used a detailed procedure for classifying the linguistic content of the tests they examined (see also Bachman, Kunnan, Vanniarajan, & Lynch, 1988). Alderson (this volume, chap. 3) found little agreement among experts on the content and difficulty of test items; he questioned validity on the grounds of this negative content evidence. These studies demonstrate the significance of content-related evidence and exhibit the need for future research.

Research on content evidence will be directed toward reliably identifying salient elements of item content. Experimental work on a nonlinguistic test offers an example of item content so well characterized that researchers were able to specify a "generative psychometrics, . . . a grammar capable of assigning a psychometric description to every item in the universe of items *and* . . . also capable of generating all the items in that universe of items" (Bejar & Yocom, 1986, p. 4). Bejar and Yocom's generative description was explicit enough to be operationalized as a computer program that generated items with predictable difficulty levels. It seems doubtful that the integrative nature of linguistic content could be formalized to this extent; however, to what extent researchers can sufficiently agree on and specify linguistic item content is as yet unknown.

Item and task analysis.   Item analysis and task analysis add an empirical dimension to judgmental content evidence, entailing "a veritable confrontation between judged content relevance and representativeness on the one hand, and empirical response consistency on the other" (Messick, 1989, p. 42). Language testing research using both qualitative (e.g., Cohen, 1984; Grotjahn, 1987; Feldmann & Stemmer, 1987) and quantitative (e.g., Kirsch & Mosenthal, 1988; Perkins & Linnville, 1987; Brown, 1988) methods has examined item performance. One outcome has been an appreciation for the role of individual differences in cognitive processing and strategic competence in test contexts, thereby bringing into question the assumption that a given test score should yield the same interpretation for each individual taking the test. Perkins and Brutten (this volume, chap. 5) follow up on this finding by investigating the suitability of various item statistics in identifying misfitting language test items for groups of students at different proficiency levels.

Language testing researchers recognize the need for continued research on item-level performance (e.g., Grotjahn, 1987; Alderson, this volume, chap. 11). Such research might adopt experimental information-processing models, which "are based on experimental task manipulations" or are constructed as computer programs that simulate task performance (Snow & Lohman, 1989, p. 267). In short, these methods build on Carroll's (1976) notion that test items are cognitive tasks that should be studied experimentally to understand the components of ability that contribute to successful performance. Then researchers can examine the components shown empirically to contribute to performance next to the theoretical definition of the construct the item is supposed to measure, thereby providing validity evidence. Methodologies for conducting such research were introduced in the late 1970s (Sternberg, 1977) and have been refined for testing research during the 1980s (e.g., Embretson, 1983, 1985). Some researchers have suggested information-processing methodologies for second language testing research (Vollmer, 1983; Grotjahn, 1986), but this approach to validation research is for the most part an uncharted course inviting empirical research in the 1990s.

   Internal structure of tests. Validity evidence concerning the internal structure of tests demonstrates empirically that test items adhere to the same structural relations as those hypothesized for the construct they represent. In other words, in theory each item measures some aspect of an overall construct, and empirical data should support the presumed item structure. Research investigating internal structure has used factor analysis (Bachman, 1982) and item response theory (IRT) (MacNamara, 1990) to yield evidence concerning the internal structure of tests. Hudson (this volume, chap. 4) uses IRT statistics to examine the characteristics of individual items designed to measure skills within the ability of reading comprehension. He examines item variance, difficulty, and discrimination in view of each skill's theoretical position among various skills (as represented by groups of items) in the overall construct of reading comprehension, thereby leading to a better understanding of the structure of the test and raising questions about the theoretical definition of reading comprehension.

   Fundamental to research on internal structure is the explicit specification of elements that comprise a construct. This challenges language testing researchers to use theoretical descriptions defined by colleagues and to contribute to theories with empirical results. Moreover, the study of internal item structure should ultimately provide justification for the way items are scored and their scores are combined. Much item-level research remains to be done to produce evidence for consistency among the levels of construct definition, item content and scoring, and test scores.

   External structure of tests. Examination of the external structure of a test, that is, the test's relationship to other tests, remains a relevant source of validity evidence. Messick (1989) distinguished two types of questions on external structure that correlational research can address. One is trait evidence for validity, "the extent to which a measure relates more highly to different methods for assessing the same construct than it does to measures of different constructs assessed by the same method" (p. 46). To identify the influence of test methods on performance, the multitrait, multimethod research design (one correlational method) has been used in language testing research (Stevenson, 1981; Bachman & Palmer, 1982) to provide validity evidence. A second type of correlational research investigates nomothetic span, "the network of relationships of a test to other measures" (Embretson, 1983, p. 180). In this type of study the researcher hypothesizes the strengths of correlations (based on distances in the nomothetic span of constructs) with other measures (e.g., Chapelle & Abraham, 1990). The results of this type of research can refine theories of constructs and their relationships to other constructs.

   For researchers to reap the benefits of trait and nomothetic span studies, however, they must be clear about the theoretical basis of the correlational research. Fundamental to both types of research is a theoretical definition of the language trait(s) measured by the test under investigation and the hypothesized strengths of relationships expected between that trait (measured by the given test method) and the others in the study. Only with a sufficiently specified theory of the relationships expected to occur in a study can the observed correlations be interpreted as trait evidence (relationships between different measures of the same trait) or nomothetic span evidence (relationships between distinct but correlated traits). Because theory is fundamental to this type of research, studies investigating the external structure of tests will continue to benefit from the theoretical foundations laid by Canale and Swain.

Experimental manipulations. As properties of constructs and their measurement are better understood, it is informative to observe whether predictable effects can be obtained by manipulating facets of the testing process (e.g., aspects of the test or the test takers). Observing test performance under systematically manipulated conditions can make the meaning of test scores clearer. In this volume, studies by Cohen (chap. 8) and Spaan (chap. 6) produce some evidence concerning performance on language tests under varied conditions. Examination of the effects of such test facets under real or experimental conditions promises to provide a better understanding of score meaning and, therefore, the valid interpretation and use of test scores.

Canale (1988), among others, argued that an understanding of the systematic effects of these facets of language tests on performance is an essential element of test validity evidence. Bachman's (1990) language test method facets, hypothesized to influence test performance, will facilitate future experimental research in this area. This work represents an important transition from globally defined test methods (i.e., multiple choice versus essay) to the characterizations of the specifics of a test task, thereby providing concrete suggestions for future research using experimental manipulations.

Social consequences. Messick's final source of validity evidence, tracing the social consequences of test score use, converges with Canale's "ethical" element of the naturalistic-ethical tradition in language testing. Both Canale and Messick recognized that values play a role in all scientific inquiry and that explicitly acknowledging that role is therefore necessary. Values are an integral part of the ways theories are defined as well as the ways test scores are interpreted and used. The study by Bachman, Davidson, and Foulkes in this volume (chap. 2) demonstrates testing practices resulting from ideologies of the British and American systems. Language testing researchers still have much ground to explore with respect to understanding the values on which testing practices rest. The 1990s hold potential for further clarifying those values in all corners of the language testing world. Canale's sociological perspective to language testing, which he discusses under "why to test?", provides a window for this future work.

Why to Test?

Canale's naturalistic-ethical tradition refers to educators' ethical responsibilities in the testing process. He emphasized that language testers' responsibilities extend beyond constructing and administering tests: "Once one has been involved in gathering information, one becomes responsible in some way to see that it is used ethically" (Canale, 1988, p. 75). Canale's collective work illuminates the sociological dimension of language testing by portraying a test as an event, conceived of socioacademic beliefs, implemented in academic society where it conveys to test takers and instructors messages about language and learners' roles (Canale, 1987) and where it is used to gain information with social consequences.

Conceptions of what language tests can and should do derive from a socioacademic consensus on the nature of language and appropriate methods of measurement as well as the perceived necessity for particular types of information. Spolsky's summary of "traditions" in language testing illustrates how to see testing practices in light of their linguistic and measurement foundations—foundations rooted in contemporary academic beliefs. Spolsky's and Canale's traditions summarize the academic field as they appeared diachronically;[5] in contrast, the cross-cultural research of Bachman, Davidson, and Foulkes (this volume, chap. 2) demonstrates the divergent foundations of current language tests from different countries. Differences in underlying assumptions, which Bachman, Davidson, and Foulkes address explicitly, have a great impact on the testing practices compared in the study and are therefore relevant to the findings. Language testers of the 1990s are challenged to identify and present the beliefs that guide them to decisions on what to measure and how to measure.

Language tests also create beliefs, or in Canale's words, "tests create images for test takers" (Canale, 1987). Canale pointed out that language tests communicate a message to those who take part in them. Among the most dangerous messages conveyed by some tests is that the learner is an "unwilling victim" (p. 250) in the process of language assessment. Other negative effects created by tests in some settings are learners' confusion and frustration because of mismatches between tests and classroom activities. To address the image problem, Canale suggested that researchers be guided by classroom learning activities in their search for more suitable assessment (1987, p. 252). Images might improve, he speculated, through classroom activities with built-in assessment, learner-instructor collaboration in assessment, project-based programs with inherent, collaborative evaluation, and computer activities as mentioned above. In searching for more suitable images, he suggested that test writers give priority not to "reliability, and practicality" but instead to what he called "test acceptability and feedback potential," the former referring to the test taker's acceptance of the test task as fair, important, and interesting, and the latter indicating the test's potential for giving test takers and other score users clear and relevant information (Canale, 1984, p. 353).

Images created by language tests also affect instructors' perceptions and, in fact, the entire instructional process. The washback effects of large-scale testing programs on instruction are widely discussed. In the view of instructors and students, such tests contain what students must learn and therefore what must be taught—a reasonable view, given that the tests in many cases represent the language hurdle students must clear before continuing their academic careers. Because of the relationship between testing and instruction, a challenge of the 1990s is to integrate tests and the process of test development with instructional programs so as to ensure maximum input from those involved with instruction (Nitko, 1989). The test programs described by Brown (chap. 9) and by Shohamy (chap. 10) in this volume exemplify such language testing programs. Brown's program, by coordinating testing with instruction, allows for the use of criterion-referenced tests. Integrated testing and teaching requires collaboration between teachers and testers, and in fact requires teachers to understand principles of language testing.

Also part of the ethical responsibility of language testers is the appropriate use of test scores—another responsibility that encompasses the need to understand the meaning of test scores and their consequences as well as the need to educate others concerning the same. The latter need is in concert with the aforementioned desirability of having instructors involved in the testing process. The former—understanding the meaning and use of test scores—underlies the essence of the definition of validity that will shape the testing research of the 1990s. Validity is the evidential basis for justifying test score interpretation and use. A validity that encompasses both score interpretation and score use must include the sociological dimension of the real-world consequences of test score use—consequences that include the images Canale described. The evidential basis of score interpretation and use also extends beyond the language-theoretic constructs and psychometric techniques that characterized the construct validity studies of a decade ago. Although those techniques offer admissible justification, they are incomplete. Other justification must come from the social context in which test score use is a consequence.

A New Decade of Language Testing Research

We began the 1990s with a more sophisticated understanding of both language and the scope and significance of validity relative to a decade ago. Canale's cumulative work over the 1980s contributed greatly to that understanding, which will affect language testing and teaching for the foreseeable future. The papers in this volume reflect the impact of Canale's work. Each paper contributes to the field in a number of ways; we have classified them below to reflect the primary focus of each.

The papers in Part I focus on recent developments in the production of validity evidence from a number of points of view. Bachman, Davidson, and Foulkes (chap. 2) present a major study comparing performance on two of the most important international English language tests, the Test of English as a Foreign Language, including the Test of Spoken English and the Test of Written English, and the Cambridge First Certificate in English. Using factor analytic techniques, the authors refine the interpretation of test scores from the two test batteries and inform our understanding of the construct of communicative language ability. Alderson's first paper in this volume (chap. 3) explores the relationship between professional judgments of applied linguists on the nature of language, learning, and achievement in the construction of language tests and the empirical data produced by the tests. He questions the validity of such judgments, given the low level of reliability obtained as well as the current state of knowledge about the components of language ability and the processes of second language acquisition.

The next two papers deal with aspects of item analysis and the interpretation of performance on items. Hudson (chap. 4) investigates specific-purpose tests through the application of item response theory. He considers the implications for criterion-referenced testing of differential item difficulty for groups of items on science reading tests. Perkins and Brutten (chap. 5) explore a different aspect of item analysis: the comparative utility of a number of different approaches to identifying misfitting items for students at varying proficiency levels.

The remaining three chapters in Part I explore the effects of manipulating method facets in language tests. Spaan (chap. 6) analyzes the effect on performance of two types of essay examination prompts and makes suggestions for the interpretation of results on writing tests. Henning, Anbar, Helm, and d'Arcy (chap. 7) investigate the difference between multiple-choice and open-ended reading comprehension questions. Cohen (chap. 8) investigates the effect of providing specific instructions versus providing minimal instructions in a summary writing test, finding that for some subjects overspecification of the task detracted from performance.

Part II contains papers on developing new tests of communicative language ability. The studies by Brown (chap. 9) and by Shohamy (chap. 10) deal with the development of tests in educational contexts: a university-level academic English program and foreign language programs in secondary schools, respectively. Brown discusses the development of criterion-referenced tests in the context of overall curriculum development. Shohamy reports on implementing an assessment model in schools, involving the integration of input from teachers, principals, and a team of assessors.

The next two papers describe the revision of a major British test, the English Language Testing Service test to be known in the future as the IELTS, the International English Language Testing System. Alderson (chap. 11) reports on the analysis of results on the grammar and reading subtests in the IELTS, charting the process leading to the decision to drop the grammar component from the battery. Ingram and Wylie (chap. 12) discuss the speaking component of the IELTS, focusing on the testing of practical skills in everyday situations within an academically oriented test battery.

The final two papers in Part II address the effects of specific-purpose contexts on test performance. Douglas and Selinker (chap. 13) find both quantitative and qualitative evidence that subjects perform differently on a general test of speaking proficiency than on a field-specific measure. Clapham (chap. 14), on the other hand, finds no measurable difference across three specific-purpose content areas in reading test performance. Both papers raise theoretical issues concerning specific-purpose language ability.

Notes

1. The need to understand communicative competence is also relevant for language teaching; however, we focus on testing issues here.

2. Canale and Swain had been working on their framework for communicative competence before the conference in 1979 even though their paper was not published until 1980.

3. See Henning, Hudson, and Turner (1985) for a discussion of the unidimensionality assumption associated with IRT statistics.

4. Other justifications include relevance and utility, value implications, and social consequences (Messick, 1989).

5. Although the traditions appeared somewhat diachronically, they coexist today.

References

Ahmad, K., Corbett, G., Rogers, M. & Sussex, R. (1985). *Computers, language learning, and language teaching*. Cambridge: Cambridge University Press.

Alderson, J. C., & Urquhart, A. H. (1985). This test is unfair; I'm not an economist. In P. C. Hauptman, R. LeBlanc, & M. B. Wesche (Eds.), *Second language performance testing* (pp. 25–43). Ottawa: University of Ottawa Press.

American Council on the Teaching of Foreign Languages. (1986). *ACTFL proficiency guidelines*. New York: Author.

Bachman, L. F. (1982). The trait structure of cloze test scores. *TESOL Quarterly, 16*, 61–70.

Bachman, L. F. (1990). *Fundamental considerations in language testing*. Oxford: Oxford University Press.

Bachman, L. F., Kunnan, A., Vanniarajan, S., & Lynch, B. (1988). Task and ability analysis as a basis for examining content and construct comparability in two EFL proficiency tests. *Language Testing, 5*, 128–159.

Bachman, L. F., & Palmer, A. S. (1982). The construct validation of some components of communicative competence. *TESOL Quarterly, 16*, 449–465.

Bachman, L. F., & Savignon, S. J. (1986). The evaluation of communicative language proficiency: A critique of the ACTFL oral interview. *Modern Language Journal, 70*, 380–390.

Bejar, I. I., & Yocom, P. (1986). *A generative approach to the development of hidden-figures items* (Report No. ETS RR-86-20-ONR). Princeton, NJ: Educational Testing Service (ETS).

Bennett, R. E., Ward, W. C., Rock, D. A., & LaHart, C. (1990). *Toward a framework for constructed-response items* (Report No. ETS RR-90-7). Princeton, NJ: ETS.

Berns, M. (1990). *Contexts of competence—Social and cultural considerations in communicative language teaching.* New York: Plenum Press.

Bialystok, E. (1990). *Communication strategies: A psychological analysis of second-language use.* Cambridge, MA: Basil Blackwell.

Bialystok, E., & Ryan, E. B. (1985). A metacognitive framework for the development of first and second language skills. In D. L. Forrest-Presley, G. E. MacKinnon, & T. G. Waller (Eds.), *Metacognition, cognition and human performance: Theoretical perspectives* (vol. 1, pp. 207–252). New York: Academic Press.

Brown, J. D. (1988). What makes a cloze item difficult? *University of Hawai'i Working Papers in ESL, 7*, 17–39.

Burton, R. R., & Brown, J. S. (1982). An investigation of computer coaching for informal learning activities. In D. H. Sleeman & J. S. Brown (Eds.), *Intelligent tutoring systems* (pp. 79–98). London: Academic Press.

Canale, M. (1983a). On some dimensions of language proficiency. In J. W. Oller Jr. (Ed.), *Issues in language testing research* (pp. 333–342). Rowley, MA: Newbury House.

Canale, M. (1983b). From communicative competence to communicative language pedagogy. In J. Richards & R. Schmidt (Eds.), *Language and communication* (pp. 2–27). London: Longman.

Canale, M. (1984). Considerations in the testing of reading and listening proficiency. *Foreign Language Annals, 17*, 349–357.

Canale, M. (1985). A theory of strategy-oriented language development. In S. Jaeger (Ed.), *Issues in English language development* (pp. 15–20). Washington, DC: National Clearinghouse on Bilingual Education.

Canale, M. (1986). The promise and threat of computerized adaptive assessment of reading comprehension. In C. Stansfield (Ed.), *Technology and language testing* (pp. 30–45). Washington, DC: Teachers of English to Speakers of Other Languages (TESOL).

Canale, M. (1987). Language assessment: The method is the message. In D. Tannen & J. E. Alatis (Eds.), *The interdependence of theory, data, and application* (pp. 249–262). Washington, DC: Georgetown University Press.

Canale, M. (1988). The measurement of communicative competence. *Annual Review of Applied Linguistics, 8*, 67–84.

Canale, M., & Swain, M. (1980). Theoretical bases of communicative approaches to second language teaching and testing. *Applied Linguistics, 1*, 1–47.

Carroll, J. B. (1976). Psychometric tests as cognitive tasks: A new "structure of intellect." In L. B. Resnick (Ed.), *The nature of intelligence* (pp. 27–56). Hillsdale, NJ: Lawrence Erlbaum Associates.

Carroll, J. B. (1989). Intellectual abilities and aptitudes. In A. Lesgold & R. Glaser (Eds.), *Foundations for a psychology of education* (pp. 137–197). Hillsdale, NJ: Lawrence Erlbaum Associates.

Chapelle, C. A., & Abraham, R. G. (1990). Cloze method: What difference does it make? *Language Testing, 7,* 121–146.

Cohen, A. (1984). On taking language tests: What the students report. *Language Testing, 1,* 70–81.

Connor-Linton, J. (1991, January). Questions, power, and crosstalk in Soviet-American spacebridges. Paper presented at the conference of the Linguistic Society of America, Chicago, IL.

Cummins, J. (1983). Language proficiency and academic achievement. In J. W. Oller Jr. (Ed.), *Issues in language testing research* (pp. 108–129). Rowley, MA: Newbury House.

Cziko, G. (1981). Psychometric and edumetric approaches to language testing: Implications and applications. *Applied Linguistics, 5,* 23–38.

Cziko, G. (1982). Improving the psychometric, criterion-referenced, and practical qualities of integrative language tests. *TESOL Quarterly, 16,* 367–379.

van Dijk, T. (1977). *Text and context.* London: Longman.

Douglas, D. (1988). Testing listening comprehension in the context of the ACTFL Proficiency Guidelines. *Studies in Second Language Acquisition, 10,* 245–262.

Douglas, D. (1989, August). Context in SLA theory and language testing. Paper presented at the Educational Testing Service Invitational Symposium, Princeton, NJ.

Educational Testing Service. (1990). *Test of Spoken English: Manual for score-users.* Princeton, NJ: Author.

Embretson, S. (1983). Construct validity: Construct representation versus nomothetic span. *Psychological Bulletin, 93,* 179–197.

Embretson, S. (Ed.) (1985). *Test design: Developments in psychology and psychometrics.* Orlando: Academic Press.

Erickson, F. (1986). Listening and speaking. In D. Tannen & J. E. Alatis (Eds.), *The interdependence of theory, data, and application* (pp. 394–419). Washington, DC: Georgetown University Press.

Erickson, F., & Schultz, J. (1981). When is a context? Some issues in the analysis of social competence. In J. Green & C. Wallat (Eds.), *Ethnography and language in educational settings* (pp. 147–160). Norwood, NJ: Ablex.

Faerch, C., & Kasper, G. (Eds.). (1983). *Strategies in interlanguage communication.* London: Longman.

Feldmann, U., & Stemmer, B. (1987). Thin___ aloud a___ retrospective da___ in C-te___ taking: diffe___ languages—diff___ learners—sa___ approaches? In C. Faerch & G. Kasper (Eds.), *Introspection in second language research* (pp. 251–267). Philadelphia: Multilingual Matters.

Gass, S. (1987). L2 vocabulary acquisition. In A. Valdman (Ed.), *Proceedings from the symposium on the evaluation of foreign language proficiency* (pp. 231–245). Bloomington, IN: Indiana University.

Goffman, E. (1974). *Frame analysis.* New York: Harper & Row.

Grotjahn, R. (1986). Test validation and cognitive psychology: Some methodological considerations. *Language Testing, 3,* 159–185.

Grotjahn, R. (1987). On the methodological basis of introspective methods. In C. Faerch & G. Kasper (Eds.), *Introspection in second language research* (pp. 54–81). Philadelphia: Multilingual Matters.

Gumperz, J. J. (1976). Language, communication and public negotiation. In P. R. Sanday (Ed.), *Anthropology and the public interest* (pp. 273–292). New York: Academic Press.

Halliday, M. A. K. (1978). *Language as social semiotic: The social interpretation of language and meaning.* London: Edward Arnold.

Henning, G., Hudson, T., & Turner, J. (1985). Item Response Theory and the assumption of unidimensionality. *Language Testing, 2,* 141–154.

Hymes, D. (1972). *Towards communicative competence.* Philadelphia: University of Pennsylvania Press.

Kirsch, I. S., & Mosenthal, P. B. (1988). *Understanding document literacy: Variables underlying the performance of young adults* (Report no. ETS RR-88-62). Princeton, NJ: ETS.

Lowe, P. Jr. (1982). *ILR handbook on oral proficiency testing.* Washington, DC: DLI/LS Oral Interview Project.

MacNamara, T. F. (1990). Item Response Theory and the validation of an ESP test for health professionals. *Language Testing, 7,* 52–75.

Messick, S. (1989). Validity. In R. L. Linn (Ed.), *Educational measurement* (3rd ed., pp. 13–103). New York: Macmillan.

Nitko, A. J. 1989. Designing tests that are integrated with instruction. In R. L. Linn (Ed.), *Educational measurement* (3rd ed., pp. 447–474). New York: Macmillan.

Olshtain, E., & Blum-Kulka, S. (1985). Crosscultural pragmatics and the testing of communicative competence. *Language Testing, 2,* 16–30.

Oxford, R. L. (1990). *Language learning strategies: What every teacher should know.* New York: Newbury House.

Palmer, A. S., & Groot, P. J. M. (1981). An introduction. In A. S. Palmer, P. J. M. Groot, & G. Trosper (Eds.), *The construct validation of tests of communicative competence* (pp. 1–11). Washington, DC: TESOL.

Perkins, K., & Linnville, S. (1987). A construct definition study of a standardized ESL vocabulary test. *Language Testing, 4,* 125–141.

Pienemann, M., Johnson, M., & Brindley, G. (1988). Constructing an acquisition-based procedure for second language assessment. *Studies in Second Language Acquisition, 10,* 217–243.

Rumelhart, D. (1980). Schemata: The building blocks of cognition. In R. J. Spiro, B. C. Bruce, & W. E. Brewer (Eds.), *Theoretical issues in reading comprehension* (pp. 33–58). Hillsdale, NJ: Lawrence Erlbaum Associates.

Sanders, A. F., & Sanders, R. H. (1989). Syntactic parsing: A survey. *Computers and the Humanities, 23,* 13–30.

Savignon, S. (1983). *Communicative competence: Theory and classroom practice.* Reading, MA: Addison-Wesley.

Schank, R. C., and Abelson, R. P. (1977). *Scripts, plans, goals and understanding.* Hillsdale, NJ: Lawrence Erlbaum Associates.

Smith, J. (1989). Topic and variation in ITA oral proficiency: SPEAK and field-specific oral tests. *English for Specific Purposes, 8,* 155–168.

Snow, R. E., & Lohman, D. F. (1989). Implications of cognitive psychology for educational measurement. In R. L. Linn (Ed.), *Educational Measurement* (3rd ed., pp. 263–331). New York: Macmillan.

Spolsky, B. (1978). Introduction: Linguists and language testers. In B. Spolsky (Ed.), *Advances in language testing research: Approaches to language testing 2* (pp. v–x). Washington, DC: Center for Applied Linguistics.

Spolsky, B. (1985). The limits of authenticity in language testing. *Language Testing, 2*, 31–40.

Stansfield, C. W., & Ross, J. (1988). A long-term research agenda for the Test of Written English. *Language Testing, 5*, 160–186.

Sternberg, R. J. (1977). *Intelligence, information processing, and analogical reasoning: The componential analysis of human abilities*. Hillsdale, NJ: Lawrence Erlbaum Associates.

Stevenson, D. K. (1981). Beyond faith and face validity: The multitrait-multimethod matrix and the convergent and discriminant validity of oral proficiency tests. In A. S. Palmer, P. J. M. Groot, & G. A. Trosper (Eds.), *The construct validation of tests of communicative competence* (pp. 37–61). Washington, DC: TESOL.

Vollmer, H. (1983). The structure of foreign language competence. In A. Hughes & D. Porter (Eds.), *Current developments in language testing* (pp. 3–29). London: Academic Press.

Wesche, M. (1987). Second language performance testing: The Ontario Test of ESL as an example. *Language Testing, 4*, 28–47.

Widdowson, H. (1983). *Learning purpose and language use*. Oxford: Oxford University Press.

Part I

Producing Validity Evidence for Language Tests

2

A Comparison of the Abilities Measured by the Cambridge and Educational Testing Service EFL Test Batteries[1]

Lyle F. Bachman
University of California at Los Angeles

Fred Davidson
University of Illinois at Urbana-Champaign

John Foulkes
University of Cambridge Local Examinations Syndicate

The First Certificate in English (FCE), administered by the University of Cambridge Local Examinations Syndicate (Cambridge), and the Test of English as a Foreign Language (TOEFL), administered by Educational Testing Service (ETS), are widely used as measures of proficiency in English as foreign language (EFL) throughout the world. Hundreds of thousands of individuals take these tests each year, and it is likely that the majority of these individuals make some sort of personal decision, such as seeking employment, advancement in a career, or admission to an educational program, that is determined partly by their scores on these tests. Furthermore, because many of these individuals will submit job or educational program applications to more than one employer or institution, it is probably safe to say that the number of individual career decisions affected in some degree by the results of these tests number well over 1 million annually.

Although the EFL proficiency test batteries developed by Cambridge and ETS are designed to measure many of the same abilities, they nevertheless represent radically different approaches to language test development. The TOEFL is perhaps the prototypical "psychometric/structuralist" language test (Spolsky, 1978), representing the best qualities of this approach, which emphasizes reliability and item analysis. Its complements, the Test of Spoken English (TSE) and Test of Written English (TWE), though still developed in the psychometric tradition, represent an expansion of the structuralist linguistic framework and incorporate features associated with a broader range of language abilities and test methods. The FCE, on the other hand, has been designed and developed largely in the tradition of the British examinations system, which places more emphasis on expert judgment and institutional experience in the production, scoring, and interpretation of test results.

In short, there are important differences in the approaches to educational measurement that characterize the FCE and the ETS tests of EFL. In conducting this study, we became increasingly aware of these differences, because they affected the way we processed and analyzed the data. But rather than causing us to prejudge one approach or the other, our awareness of these differences has, we believe, enriched our treatment of the data and, we hope, enlightened our interpretation of the results.

Objectives

The results reported in this paper were obtained as part of a larger study, the Cambridge-TOEFL Comparability Study (CTCS), which was commissioned by Cambridge to examine the comparability of the Cambridge EFL tests (both the FCE and the Certificate of Proficiency in English) and the ETS tests of EFL (Bachman, Davidson, Ryan, & Choi, forthcoming). The first goal of the CTCS was short term: to examine the comparability of abilities measured by these two EFL proficiency test batteries. This involved two different but complementary approaches: (a) the qualitative content analysis of the two tests, including the specific language abilities and the types of test tasks employed, and (b) the quantitative investigation of patterns of relationships in examinee performance among the different tests. The results of the content analysis have been reported elsewhere (Bachman, Davidson, & Lynch, 1988; Bachman, Kunnan, Vanniarajan, & Lynch, 1988). This paper will thus focus on the results of the quantitative analyses of performance on the FCE and the ETS tests of EFL.

The second goal of the study is long term—to initiate a program of research and development with two aims: (a) improving both the content and measurement characteristics of the Cambridge EFL examinations by understanding better what language abilities they measure and (b) investigating the nature of communicative language ability and its measurement. This long-term goal will be accomplished in a number of ways, including, but not limited to, the following:

1. routine monitoring of the reliability of Cambridge EFL examinations, and refinement of procedures for maximizing reliability
2. research into the patterns of performance across the various parts of the Cambridge EFL examinations
3. research into the relationships between test-taker characteristics and test performance
4. research into the analysis of test content and the subsequent refinement of the models on which this study is based and of the procedures for operationalizing these models in test design and specifications

5. research into the relationships between aspects of test content and test performance.

These last two areas represent a particularly important concern for both test developers and test users, as recent work has indicated a poor relationship between what "experts" believe a given test item measures and test takers' performance (Alderson & Lukmani, 1986; Alderson, Henning, & Lukmani, 1987; Perkins & Linnville, 1987; Bachman, Davidson, Lynch, & Ryan, 1989; Alderson, this volume, chap. 3).

Procedures

Subjects

Characteristics of Typical FCE Candidates

Candidates for the FCE represent a widely varied population and have many reasons for seeking FCE certification. For example, if a candidate is working in a clerical or support position where English proficiency is required in a business or in the government service, an FCE certificate might be one criterion for promotion or salary increase. In addition to these adult candidates, large numbers of FCE takers are of school age; in many parts of the world, particularly in countries without formal institutional examinations for school-leaving, the FCE is taken as a de facto school-leaving examination. It is definitely not the case that candidates take the FCE for purposes of university entrance, a function served by the Certificate of Proficiency in English.

Although systematic data on native language background, educational status, age, sex, and amount of non-FCE prior English study are not available, it is probably safe to assume that among the FCE population there is a wide variation in background variables. It is also likely that candidates are familiar with the FCE format, as the vast majority of FCE candidates have undergone a prior course of instruction covering the syllabus on which the FCE is based.

Characteristics of Typical TOEFL Takers

Extensive information about TOEFL takers is available in several published ETS reports (ETS, 1987; Wilson, 1982; Wilson, 1987). According to these reports, typical TOEFL takers, in contrast to typical FCE candidates, are largely "degree planners"—individuals planning to enter a college or university degree program in the United States or Canada (80%)—are male (72%), and have median ages of 20.6 and 25.4 for undergraduate- and graduate-level degree planners, respectively. Furthermore, 28% of the individuals who took the TOEFL for the first time in 1977 and 1978 had taken the test two or more times by 1982, with much higher percentages of test repeaters (40–50%) being reported for three CTCS sites: Hong Kong, Thailand, and Japan.

Sampling Procedures

The sampling procedures followed in the study were intended to ensure that sites and subjects would constitute a representative sample of the operational worldwide populations of the TOEFL and FCE. The first consideration in selecting sites was the need to represent different geographic regions and native languages in the sample. Based on the geographic distributions of the Cambridge and TOEFL operational populations, we decided to include sites in the Far East, Middle East, Europe, and South America. Within each of these regions we attempted to obtain representative samples of different language groups: Chinese, Japanese, and Thai for the Far East; Arabic for the Middle East; Spanish, French, and German for Europe; Spanish and Portuguese for South America.

The second consideration in selecting sites for the study was the need to obtain a representative sample both of typical FCE candidates and of typical TOEFL takers. We identified two types of sites: (a) "Cambridge-dominant," which were identified from Cambridge records as having large numbers of FCE candidates, and (b) "TOEFL-dominant," which generally had small numbers of FCE candidates and, according to published ETS reports (e.g., ETS, 1987) relatively large numbers of TOEFL takers.

Finally, the availability of local persons to participate as Site Coordinators, who could assure that they were able to administer both sets of tests under operational conditions, and the availability of adequate numbers of subjects obviously had to be taken into account. After lengthy discussions revolving around these areas of concern, and considerable negotiation, the following eight sites were agreed on: (a) TOEFL-dominant sites: Bangkok, Cairo, Hong Kong, Osaka; and (b) Cambridge-dominant sites: Madrid, São Paulo, Toulouse, Zürich.

At the Cambridge-dominant sites, the Site Coordinator was the examinations officer in charge of Cambridge EFL tests, and the Site Coordinator at the TOEFL-dominant sites was a staff member of an institution of higher education who was not only familiar with the local population of "typical" TOEFL takers but also had access to adequate numbers of these individuals from which to draw a sample. This individual generally worked closely with the local Cambridge examinations officer in arranging the schedule for test administration.

Characteristics of the Sample Subjects

Test performance.   Summary descriptive statistics for test or paper scores for the sample subjects are given in Table 2-1. Inspection of these score distributions indicated that all the measures were reasonably normally distributed and that the distributional assumptions for parametric statistical analyses were warranted. In order to examine the extent to which the sample subjects were typical of their respective operational populations, the sample means were compared with relevant norm groups. For the FCE, the norm group was all individuals who took the

Table 2-1

Score Distributions, All Measures

Variable	M	SD	Minimum	Maximum	N
TOEFL					
1	49.62	6.67	29	68	1,448
2	51.12	6.90	25	68	1,448
3	51.49	6.70	28	66	1,448
Total	507.43	58.86	310	647	1,448
TEW	3.93	.89	1	6	1,398
SPEAK					
Grammar	1.93	.45	0	3	1,304
Pronunciation	2.13	.38	0	3	1,314
Fluency	1.95	.44	0	3	1,304
Comprehensibility	201.57	40.91	50	300	1,304
FCE					
Paper 1	25.95	4.90	10	40	1,359
Paper 2	24.30	6.04	0	40	1,357
Paper 3	24.86	5.71	1	40	1,353
Paper 4	13.60	3.18	4	20	1,344
Paper 5	27.20	5.95	1	40	1,381

FCE in December 1988 (University of Cambridge Local Examinations Syndicate, 1988), and for the ETS tests the norm groups were those reported in the most recent editions of the *TOEFL Test and Score Manual* (ETS, 1987), the *Test of Spoken English: Manual for Score Users* (ETS, 1982) and the *Test of Written English Guide* (ETS, 1989).

The sample means and standard deviations on the FCE and the ETS tests and those of the FCE and ETS norm groups are presented in Tables 2-2 and 2-3, respectively. Although virtually all of the differences between the sample and norm group means were statistically significant, this is primarily a function of the large sample sizes, and thus it makes more sense to consider the practical importance of the differences. Looking at Table 2-2, we see that the largest difference between the sample and FCE norm group means is for Paper 2: 1.77 points on a scale of 40. The differences between the sample and ETS norm group means, presented in Table 2-3, are also small, relative to the standard deviations of the ETS norm group. The largest difference here was for the TSE/SPEAK Comprehensibility rating, with a mean difference of 19.4 on a scale of 300. Thus, although the sample means tend to be slightly lower than those of their relevant norm groups, these differences are too small to be of practical importance, and it can be concluded that the sample subjects constitute a representative sample of the FCE and ETS operational populations in terms of their test performance.

Test takers' characteristics. Information on the subjects' age and sex was obtained from responses to questions on their TOEFL answer sheets, and informa-

Table 2-2

Differences Between CTCS Group Means, Standard Deviations, and FCE Norms

	N		M		SD	
Test	CTCS	Norm	CTCS	Norm	CTCS	Norm
Paper 1	1,359	30,816	25.95	27.19	4.90	5.19
Paper 2	1,357	30,818	24.30	26.07	6.04	5.22
Paper 3	1,353	30,805	24.86	26.30	5.71	5.26
Paper 4	1,344	30,936	13.60	14.47	3.18	3.25
Paper 5	1,381	31,040	27.20	28.04	5.95	5.72

tion on their current educational status was obtained from responses to questions on a background questionnaire. The majority of the CTCS subjects were enrolled as students, either at the secondary school level (21.3%) or at the college level (full-time, 27.6%; part-time, 10.4%) or in a language institute or other English course (17%), and 23.7%) indicated that they were not enrolled as students. The median age was 21, with the youngest test taker 14 years of age and the oldest 58. Slightly over half (59.4%) were female.

Information on the characteristics of TOEFL examinees from 1977–1979, provided by Wilson (1982), was used as a basis for comparing the sample subjects' characteristics with those of the operational TOEFL population. Because no such information is available for the operational FCE population, no comparisons could be made. Wilson did not include current educational status in his study, but the mean age for his population was 21.4 for individuals intending to apply to an undergraduate degree program ("undergraduate level degree planners") and 26.3 for graduate-level degree planners, compared with 22.7 for the

Table 2-3

Differences Between CTCS Group Means, Standard Deviations, and ETS Norms

	N		M		SD	
Test	CTCS	Norm	CTCS	Norm	CTCS	Norm
TOEFL						
1	1,448	714,731	49.62	51.2	6.67	6.9
2	1,448	714,731	51.12	51.3	6.90	7.7
3	1,448	714,731	51.49	51.1	6.70	7.3
Total	1,448	714,731	507.43	512.0	58.86	66.0
TWE/TEW	1,398	230,921	3.93	3.64	0.89	0.99
TSE/SPEAK						
Grammar	1,304	3,500	1.93	2.43	0.45	0.39
Pronunciation	1,314	3,500	2.13	2.10	0.38	0.49
Fluency	1,304	3,500	1.95	2.15	0.44	0.45
Comprehensibility	1,304	3,500	201.57	221.0	40.91	45.0

sample group. A larger difference between the operational TOEFL population and the sample can be seen in the sex of the test takers, with Wilson reporting that 72% of his group was male, compared with about 41% for the sample subjects.

In summary, the sample subjects appeared to be quite similar to the operational populations of both the TOEFL and the FCE in terms of their test performance. With respect to test-taker characteristics, the sample was quite close in age to TOEFL undergraduate degree planners but had a higher proportion of females than is typical of TOEFL test takers.

Test Instruments

First Certificate in English (FCE)

FCE Paper 1, entitled "Reading Comprehension," includes two sections of four-choice multiple-choice items: 25 items that appear to test use or usage and 10 items based on reading passages. FCE Paper 2, entitled "Composition," consists of five prompts from which the candidate chooses two, writing 120–180 words in response to each. FCE Paper 3, entitled "Use of English," includes items that appear to test various aspects of lexicon, register, and other elements of English usage. Paper 4 is a tape-recording-plus-booklet test entitled "Listening Comprehension," for which candidates listen to several passages and respond to items on each passage. Paper 5 consists of a face-to-face oral interview conducted as either a "one-on-one," with one examiner and one candidate, or as a "group" interview, with more than one candidate and two examiners.

Test of English as a Foreign Language

Early in the planning of the study it was obvious that we would not be able to synchronize the operational administrations of the two test batteries; we therefore decided to use the institutional versions of the TOEFL and the TSE as well as a composition test similar to the TWE. The institutional TOEFL consists of those official international forms of the TOEFL that have been retired from operational use. Although ETS does not report scores on the institutional TOEFL to other institutions, it does guarantee content and statistical equivalence of the institutional and international forms of the TOEFL. There are three sections to the test: Section 1—Listening Comprehension; Section 2—Structure and Written Expression; Section 3—Vocabulary and Reading Comprehension. Item types vary somewhat, but all follow a four-option multiple-choice format.

Speaking Proficiency in English Assessment Kit (SPEAK)

The SPEAK is a semidirect test of oral performance and is the institutional counterpart of the Test of Spoken English (TSE), consisting of retired forms of the operational TSE. It consists of a complete kit, including materials for training raters in the scoring procedure, and is administered entirely by tape recorder, with candidates listening to a number of prompts from a cassette source tape, looking at verbal and graphic stimulus material in an accompanying booklet, and responding on a target cassette tape, which also records the prompts from the source tape.

Test of English Writing (TEW)

ETS produces a composition test called the Test of Written English (TWE), which, because it was still considered experimental by ETS at the time the study began, had no institutional counterpart. An experienced TWE rater was therefore asked to produce a prompt similar to example prompts that ETS makes available in its information to prospective TWE takers. We called this test the "Test of English Writing." The TEW test booklet contained two printed sheets: on the first were the instructions, and the second contained the single prompt, including both verbal and graphic information, to be answered by all candidates in the study.

Test Administration

Because it was not possible to synchronize operational administrations of the FCE and the ETS tests, we decided to administer all tests within the schedule of an operational FCE administration (December 1988). This meant that candidates generally took the FCE and ETS pencil-and-paper sections (i.e., FCE Papers 1, 2, and 3, TOEFL and TEW) on adjacent days. FCE Papers 4 and 5 were administered within the 5 weeks devoted to Cambridge Papers 1, 2, and 3, and at most sites the SPEAK was given in the same 2-day period as the pencil-and-paper tests. Operational procedures and time allocations prescribed by all tests were strictly adhered to.

Scoring Procedure

All tests were scored according to operational procedures prescribed by Cambridge and ETS. FCE Paper 1 was scored by optical scanner at Cambridge, and answers to Papers 3 and 4 were hand scored using scoring keys or "marking schemes" prepared by examiners. Papers 2 and 5 were rated subjectively by trained examiners, using rating scales developed by Cambridge. The TOEFL was scored by optical scanner at Illinois, and the SPEAK and TEW were rated subjectively by trained raters in North America, according to rating scales developed by ETS.

Data Preparation and Analyses

Data from all the FCE papers were prepared in Cambridge. Paper 1 answer sheets were optically scanned, but the majority of the data from the other papers were manually entered into computer files. The machine-scorable answer sheets for the TOEFL and SPEAK were optically scanned, and the TEW ratings were manually entered into computer files at the University of Illinois at Urbana-Champaign. Subsequent data merging and data file assembly were performed using SAS or PC-SAS (SAS, 1988). Statistical analyses were performed using SPSSX Version 3.0 (SPSS, 1988a), SPSS/PC+ Version 2.1 (SPSS, 1988b; SPSS, 1988c), GENOVA (Crick & Brennan, 1983), and factor analysis programs written for the PC by Carroll (1989).

Measurement Characteristics of the Two Test Batteries

Reliability

Classical internal consistency estimates (coefficient alpha) were calculated for the discrete item tests (FCE Papers 1, 3, and 4 and TOEFL). Because 2 forms of FCE Paper 1 and 10 forms of Paper 4 were administered in the study, the reliabilities reported here for these papers are the weighted averages (using Fisher's z transformation) of the coefficient alphas for the different forms of each paper. Interrater reliabilities for the TWE and SPEAK ratings were estimated using generalizability theory. The values reported here were obtained from a single facet G-study design with raters as the facet. Because multiple independent ratings are not done as part of the operational FCE, inter- and intrarater reliabilities could not be estimated for FCE Papers 2 (composition) and 5 (oral interview).

Reliability estimates for the sample, along with their respective population norms, are reported in Table 2-4. The norm for FCE Paper 1 is the reported Kuder-Richardson Formula 20 (KR-20) for operational examinees who took the FCE between December 1988 and December 1989, and the norms for FCE Papers 3 and 4 consist of average KR-20s (using Fisher's z transformation) across samples of operational examinees who took the FCE in December 1989. Norms for the ETS tests are those reported in the ETS score and interpretative manuals cited above. In general, the FCE reliabilities for our sample are slightly lower than those generally obtained operationally by Cambridge and somewhat below the norms reported for the ETS tests. The reliability estimate obtained for Paper 3 is within acceptable limits, but those obtained for Papers 1 and 4 are lower than normally acceptable for standardized tests.

Comparability of Abilities Measured

To determine whether and to what extent the two test batteries (FCE and ETS) might be comparable, it was first necessary to investigate the extent to which patterns of performance support interpretations of similar abilities. This was done

Table 2-4

Reliability Estimates

Test	k	N	α	Norm
FCE				
Paper 1[a]	40	1,394	.791	.901[a]
Paper 2	NA	NA	NA	NA
Paper 3	52	995	.847	.870[a]
Paper 4[a]	27	759	.616	.705[a]
Paper 5	NA	NA	NA	NA.
TOEFL				
1	50	1,467	.889	.90
2	34	1,467	.834	.86
3	58	1,467	.874	.90
TEW	—	1,399	.896[b]	.86[c]
SPEAK Comprehensibility	—	1,318	.970[b]	.88[c]

[a]Weighted average coefficient alphas across more than one test form. [b]Generalizability coefficients. [c]Interrater correlation.
NA = not available.

primarily by examining the patterns of correlations within and across the two test batteries through exploratory factor analysis.

Three correlation matrices were analyzed: (a) intercorrelations among the scaled scores for the 5 FCE papers, (b) intercorrelations among the 8 ETS standard scores, and (c) intercorrelations among all 13 of these measures. These correlation matrices are given in Appendixes 2A, 2B, and 2C, respectively. The matrix of product-moment correlations among the various test scores to be analyzed was examined for appropriateness of the common factor model in several ways. Principal axes were extracted with squared multiple correlations on the diagonal as initial communality estimates. A consideration of the eigenvalues obtained from the initial extraction and of the parallel analysis criterion (Montanelli and Humphreys, 1976) led to an initial decision about the appropriate number of factors to extract. Specified numbers of principal axes, generally including one fewer and one more than the number initially decided on for a given correlation matrix, were then successively extracted and rotated. Two rotated factor structure matrices were obtained for each number of principal axes extracted: an orthogonal solution with the normal varimax procedure and an oblique solution with Tucker and Finkbeiner's (1981) least-squares hyperplane fitting ("DAPPFR"). The final determination of the number of factors and the "best" solution was made on the basis of simplicity and interpretability, these qualities being judged, of course, subjectively. Simplicity was evaluated by examining both the patterns of salient loadings for the orthogonal and oblique solutions and the scatter plots of loadings on the rotated axes. Interpretability was evaluated with reference to the extent to

Table 2-5

Exploratory Factor Analysis of FCE Papers

Variable	Communality
Paper 1	.54835
Paper 2	.48888
Paper 3	.62272
Paper 4	.41468
Paper 5	.32595

Factor	Eigenvalue	% of variance	Cumulative %
1	3.18529	63.7	63.7
2	.63769	12.8	76.5
3	.48866	9.8	86.2
4	.41719	8.3	94.6
5	.27117	5.4	100.0

Orthogonolized Factor Matrix With Second-Order General Factor

	General factor	Factor 1	Factor 2	h^2
Paper 1	.733	.275	.062	.617
Paper 2	.689	.260	.057	.546
Paper 3	.809	.433	.061	.846
Paper 4	.679	.071	.241	.524
Paper 5	.622	.024	.310	.484
Eigenvalue	2.515	.336	.165	3.016
% of h^2	50.3	6.7	3.3	60.3

which the salient factor loadings and factor correlations reflected the nature of the tasks and abilities thought to be operationalized in the different measures.

Within-Paper/Test Factor Structures

The results of the exploratory factor analysis for the FCE paper scores are given in Table 2-5; those for the ETS test scores appear in Table 2-6. The scree plots and the parallel analyses suggested that two factors underlay both sets of test scores, and the oblique rotations yielded factors that were highly correlated for both sets of tests. Because both of these factor solutions were highly oblique, with correlations between factors of .826 for the FCE and .601 for the ETS tests, a Schmid-Leiman transformation to orthogonal primary factors with a second-order general factor was performed on each (Schmid & Leiman, 1957).

All the FCE papers loaded most heavily on a higher-order factor, which accounted for 50.3% of the common variance. The first primary factor was

Table 2-6

Exploratory Factor Analysis of ETS Tests.

Variable	Communality
TOEFL 1	.53783
TOEFL 2	.57999
TOEFL 3	.57389
TEW	.37389
SPEAK Grammar	.80099
SPEAK Pronunciation	.60725
SPEAK Fluency	.77096
SPEAK Comprehensibility	.89596

Factor	Eigenvalue	% of variance	Cumulative %
1	4.93914	61.7	61.7
2	1.17112	14.6	76.4
3	.55103	6.9	83.3
4	.39869	5.0	88.2
5	.38118	4.8	93.0
6	.28032	3.5	96.5
7	.20493	2.6	99.1
8	.07357	.9	100.0

Orthogonolized Factor Matrix With Second-Order General Factor

	General factor	Factor 1	Factor 2	h^2
TOEFL 1	.654	.275	.258	.569
TOEFL 2	.648	−.004	.532	.703
TOEFL 3	.642	−.036	.559	.726
TEW	.534	.094	.341	.410
SPEAK Grammar	.668	.576	−.032	.779
SPEAK Pronunciation	.651	.404	.126	.603
SPEAK Fluency	.684	.567	−.009	.791
SPEAK Comprehensibility	.750	.650	−.038	.986
Eigenvalue	3.444	1.325	.798	5.567
% of h^2	43.1	16.6	9.9	69.6

characterized by high loadings on Papers 1, 2, and 3, whereas Papers 4 and 5 had high loadings on the second primary factor. This suggests that the FCE Papers all tend to measure a common component of the subjects' English language ability, with two specific ability factors, "reading, structure and writing" and "speaking and listening," being identified.

This pattern of loadings was repeated for the ETS tests, with all tests loading most heavily on a second-order general factor that accounted for 43.1% of the common variance. The ETS tests, except perhaps TOEFL Section 1, also had high loadings on the two primary factors, with TOEFL Section 1 and the SPEAK ratings loading most heavily on the first, and with TOEFL Sections 2 and 3 and the TEW loading on the second. These results suggest that the ETS tests also tend to measure a common component of the subjects' language ability, with specific factors associated with listening and speaking on the one hand and reading, structure and writing on the other being identified. These two sets of test scores show remarkable similarities in their factor structures, with higher-order general factors accounting for large portions of the common variances in the two test batteries. On the other hand, whereas relatively little common variance in the FCE papers is accounted for by first-order factors (10%), in the ETS tests the two first-order factors account for a considerable proportion (26.5%) of the common variance. This suggests that whereas each test battery appears to measure a single language ability, the ETS tests provide relatively more information about specific language abilities than the FCE papers do. Although these similarities in factor structures would appear to reflect similarities in the abilities of the subjects in the study, they also suggest that these two sets of tests measure these abilities in much the same way.

Across-Battery Factor Structures

To examine the relationships between the two test batteries, the correlations among the scaled scores for the five FCE Papers and for the eight ETS test scores were analyzed using the procedures described above. Although the scree test suggested that only two or three factors should be extracted, the parallel analyses criterion indicated five. Therefore, orthogonal and oblique solutions with two, three, four, and five principal axes were examined. The solution that appeared to optimize the simplicity and interpretability criteria was a four-factor oblique solution with highly correlated factors. The higher-order solution produced by the Schmid-Leiman transformation is presented in Table 2-7. As would be expected with very high correlations among the first-order factors, all the measures have salient loadings on the second-order general factor, which accounts for 49.2% of the common variance. The first-order factors can be characterized as follows: Factor 1 (10.6% of common variance)—SPEAK ratings and FCE Paper 5; Factor 2 (4.4%)—TOEFL Sections 2 and 3 and TEW; Factor 3 (1.9%)—FCE Papers 1, 2, and 3; and Factor 4 (1.5%)—FCE Paper 4 and TOEFL Section 1.

These loadings suggest that all of these tests measure, to a considerable degree, a common portion of the language abilities that characterize the test takers in the sample. After this general or common ability, the next largest component appears to be associated with speaking ability. This is followed by two components that appear to be combinations of ability (reading, structure, and writing) and test method ("ETS test method" and "FCE test method"). Finally, there is a relatively small component associated with listening ability. Given that all of the measures examined load most heavily on a higher-order general factor and that two of the first-order factors appear to be associated with aspects of language ability (speaking and listening) across both tests, these tests do, in general, measure the same abilities. That the other two factors appear to be associated in part with specific

Table 2-7

Exploratory Factor Analysis of FCE Papers and ETS Tests

Variable	Communality	Variable	Communality
FCE Paper 1	.58958	TOEFL 3	.61938
FCE Paper 2	.52228	TEW	.39597
FCE Paper 3	.66459	SPEAK Grammar	.80465
FCE Paper 4	.48009	SPEAK Pronunciation	.62949
FCE Paper 5	.42786	SPEAK Fluency	.77734
TOEFL 1	.59892	SPEAK Comprehensibility	.89563
TOEFL 2	.60101		

Factor	Eigenvalue	% of variance	Cumulative %
1	7.48415	57.6	57.6
2	1.32523	10.2	67.8
3	.65258	5.0	72.8
4	.57734	4.4	77.2
5	.55311	4.3	81.5
6	.50183	3.9	85.3
7	.38833	3.0	88.3
8	.37212	2.9	91.2
9	.34312	2.6	93.8
10	.27587	2.1	96.0
11	.25262	1.9	97.9
12	.20044	1.5	99.4
13	.07325	0.6	100.0

Orthogonolized Factor Matrix With Second-Order General Factor

	General factor	Factor 1	Factor 2	Factor 3	Factor 4	h^2
FCE						
Paper 1	.754	−.031	.078	.175	.104	.617
Paper 2	.711	.074	−.023	.270	.002	.584
Paper 3	.820	−.026	.028	.341	−.004	.789
Paper 4	.704	−.004	−.048	.053	.236	.556
Paper 5	.621	.173	−.028	.015	.165	.443
TOEFL						
1	.776	.058	.059	−.043	.284	.692
2	.680	.049	.573	−.004	.010	.793
3	.711	−.085	.419	.032	.102	.699
TEW	.581	.074	.223	.097	.012	.402
SPEAK						
Grammar	.642	.621	.015	−.000	−.000	.798
Pronunciation	.707	.333	−.026	.131	.030	.630
Fluency	.676	.555	−.021	.007	.045	.767
Comprehensibility	.705	.719	.040	.011	−.034	1.018
Eigenvalue	6.401	1.377	.570	.252	.189	8.789
% of h^2	49.2	10.6	4.4	1.9	1.5	67.6

tests suggests that some of the observed differences in performance across the two test batteries are attributable to differences in the methods used in testing.

Discussion

Adequacy of Sample

In terms of test performance, the sample subjects were representative of both the December 1988 FCE candidature and "typical" ETS test takers. In terms of test-taker characteristics, the sample subjects were similar in age to ETS undergraduate degree planners, but they included a higher proportion of female test takers than the ETS population does. Because little is known about the characteristics of typical FCE candidates, no generalizations can be made in this regard.

Reliability

FCE Papers 1, 3, and 4 were somewhat less reliable than the ETS tests, and the reliabilities of Papers 2 and 5 could not be estimated. Although this does not necessarily mean that Papers 2 and 5 are unreliable, the inability to estimate their reliability is a recognized deficiency that will be remedied through the ongoing program of research and development described below.

Comparability of Abilities Measured

The factor structure for any given set of test scores will be a function of both the profile of language abilities of the specific group(s) of individuals tested and the characteristics of the specific tests used. The large proportions of variance accounted for by the general factors in our analyses suggest that the FCE papers and ETS tests administered in this study appear to measure, to a large degree, the same common aspect of the language proficiency of the subjects in our sample. We feel that at present there is no basis for interpreting this general factor as anything other than a common aspect of language proficiency shared by these subjects as measured by these tests. That is, this general factor does not necessarily represent the same aspect of language proficiency as do the general factors that have been found in other sets of language tests with other groups of subjects (e.g., Oller, 1979; Carroll, 1983; Bachman & Palmer, 1982; Sang, Schmitz, Vollmer, Baumert, & Roeder, 1986).

In addition to a common, general aspect of language ability, these test batteries appear to reflect shared specific abilities and different testing formats. The primary factor that accounts for the largest proportion of variance is associated with measures of speaking, especially the SPEAK. The primary factor that accounts for the least amount of variance is associated with measures of listening. The FCE oral interview loads almost equally on these speaking and listening factors.

A third primary factor (associated with ETS measures of structure, reading, and writing) can be identified as an "ETS written test factor," and a fourth primary factor (associated with the FCE measures of structure, writing, and reading) can be identified as an "FCE written test factor."

Score Comparisons Across Test Batteries

Because the forms of the FCE and ETS tests of EFL examined in this study appear to measure nearly the same aspects of the subjects' English language proficiency, score comparisons across tests are justified and could be made in a meaningful way. However, because of differences in levels of reliability across the two test batteries, as well as lack of demonstrated equivalence of different FCE forms, such score comparisons could best be made on the basis of subsequent studies, once reliability and equivalence are better assured.

Future Research

This study has provided an opportunity for Cambridge to study its EFL examinations in a way that has not generally been done in the past, which includes an ongoing program of research and development that is consistent with the long-range objectives of the study. This research, which will address both practical test development issues and research questions that are of theoretical interest to the field of language testing, currently includes the following specific projects:

1. *The investigation into the reliability of Paper 2 and Paper 5 ratings.* This will involve a three-facet G-study for Paper 2, with rater, occasion, and topic as facets, using papers from several different administrations, as well as a three-facet G-study for Paper 5, with interview mode (individual versus group), rater, and occasion as facets, using taped interviews from the June 1990 administration.
2. *The investigation into the comparability of FCE forms.* This will involve two stages: (a) investigation of content and comparability, followed by the establishment of procedures for ensuring comparability of content across forms, and (b) investigation of statistical equivalence of forms.
3. *The investigation into the relationship between test content and test performance.* This will involve both a continuation and extension of the type of analyses of this study's data that have been reported elsewhere and the content analysis of new forms of the FCE.
4. *The investigation into the relationship between test-taker characteristics and test performance.* This will involve the analysis of data on test-taker characteristics in this study as well as the development of a questionnaire to be used to gather such information operationally on a regular basis.

5. *The investigation into the relationship between self-reported test-taking strategies and test performance.*
6. *The setting of standards for the content, design, development, and use of language proficiency tests.* These would initially be standards to be used by Cambridge for its own EFL exams, but would, we hope, provide a basis for developing more general standards for language tests.

Contributions of This Study to the Field of Language Testing

One of the most pressing issues in the field of foreign language testing at present is that of defining the construct "communicative competence" precisely enough to permit its assessment. A related issue involves defining what we mean by a "communicative" or "authentic" test and determining whether test takers perform differentially on "communicative" and "noncommunicative" language tests. These issues are of crucial importance for the development and use of language tests, as considerable effort is currently being expended in developing "communicative" language tests to measure "communicative competence" or "communicative language ability." The content analysis instruments developed as part of the CTCS, based on theoretical models of communicative language ability and test method facets (Bachman, 1990), provide a starting point for accurately describing the content of language tests and for investigating the relationship between test content and test performance.

Furthermore, whereas the focus of the CTCS was not on construct validation, much of the information that was gathered about the measures examined is relevant to the validity of construct interpretations. In this regard, the finding that measures as diverse as those examined in the CTCS tap virtually the same sets of language abilities is remarkable, although not particularly surprising, given the long history of such findings in language testing. At the same time, it is encouraging to find both that the theoretical constructs claimed to inform the measures are reflected, to a large degree, in patterns of performance and that the methodological approaches employed are useful in making these patterns interpretable.

Because the CTCS employed a variety of empirical approaches to research, both qualitative and quantitative, the experience gained may thus be useful not only for continued multimodal research, as has been proposed by Bachman and Clark (1987), but also for future test comparison studies. Although some operational procedures that were planned had to be either changed or abandoned in the course of the study, we believe that in general the CTCS design, procedures, and analyses provide a useful model for the comparison of different batteries of language tests.

Finally, the CTCS explored the complexities of cross-national comparative research, which involve issues such as the types of negotiations and compromises that are necessary in such studies, whether these compromises vitiate or enrich the results of cross-national research, and whether the results are worth the effort.

This complex topic is taken up in Davidson and Bachman (1990). Suffice it here to say that although we feel the CTCS illustrates the benefits to be derived from cross-national comparison studies, we have no delusions of having resolved these issues in this study. However, by bringing them to the fore we believe we have made some contribution to a better understanding of the similarities and differences between two approaches to EFL proficiency testing, an understanding that we hope will spur collaborative projects in which the subjective, qualitative judgments of "experts" are complemented by objective, quantitative research and development methods.

Note

1. Reprinted with permission from *Issues in Applied Linguistics, 1* (1990), 30–55, and based on a paper presented at the 12th Annual Language Testing Research Colloquium, San Francisco, March 1990. The tables also appear in J. H. A. L. DeJong (Ed.), 1990, "The Cambridge-TOEFL Comparability Study: An Example of the Cross-National Comparison of Language Tests," *AILA Review, 7, Standardization in Language Testing*.

References

Alderson, J. C., Henning, G., & Lukmani, Y. (1987, April). *Levels of understanding in reading comprehension tests*. Paper presented at the Ninth Annual Language Testing Research Colloquium, Miami, FL.

Alderson, J. C., & Lukmani, Y. (1986, March). *Reading in a second language*. Paper presented in the Fourth Colloquium on Research on Reading in a Second Language, TESOL convention, Anaheim, CA.

Bachman, L. F. (1990). *Fundamental considerations in language testing*. Oxford: Oxford University Press.

Bachman, L. F., & Clark, J. L. D. (1987). The measurement of foreign/second language proficiency. *Annals of the American Academy of Political and Social Science, 490*, 20–33.

Bachman, L. F., Davidson, F., & Lynch, B. (1988, December). Test method: The context for performance on language tests. Paper presented at the annual meeting of the American Association for Applied Linguistics, New Orleans, LA.

Bachman, L. F., Davidson, F., Lynch, B., & Ryan, K. (1989, March). Content analysis and statistical modeling of EFL proficiency tests. Paper presented at the 11th Annual Language Testing Research Colloquium, San Antonio, TX.

Bachman, L. F., Davidson, F., Ryan, K., & Choi, I.-C. (Forthcoming). *An investigation into the comparability of two tests of English as a foreign language: The Cambridge-TOEFL comparability study: Final report*. Cambridge: University of Cambridge Local Examinations Syndicate.

Bachman, L. F., Kunnan, A., Vanniarajan, S., & Lynch, B. (1988). Task and ability analysis as a basis for examining content and construct comparability in two EFL proficiency test batteries. *Language Testing, 5*, 128–159.

Bachman, L. F., & Palmer, A. S. (1982). The construct validation of some components of communicative proficiency. *TESOL Quarterly, 16*, 449–465.

Carroll, J. B. (1983). Psychometric theory and language testing. In J. W. Oller (Ed.), *Issues in language testing research* (pp. 80–107). Rowley, MA: Newbury House.

Carroll, J. B. (1989). *Exploratory factor analysis programs for the IBM PC (and compatibles)*. Chapel Hill, NC: Author.

Crick, J. E., & Brennan, R.L. (1983). *Manual for GENOVA: A generalized analysis of variance system* (ACT Technical Bulletin No. 43). Iowa City, IA: American College Testing Program.

Davidson, F.,& Bachman, L. F. (1990). The Cambridge-TOEFL comparability study: An example of the cross-national comparison of language tests. *AILA Review, 7*.

Educational Testing Service. (1982). *Test of Spoken English: Manual for score users*. Princeton, NJ: Author.

Educational Testing Service. (1987). *TOEFL test and score manual, 1987-88 edition*. Princeton, NJ: Author.

Educational Testing Service. (1989). *Test of Written English guide*. Princeton, NJ: Author.

Montanelli, R. G., & Humphreys, L. G. (1976). Latent roots of random data correlation matrices with squared multiple correlations on the diagonal. *Psychometrika, 41*, 341–348.

Oller, J. W. Jr. (1979). *Language tests at school: A pragmatic approach*. London: Longman.

Perkins, K., & Linnville, S. E. (1987). A construct definition study of a standardized ESL vocabulary test. *Language Testing, 4*, 125–141.

Sang, F., Schmitz, B., Vollmer, H. J., Baumert, J., & Roeder, P. M. (1986). Models of second language competence: A structural equation approach. *Language Testing, 3*, 54–79.

SAS Institute, Inc. (1988). *SAS guide to personal computers: Language* (Version 6). Cary, NC: Author.

Schmid, J., & Leiman, J. M. (1957). The development of hierarchical factor solutions. *Psychometrika, 22*, 53–61.

Spolsky, B. (1978). Introduction: Linguists and language testers. In B. Spolsky (Ed.), *Approaches to Language testing* (pp. v–x). Arlington, VA: Center for Applied Linguistics.

SPSS Incorporated. (1988a). *SPSS-X user's guide* (3rd ed.). Chicago: Author.

SPSS Incorporated. (1988b). *SPSS/PC+ V2.0 base manual*. Chicago: Author.

SPSS Incorporated. (1988c). *SPSS/PC+ advanced statistics V2.0*. Chicago: Author.

Tucker, L. R., & Finkbeiner, C. T. (1981). *Transformation of factors by artificial personal probability functions* (Research Report 81-58). Princeton, NJ: Educational Testing Service.

University of Cambridge Local Examinations Syndicate. (1988). *Cambridge examinations in English: Survey for 1988*. Cambridge, England: Author.

Wilson, K. M. (1982). *A comparative analysis of TOEFL examinee characteristics, 1977–1979* (TOEFL Research Report 11). Princeton, NJ: Educational Testing Service.

Wilson, K. M. (1987). *Patterns of test taking and score change for examinees who repeat the Test of English as a Foreign Language* (TOEFL Research Report 22). Princeton, NJ: Educational Testing Service.

Appendix 2A:

Correlations Among FCE Papers

	Paper 1	Paper 2	Paper 3	Paper 4	Paper 5
Paper 1	1.00000	—	—	—	—
Paper 2	.58054	1.00000	—	—	—
Paper 3	.70730	.66754	1.00000	—	—
Paper 4	.53710	.49427	.56614	1.00000	—
Paper 5	.46457	.44448	.47369	.49554	1.00000

Note. Listwise $N = 1,332$. All correlations significant at $p \leq .001$.

Appendix 2B:

Correlations Among ETS Tests

	TOEFL 1	TOEFL 2	TOEFL 3	TOEFL TEW	SPEAK Gr.	SPEAK Pr.	SPEAK Fl.	SPEAK Co.
TOEFL 1	1.00000	—	—	—	—	—	—	—
TOEFL 2	.55197	1.00000	—	—	—	—	—	—
TOEFL 3	.56483	.71597	1.00000	—	—	—	—	—
TEW	.44761	.54038	.51739	1.00000	—	—	—	—
SPEAK Gr.	.58395	.43680	.38214	.38866	1.00000	—	—	—
SPEAK Pr.	.58779	.46374	.47350	.45019	.64165	1.00000	—	—
SPEAK Fl.	.61484	.41868	.41163	.43372	.78437	.67494	1.00000	—
SPEAK Co.	.64026	.47326	.44279	.43503	.89268	.75249	.87286	1.00000

Note. Listwise $N = 1,283$. All correlations significant at $p \leq .001$.

Appendix 2C:

Correlations Among FCE Papers and ETS Tests

	TOEFL 1	TOEFL 2	TOEFL 3	TEW	SPEAK Gr.	SPEAK Pr.	SPEAK Fl.	SPEAK Co.	FCE 1	FCE 2	FCE 3	FCE 4	FCE 5
TOEFL 1	1.00000	—	—	—	—	—	—	—	—	—	—	—	—
TOEFL 2	.55354	1.00000	—	—	—	—	—	—	—	—	—	—	—
TOEFL 3	.56500	.71801	1.00000	—	—	—	—	—	—	—	—	—	—
TEW	.43919	.54284	.51782	1.00000	—	—	—	—	—	—	—	—	—
SPEAK Gr.	.58721	.43657	.38292	.38729	1.00000	—	—	—	—	—	—	—	—
SPEAK Pr.	.58578	.47240	.47637	.44754	.64102	1.00000	—	—	—	—	—	—	—
SPEAK Fl.	.61371	.42348	.40753	.42906	.78855	.66837	1.00000	—	—	—	—	—	—
SPEAK Co.	.64193	.47819	.44714	.43305	.89324	.74693	.87416	1.00000	—	—	—	—	—
FCE 1	.60579	.57021	.62738	.44062	.47310	.52405	.50064	.53396	1.00000	—	—	—	—
FCE 2	.53629	.51820	.50162	.47045	.50129	.52807	.48799	.53821	.57632	1.00000	—	—	—
FCE 3	.58680	.62876	.63841	.56657	.49123	.59153	.52199	.54648	.69970	.66234	1.00000	—	—
FCE 4	.61123	.44312	.49670	.42396	.49685	.52697	.52437	.53489	.52980	.49364	.56273	1.00000	—
FCE 5	.55493	.40958	.40419	.36558	.54278	.53077	.56055	.57177	.45530	.45189	.47376	.49156	1.00000

Note. Listwise $N = 1,227$. All correlations significant at $p \leq .001$.

3

Judgments in Language Testing

J. Charles Alderson
University of Lancaster

Language testing is an area of applied linguistics that combines the exercise of professional judgment about language, learning, and the nature of the achievement of language learning with empirical data about students' performances and, by inference, their abilities. This paper addresses the relationship between judgments and empirical data in language testing by reporting on three studies.

The first study investigates the judgments of language professionals about test content and the skills and abilities supposedly tested by certain test items, and compares these judgments with the results of test administrations and the introspections of test takers. The second study compares the judgments that experienced test writers and examination markers make about the difficulty of items with the results of an administration of the items. The third study gathers judgments from language testers and teachers about standards of performance of a given population in a so-called standard-setting exercise, aimed at determining grade boundaries for a public examination. The discussion that follows addresses the value of professional judgments in determining test content, test difficulty, and criterial cutoffs.

The Importance of Judgments in Language Testing

Language testers are frequently required to make professional judgments about test content and test method, and their appropriateness for a given purpose or the extent to which they reflect particular theoretical approaches. Indeed, language testing is an area of applied linguistics that requires judgments at every level of activity and every stage in test development and validation. Testers have to judge whether test specifications are fit for their purpose, whether test content reflects the test's specifications, whether the test method is appropriate for the test's purpose, whether scoring criteria are appropriate, and whether candidates' performances meet those criteria. Judgments abound in language testing and are inevitable, even, as Pilliner pointed out in 1968, in so-called "objective" tests.

Language testing is characterized by its attempts, indeed its determination, to corroborate judgments in some areas—as when scorers make subjective judgments on candidates' performances. In such cases, the usual practice is to estimate the intra- and interrater reliability of the judges' opinions. It is generally recognized that the reliability of professional judgments may vary and that therefore it is important to assess the consistency of these judgments. In other areas of language testing, empirical data commonly replace judgment—as, for example, in the practice of piloting test items to determine their difficulty levels rather than relying on the test constructor's judgments.

Even though studies of the reliability of scorers' judgments—the inter- and intrarater reliability studies referred to above—are common in language testing research, it is unusual to find studies investigating the consistency of other aspects of judgments that constructors have to make. Yet, if judgments pervade the whole process of test design, construction, trialing, validating, and operation, then the potential variability of these judgments is a serious source of error in test measurement and test validity.

In this paper I attempt to add to the understanding of the nature of judgments in language testing by examining underresearched areas where judgments are important. I argue, and demonstrate, that so-called professional judgments are frequently flawed or in serious conflict with other professionals' judgments, and that language testers must be alert to the need to corroborate and validate the professional judgments we so frequently make. The exercise of judgment and the variability of judgments are illustrated in three areas: test content, test and item difficulty, and decisions on grade boundaries.

Study One: Test Content

Part of the process of test construction involves turning intentions into actions: having decided what they want to test, test constructors have to produce items that embody those intentions. Test specifications have to be translated into test items, and an important part of the judgmental process in testing is deciding whether the test adequately realizes the specifications: whether a test item does indeed test what the specifications say it tests.

Alderson and Lukmani (1989) reported on a study in which 10 native speaker judges were asked to decide what skills items in a reading test were testing and whether those skills were higher- or lower-order reading skills. The judges were all experienced teachers of English as a foreign language working at the University of Lancaster, with at least master's-level qualifications in their profession. After an introductory discussion of the notion of reading skills—a concept familiar to all the judges—and of the notion of skill level, whether "lower-order" or "higher-order," all judges completed the same task, which involved them in three separate judgments. First, they read through a test of reading comprehension designed to test a specific set of reading skills and described in their own words the skill tested by each item. Second, they decided whether each item was testing "lower-order" or "higher-order" skills. Third, they received a list of the skills supposedly being tested by the items and were asked to decide, for each item, which of the listed skills was being tested. (For further details, see Alderson and Lukmani, 1989.)

In more than half the items judged, little or no agreement emerged on which skills were being tested or what "level" of skill was involved. For example, Alderson and Lukmani reported, some judges claimed that a given item tested the skill of vocabulary recognition; others, the ability to distinguish and discriminate elements in a context; others, the ability to break entities down into their constituent parts and to perceive relationships; others, the ability to clarify the meaning of complex ideas; and still others, the ability to synthesize and recognize patterns. The 10 judges' descriptions for one item follow.

- Judge 1: Recognition of vocabulary and grammar
- Judge 2: The words "where," "bottom," "Atlantic"; knowledge that settings are early in a narrative
- Judge 3: Scan for specifics, relations in a sentence
- Judge 4: Detailed information, recognize prepositions, links between parts of complex
- Judge 5: Word meaning, text organization, accessibility of "sea-bed" schema
- Judge 6: Inferred meaning; discourse rules regarding mentions
- Judge 7: Direct verbatim extraction of information
- Judge 8: Establish context, lift a phrase direct from text
- Judge 9: Direct reference, intersentence connections
- Judge 10: Understand text links

(Alderson & Lukmani, 1989, p. 263)

The authors concluded that the judges had difficulty agreeing on the skills being tested by particular test items. They recognized, moreover, that there was likely to be a degree of intrarater unreliability in the judgments. If the judges had been asked to repeat their judgments after some lapse of time, they might well have assigned different descriptions to particular items.

In a subsequent study (Alderson, 1988) 17 experienced EFL teachers taking a master's degree in linguistics for English language teaching at Lancaster University were asked to identify which skill from a list of 14 (adapted by Weir, 1983, from Munby, 1978) each item in a 15-item reading test designed by Weir (1983) was testing. The judges also decided whether the skill tested by each item was a higher- or a lower-order skill. Again, the results showed considerable disagreement among the judges as to which skill was being tested by each item. Indeed, in one case no judge agreed with the test constructor on the skill tested by an item, and in no case was there complete agreement, either among the judges or between the judges and the test constructor, on the skill being tested.

Judges also disagreed on the level of skill each item was testing. Some evidence indicated changes of mind as to whether a particular skill was lower or higher order: a judge might say a particular skill as described in the test specifications was lower order but make a different judgment about the level of the item he thought tested that particular skill. The conclusion was that judges could agree neither on what an item was testing nor on what particular skill to assign to a particular test item. Moreover, an examination of the relationship between the judgments of what test items were testing and the empirical item difficulties and discriminations led to the conclusion that no relationship existed between item statistics and what judges claimed an item was testing.

As noted, testing assumes that it is possible to discover what ability a test or an item measures. If, however, judges cannot agree on what an item or test is testing, then we must seriously question the validity of a judgmental approach to content validation. In this event, a strong case exists for seeking other sources of information on a test's content validity, such as the introspective accounts of test takers.

Study Two: Test and Item Difficulty

To examine whether experienced teachers, examiners, and test constructors could accurately predict item and test difficulty from an inspection of items, I enlisted the cooperation of 21 Sri Lankan teachers of English with varying degrees of familiarity with and responsibility for a new National Certificate in English (NCE) test in Sri Lanka. The new test, introduced into Sri Lanka by the Ministry of Education in 1986, was intended to provide a prestigious qualification of proficiency in English for adults outside the formal educational system who wished to enhance their employment prospects by producing evidence of their level of English. (Another purpose of the new test was to provide the opportunity to experiment with innovative testing methods before the introduction of examination reform within the secondary school system.) A restricted number of teachers on the staff of the Curriculum Development Division of the Ministry designed the test, and raters trained and supervised by team leaders scored the examinees' performances.

The 21 teachers who took part in the judgmental task included three highly experienced testers who had been responsible for designing the test paper that was the object of the study, for training markers, and for supervising marking of this test paper; five testers who had written some test items and taken part in the supervision of markers; five testers who had been team leaders during the marking; five minimally trained testers who had been involved in marking the test as part of a team; and three testers with no experience in writing items for the NCE nor in marking the 1986 paper.

Several weeks after marking the examination paper and returning to their normal duties, the testers were given a copy of the 1986 test paper and asked to indicate, against each item, what approximate percentage of the candidates taking the examination they thought would have answered that item correctly. (The test paper consisted of 30 reading items across five subtests, 75 C-test items on three passages, and 60 cloze test items on three passages.) The estimated probability values for each item were then totaled to arrive at estimated subtest difficulties.

The estimated difficulties could thus be compared with the actual difficulties of the items and subtests. The hypothesis was that experienced test designers and examiners would be able to predict item and test difficulty in advance of a test administration. If so, there would be no need to pretest the test items—a finding that would have greatly convenienced the system, as item pretesting was virtually unknown in Sri Lanka. Note that judges were asked not to predict item difficulty but to judge item difficulty after, in most cases, gaining considerable familiarity with candidates' performances on the 1986 paper being studied. Their ability to make accurate judgments would not itself prove their ability to predict difficulty, but their inability to make accurate judgments despite considerable experience with the test's performance would certainly argue against their ability to predict difficulty in advance of test administration!

Table 3-1 presents the correlation matrix for judges' estimates and the empirical item difficulties. Clearly, there was no marked agreement between the judges

Table 3-1

Correlations Between Judges' Estimates of Item Difficulties and Actual Item Difficulties

		Test						
		C-test			Cloze			
Judge	Reading	1	2	3	1	2	3	All tests
1	.38	.67	.60	.41	.58	NS	NS	.49
2	NS	.51	.52	.52	.51	NS	NS	.49
3	.71	.35	.56	.57	.52	NS	.51	.64
4	.61	NS	NS	NS	NS	.46	NS	.52
5	.70	.47	NS	.65	.52	NS	.75	.58
6	.49	.36	.56	.37	NS	.39	.47	.54
7	.35	.44	NS	NS	.50	NS	NS	.51
8	.68	NS	.58	.48	NS	NS	NS	.37
9	.68	NS	.34	.44	NS	NS	NS	.28
10	.32	.39	NS	.42	.52	NS	NS	.33
11	.63	NS	−.48	NS	NS	NS	NS	.36
12	.74	.57	.61	.62	NS	.45	NS	.64
13	.63	.54	NS	NS	NS	NS	NS	.52
14	.69	NS	NS	.57	.43	NS	NS	.45
15	.75	.48	.41	.65	NS	.48	NS	.59
16	.67	.63	.51	.44	NS	NS	NS	.56
17	.68	.51	.34	.54	.81	NS	NS	.45
18	.52	.53	.74	.49	.60	NS	NS	.41
19	.77	NS	.47	NS	.43	NS	.43	.61
20	NS	.58	.50	.48	.52	.53	NS	.52
21	.49	−.40	.53	NS	−.30	NS	NS	.27

Note. NS = not significant.

Table 3-2

Correlations Between Judgments of Highly Experienced and Inexperienced Judges

| | | Test | | | | | |
| | | C-test | | | Cloze | | |
Judges	Reading	1	2	3	1	2	3
Experienced	.79	.63	.71	.61	.68	NS	.45
Inexperienced	.67	NS	.71	.47	.51	NS	NS

Note. NS = not significant.

and the empirical difficulties. Nor was there any discernible tendency for highly experienced testers to predict difficulty better than inexperienced testers (judges 1-3 versus judges 19-21) (Table 3-2).

Although the experienced judges fared slightly better and achieved fewer very low coefficients, they were still far from accurate in their predictions. In general, the difficulties of the C-tests and the cloze tests appear to have been more difficult to predict than those of the reading tests. Nevertheless, although most judges (regardless of experience) seemed better at predicting reading test difficulty, there is no obvious reason why this should have been the case, and they were still far from perfect.

Tables 3-3 and 3-4 present the actual subtest difficulties compared with the mean item difficulties for all judges and for experienced versus inexperienced judges. Whatever patterns are (faintly) discernible in the data, and whatever tentative reasons might be advanced to account for such patterns, both very experienced and inexperienced testers clearly have problems in predicting the difficulty of items and tests. These results justify the recommendation that all test items should be pretested before incorporation into new versions of the NCE in Sri Lanka, on the grounds that the judgments of experienced testers about likely item difficulty are simply too variable and inaccurate to be trustworthy.

Study Three: Deciding on Grade Boundaries

As part of a research project to evaluate a new school-leaving examination in English (in a country whose identity must remain confidential), the principal researchers, of whom I was one, investigated ways to determine cutoff points, or grade boundaries, for the new examination (results had to be reported as Pass, Credit, Distinction, and Fail). The examination represented a radical departure in both content and method from the previous one, and the relevant authorities therefore needed advice on how to establish examination grades.[1] In an attempt to get some notion of criterion referencing into the decision-making process with respect to grade boundaries for the examination, we undertook a small study.

Nineteen individuals—all experienced teachers, and most also experienced

Table 3-3

Actual Test Difficulties and Judged Test Difficulties (%)

| | | | Test | | | | | |
| | | C-test | | | Cloze | | | |
	Reading	1	2	3	1	2	3	All tests
M	50	48	27	30	28	12	27	33
SD	23.9	18.9	18.6	22.7	22.1	11.6	18.8	23.5
Judge								
1	67	67	57	60	64	52	59	61
2	47	35	29	24	16	10	36	29
3	57	38	28	32	18	22	21	33
4	56	53	39	35	20	24	23	38
5	62	46	23	48	37	32	33	41
6	71	50	44	54	36	29	54	50
7	69	50	38	34	11	11	10	34
8	64	86	65	81	82	67	64	73
9	61	49	40	43	50	61	45	50
10	62	25	12	18	20	35	36	31
11	46	8	9	10	21	14	8	18
12	64	68	44	42	52	23	23	47
13	67	66	51	43	58	22	20	48
14	66	56	40	62	53	43	61	55
15	61	46	37	53	46	34	38	46
16	54	60	39	20	36	22	31	38
17	71	91	80	88	62	52	56	72
18	62	44	41	40	49	50	56	49
19	84	77	26	31	47	22	25	47
20	73	58	40	48	43	41	43	51
21	64	62	62	49	55	53	55	57
All judges	63	54	40	43	42	34	38	46
SD	8.7	19.2	16.7	19.3	18.6	16.7	17.1	13.6

Table 3-4

Mean Judgments of Experienced and Inexperienced Judges (%)

| | | Test | | | | | |
| | | C-test | | | Cloze | | |
Judges	Reading	1	2	3	1	2	3
Experienced	57	46	38	39	33	28	39
Inexperienced	74	66	43	42	48	39	41

test designers—were given a copy of the new examination papers (Papers One and Two) and were asked to make three sets of judgments. The judges included experienced and trained language testers, who were closely involved in the development of the new examination, and experienced teachers of English at prestigious schools in the country. The details of the experience and expertise of individuals are unknown but must have varied.

The first set of judgments related to the marks certain stereotypical candidates would gain on each paper. The instructions were as follows:

> Think of pupils you have taught. Think of people who you consider to be just barely a Pass at O-Level English Language. Call them "Bare Pass."

> Think of other pupils who you consider to be only just barely a Credit at O-Level English Language. Call them "Bare Credit."

> Think of a third group of pupils who you consider to be just barely a distinction in O Level English Language. Call them "Bare Distinction."

Judges were asked to consider what mark each category of candidate would achieve on Paper One (out of 60) and Paper Two (out of 140). These judgments were called *global* judgments. In the second set of judgments, we asked the judges to decide the percentage of the same categories of candidates that would answer each question correctly, or, in the case of the writing questions, what score (out of 5 or 10, 15 or 20, depending on the question) each category of candidates would achieve. These item-level judgments were then summed to give an *item-level total* judgment. Finally, we asked judges to say what overall total score (out of 100%) each of the three categories of pupils would achieve. These judgments were labeled *overall total*. The results showed considerable variation in the judgments, both at the global and item levels (Table 3-5). We were, however, able to pool judgments across 19 judges in the case of the global judgments and 14 judges in the case of item-level judgments.[2]

The "traditional" percentage marks are the cutoffs *believed* to have been used by the relevant authorities in determining grade boundaries. These percentages do not appear to have varied with the difficulty of the examination. Whatever variation might have existed in individual judgments, the pooled judgments

Table 3-5

Marks Judged Appropriate for Particular Grade Boundaries and Traditional
Grade Boundaries (%)

	Pass	*Credit*	*Distinction*
Current study			
Global	34	51	71
Item-level	26	51	75
Overall total	30	48	68
Traditional	30	50	75

arrived at in the three different ways agreed considerably when compared with the "traditional" cutoffs. The percentage cutoff judged appropriate, even when judgments were pooled, varied according to the method used to collect the judgments (see Table 3-5). The pooled item-level judgments resulted in an "underestimate" of the cutoff for Bare Pass, and pooled global judgments resulted in an "overestimate" of the cutoff for the same candidates.[3]

Having identified the possible cutoffs, we could then calculate the proportion of candidates gaining each grade for each of these putative decisions, to compare effects. Calculations were based on the distributions of the total population (about 200,000). The consequences of using each set of cutoffs are given in Table 3-6, along with, for comparative purposes, the actual proportions of candidates gaining each grade in three previous years. The proportions of students passing, failing, and so on have varied considerably over the years, obviously because of the rigid application of fixed grade boundaries—assumed to be 30%, 50%, and 75% respectively—without regard for the variation in the difficulty of the set of examinations. (In such a large population, levels of achievement are highly unlikely to vary much from year to year, at least until the recent provision of new textbooks and teacher training can be supposed or shown to have had some impact.) Table 3-6 also shows that the percentage of students failing or gaining a bare pass in the new examination will vary considerably depending on the method used to determine the appropriate cutoff mark.

Clearly, a decision on grade boundaries is a complex matter, and the possibilities are numerous. One can decide to award grades proportionally, so that roughly the same percentage of candidates receives a given grade each year, unless some change in circumstances warrants otherwise. This has obviously not been the practice to date.

Alternatively, one can decide to have the same percentage marks as boundaries as in previous years (i.e., 30%, 50%, 75%). That would give, as indicated above, a failure rate for the new examination of some 66%. However, such a practice

Table 3-6

Proportion of the Population Gaining Each Grade, According to Judges, and Actual Proportions, 1985-1987 (%)

	Pass	Credit	Distinction	Fail
Judgments				
Global	18.1	7.1	2.6	72.2
Item-level	35.8	7.5	2.2	54.5
Overall total	22.1	8.1	3.4	66.4
Actual proportions				
1987	28.6	5.9	2.1	63.4
1986	28.7	8.8	2.1	60.4
1985	15.2	5.0	1.4	78.4
Historical average	23.1	8.3	2.2	66.4

is theoretically justified only if one has reason to believe that the current examination is equivalent in difficulty and reliability to previous exams, which has not been established and which is fairly unlikely—as, indeed, is shown by the fluctuation over time in the proportions of candidates being awarded any given grade.

Another alternative is to take the judgments of experienced teachers and testers, who might be expected in the light of their experience of teaching and of marking exams over a period of time to have internalized a notion of difficulty in relation to candidates' ability. Interestingly, if this course were chosen, the overall total judgments would give results broadly similar to the average historical grade boundaries (66% Failure, 22% Pass, 8% Credit, and 3.4% Distinction, although overall total judgments result in a distinction cutoff mark of 68% rather than the historical 75%).

In the absence of data comparing the difficulty of the 1988 exam with that of previous exams, the assumption that candidates' abilities on the whole have not changed greatly from previous years seems reasonable. Three possible recommendations follow:

1. Trial all future draft examination items alongside equivalent or comparable items from the previous year's examination paper to enable direct comparisons of the difficulty of papers.
2. For the new 1988 examination, retain the grade boundaries of 30%, 50%, and 75%. This would give a failure rate of 66%—higher than in 1986 or 1987, but not by much, and considerably lower than in 1981–1985. Retaining the grade boundaries might be felt justified in the light of the 1988 exam's improved quality and relevance to the use of English.
3. Regard grade boundaries not as fixed for all time but as subject to change depending on the performance of candidates and the difficulty of future items and exams as a whole.

I stress, however, that this research project was intended only to throw some light on ways to gather judgments that might inform decisions on grade boundaries and on the consequences that might flow from using one method rather than another to arrive at possible cutoffs. I do not know the decisions eventually reached by the appropriate authorities, and such decisions were, of course, taken completely independently of any "outside" advice.

Despite the differences among judges in this standard-setting exercise, gathering judgments seemed to have some value: pooling the judgments did not lead to wildly different results from decisions that would have been made using traditional criteria. In this particular circumstance, corroborating data were not available: there were no candidates who had taken the new exam and the previous exam, and although item and test difficulty statistics existed, there was no independent evidence of what constituted an adequate performance at each boundary. Thus one could argue for placing considerable faith in the quality of the pooled judgments, whatever the variation in individual judgments.

Summary and Conclusion

This paper has examined the results of three studies of judgments. In the first study, considerable disagreement was found among judges on what items in reading tests were testing. Even when agreement was discernible, the judges did not necessarily agree with the test constructor on what an item supposedly tested. Nor did their claims relate in any predictable way to item difficulty and discriminations. These discrepancies highlighted the need to corroborate judgments about test content by investigating what test takers reported about their performances and their reasons for their decisions in responding to test items. In the second study, judges were unable to predict with any degree of accuracy the difficulty of test items and subtests. The results established the need to pretest items and subtests, independently of the opinions of test constructors, as to item difficulty. In the third study, the judgments gathered varied considerably, and even the pooling of judgments resulted in different recommended cutoffs depending on the method used to gather the judgments.

In the third study the judgments gathered could be accepted with some caution in the absence of other data on the appropriateness of cutoffs. In the second study the judgments had to be rejected as a basis for decisions about items. And in the first study recourse to different data sources was necessary to obtain a clearer picture of what was being tested.

In the first study, however, some of the variation in judgments admittedly could have resulted from inadequate test specifications or models of the reading process. That is, the assumption that one can isolate and test "enabling skills" separately probably was wrong. Rather, test takers most likely use a variety of skills in some as yet not-understood fashion (but probably in an integrated way) when answering reading test items. Thus gathering judgments may have led to further insights into test design and to the need for a revision of test specifications.

Similarly in the second study, the comparison of judgments with empirical difficulties highlights the need not only to pretest items to establish their difficulty levels but also to provide feedback to item writers in an attempt to train them to predict item difficulty more accurately. The third study reveals the difficulty of making criterion-referenced cutoffs for grade boundaries and highlights the need for further research in the area.

All three studies present evidence on the usefulness and limitations of gathering judgments from professional testers. There is a clear need, in all cases involving judgments, for corroboration of the accuracy of the judgments before we accept that they are valid. We need to ensure that all our judgments, not just the judgments of markers, at all stages of the test construction and validation process are open to scrutiny and challenge. It is essential to investigate and establish the reliability, validity, and accuracy of professional judgments in language testing and to identify alternative procedures and sources of information in cases where judgments have been found unsatisfactory.

Notes

1. In the operational circumstances it was impossible to administer both new and old examinations to a sample of students to determine the comparability of examinations.

2. In the latter case, obvious inconsistencies were omitted, for example, where a judge indicated that a Bare Pass pupil would receive a higher score for an item than a Bare Credit pupil would. In such cases, it was assumed that the judge had misunderstood the instructions, and the judge was omitted from the analyses.

3. However, remember that no independent data are available on what the cutoffs "should" be.

References

Alderson, J. C. (1988, March). *Testing reading comprehension skills.* Paper presented at the Sixth Colloquium on Research in Reading in a Second Language, TESOL Convention, Chicago.

Alderson, J. C., & Lukmani, Y. (1989). Cognition and reading: Cognitive levels as embodied in test questions. *Journal of Reading in a Foreign Language, 5*, 253–270.

Munby, J. (1978). *Communicative syllabus design.* Cambridge: Cambridge University Press.

Pilliner, A. E. G. (1968). Subjective and objective testing. In A. Davies (Ed.), *Language testing symposium: A psycholinguistic approach* (pp. 19–35). Oxford: Oxford University Press.

Weir, C. J. (1983). *Identifying the language problems of overseas university students in tertiary education in the UK.* Unpublished doctoral thesis, Institute of Education, University of London.

4

Testing the Specificity of ESP Reading Skills

Thom Hudson
University of Hawai'i at Manoa

The concerns addressed in this paper emerged from attempts to incorporate the interactive approach to reading into English for specific purposes (ESP) reading materials and syllabi and into testing programs in the ESP reading context. Two general issues are addressed here. First, how can we define second language reading skills, specifically in an ESP context? Second, what role can item response theory (IRT) statistical approaches play in examining the levels of skill processing involved in ESP reading skills?

Both issues are related to a growing realization that the current analogy of reading as an interaction of top-down and bottom-up processes and skills is a restricting heuristic. The processes and skills are certainly interactive, but it may be time to think about the interaction as other than top-down and bottom-up, at least for all but readers of very low ability. Instead, we may need to emphasize the overlapping parallel interactions between language skills, interactions that are independent of skill levels designated as higher or lower, top-down or bottom-up. This emphasis may simply be a recognition that there is more variation within skill levels than between levels of reading skills. As a consequence, we need to reexamine models using levels, indeed most of those using discrete categories.

This paper first discusses the background of the interactive approach to reading and its notions of top-down and bottom-up processes, as well as definitional problems in the use of terms such as *skills*, *subskills*, and *processes*. An examination follows of the role of IRT in determining which levels of skills may exist. Finally, it will report on a set of reading tests administered to a group of native Spanish-speaking chemical engineering students to examine the two concerns mentioned above.

Research Question and Background

The concern with defining reading skills comes from current interactive views of reading. As Carrell (1988) notes, schema-theory research has shown that the most efficient processing of text is interactive; that is, both top-down and bottom-up processes are incorporated. She defines the two processes in the following conventional way.

> Top-down is the making of predictions about the text based on prior experiences or background knowledge, and then checking the text for confirmation or refutation of those predictions. Bottom-up processing is decoding individual linguistic units (e.g. phonemes, graphemes, words) and building textual meaning from the smallest units to the largest, and then modifying preexisting background knowledge and current predictions on the basis of information encountered in the text. (p. 101)

As these two levels interact, according to Stanovich (1980), a pattern of comprehension is synthesized based on information from several sources. This interaction allows readers to compensate for deficits in one area by relying on strengths in other areas. He notes that "the compensatory assumption states that a deficit in any knowledge source results in a heavier reliance on other knowledge sources regardless of their level in the processing hierarchy" (Stanovich, 1980, p. 63). However, it is not assumed that a deficit in a knowledge source, or skill, necessarily represents a constant deficit in that area. That is, a deficit at one time in vocabulary or grammar that causes a heavier reliance on, say, knowledge of text structure or application of background knowledge does not mean that the vocabulary or grammar skill is a level that is unitarily deficient. Nevertheless, the reading literature implies, if only by omission, that the two types of processing represent levels of some sort. Indeed, in the quotation above Stanovich discusses the skills in terms of their "level in the processing hierarchy" as if they are ordered levels.

Two basic questions have arisen from attempts to incorporate the interactive approach into explanations of second language reading and development of course materials. The first is initially a definitional issue that can be verified empirically by answering the second question. First, what are skills, subskills, processing strategies, and knowledge sources? Second, what kinds of compensation can take place and what kinds cannot? Involved with this second question is the issue of what a level is. That is, are any of the lower-level skills prerequisite to reading, such that no compensation can occur? How can we operationally define the levels, and what is meant by level?

In attempting to answer the first question, it should be kept in mind that the terms *skills, subskills, processing strategies, ability,* and what Stanovich (1980) identifies as *knowledge* sources are terms used variably in the applied linguistics literature. In general their use depends on whether the term refers to a language component or to an individual reader or speaker's ability to perform. Richards, Platt, and Weber (1985) state that language skills are ". . . the mode or manner in which language is used. Listening, speaking, reading and writing are generally called the four language skills. . . . Often skills are divided into subskills, such as discriminating sounds in connected speech, or understanding relations within a sentence" (p. 160). Harris and Hodges (1981) define skill as "an acquired ability to perform well; proficiency" (p. 298). Thus the term *skill* can relate either to a particular language modality or to the facility with which the language user applies the language area. Additionally, the term *processing strategies* is often seen as relating to both of the above views of skills. For example, while discussing problems associated with Goodman's psycholinguistic approach, Grabe (1988) states there are questions about ". . . how and to what degree literate second language readers employ lower-level processing strategies, and how these skills interact with higher-level (top-down) strategies" (p. 57). From that point of view, skills are seen as equivalent to processing strategies and again are referred to as being embedded in levels. Harris and Hodges (1981) define subskill as "a skill which is part of a more complex skill or body of skills" (p. 316). Thus whether an area of language is a skill or a subskill may depend on how closely the language area is examined.

In this paper, the term *skill* designates areas of second language reading, such as reading comprehension, grammar knowledge, and vocabulary knowledge. The term *subskill* will be used to designate components of the skills. For example, within the skill of reading comprehension, subskills are identifying the main idea, locating specific information, using a graph or chart, and so on. Within the skill of grammar, subskills are the use of simple verb tenses, modals, or the passive voice. Within the skill of vocabulary, the subskills are identifying a particular idiom, inferring the meaning of a term from interclausal context, and so on. Additionally, the term *ability* here designates the second meaning of skill, related to the difficulty or facility the language user demonstrates in processing the skill.

The second question above involves the basic issue of compensation and its relation to levels of skill or ability. In the interactive model, "a pattern is synthesized based on information provided simultaneously from several knowledge sources (e.g., feature extraction, orthographic knowledge, lexical knowledge, syntactic knowledge, semantic knowledge)" (Stanovich, 1980, p. 35). In interactive models, "semantic processes constrain the alternatives of lower levels but are themselves constrained by lower level analyses. Thus each level of processing is not merely a data source for higher levels, but instead seeks to synthesize the stimulus based on its own analysis and the constraints imposed by both higher and lower-level processes" (Stanovich, 1980, p. 35). Again, the focus is on levels of processes assumed to exist in a hierarchy. In effect, the discussions imply that there are implicationally ordered higher and lower levels of skills, in a taxonomic sense, that can, however, interact and compensate one another in certain contexts.

This interactive process, however, is somewhat different at times for second language readers. According to many researchers, second language readers have difficulty using the interactive strategy efficiently and effectively. Carrell (1983) notes that foreign language readers tend to be linguistically bound to a text. They may process the literal language of the text, but they may not make the necessary connections between the text and the appropriate background—even when they are explicitly provided with that appropriate background information. That is, given an explicit context and a transparent text, English as a second language

(ESL) readers fail to tap their background knowledge. The reverse can happen, she notes, in that some second language readers attempt to use only a top-down approach. Consequently, the compensation on which first language readers rely apparently does not take place with many second language readers. Attempts to explain this phenomenon have claimed that perhaps too much emphasis has been placed on top-down skills in second language reading and too little on bottom-up. Eskey and Grabe (1988), for example, state that "an interactive model would suggest that reading requires a relatively high degree of grammatical control over structures that appear in whatever readings are given to ESL students" (p. 226). If so, there would appear to be prerequisite levels in second language reading, such as low-level grammar skills. That is, if reading requires a relatively high degree of grammatical control over structures that appear in readings, then grammar would constitute a lower level. For example, as Eskey and Grabe indicate, in terms of instruction:

> some time must be devoted in reading classes to such relatively bottom-up concerns as rapid and accurate identification of lexical and grammatical forms. Even students who have developed strong top-down skills in their native languages may not be able to transfer these higher-level skills to a second language context until they have developed a stronger bottom-up foundation of basic identification skills. (p. 227)

A similar question concerning ordered levels arises in terms of "reading skills." Do they constitute prerequisite levels? Researchers have had little luck in identifying particular reading levels. In their research, Alderson and Lukmani conclude that ". . . one should not be inferring from poor performance on lower order questions an inability to perform well on higher order questions. This would suggest that there is no implicational scale in reading in a second language such that one needs lower order abilities before one can progress to higher order questions" (1989, p. 269). Hudson (1989) found great overlap in the difficulty of reading tasks that had been hypothesized to represent differing levels of ability. No hierarchy of skills seemed apparent. However, the reading tasks in that study involved students from three different language and cultural groups. If cognitive skills are present, their ordering may be language or culture specific to some extent.

In the context of instruction, reading programs and ESP reading projects in particular frequently focus on specific reading skills such as locating specific information, determining vocabulary in context, and so on. However, it is not clear how the notion of "specific skills" fits within the context of interactive models of reading. That is, learners' abilities in particular skills may develop differentially, both in terms of where they are located on a continuum of difficulty and ease and in terms of how narrow or wide a spectrum of difficulty they encompass. For example, the ability to recognize correct tense or aspect from context may have a more narrow ability band than the ability to recognize logical connectors in an extended text or the ability to find main ideas in a reading passage. This differential band width has implications for ESP reading instruction and syllabus design as well as for the development of criterion-referenced and placement tests.

Thus we are left with the major theoretical issue: what precisely is meant by higher-level and lower-level skills, and how do reading abilities represent those skills? First, it would be valuable to identify the skills and levels of processing. If we cannot determine levels of processing or skills, however, we may have to abandon the terminology of top-down and bottom-up as a useful heuristic. The terminology itself may in part divert us from research into potentially more informative analogies.

Defining Skills and Skill Levels

To determine the extent to which there are narrowly defined prerequisite skills that are acquired sooner or later than other skills and the extent to which there are broader interacting and compensating skills, it is necessary to address two issues. First, it is necessary to determine whether there are reading skills that are ordered in terms of their difficulty. Second, it is necessary to determine the extent to which these skills are narrow bands or broad bands overlapping other skills. How, though, can these skills or levels, or the absence of skills or levels, be determined? Latent trait or item response theory (IRT) seems a potentially valuable approach.

Item Response Theory

IRT models are a family of probabilistic models that assume differing numbers of item parameters in item analysis and item selection. The two models used in the study described here are the two-parameter and one-parameter logistic models. IRT begins with a mathematical statement as to how each expected response depends on level of ability. This relationship is shown by the item response function, or item characteristic curve (ICC). An ICC relates an examinee's probability of answering the item correctly to the ability measured by the set of items in the test (Birnbaum, 1968; Hambleton, 1979). Essentially, the two models provide a difficulty level for each test item that is on the same scale as the ability level of the examinees. A primary advantage of the IRT difficulty estimate is that, because it presents the item difficulty in terms of the examinee's ability rather than traditional proportion-correct item facilities, the distances between any two items is on a scale relative to the difficulty levels of all possible items. This difficulty level is designated by β. Although the level theoretically extends from minus infinity to plus infinity, in practice the range of β is from about -2 to $+2$. If the value of β is -2, the items are very easy for the group of examinees; if the values are around $+2$, the items are very difficult (Hambleton & Cook,

1977). Additionally, the two-parameter model provides a measure of the item discrimination, or slope, designated by α. This measure also theoretically has a scale ranging from minus infinity to plus infinity. High values of α produce very steep ICCs, and low values produce ICCs that increase more gradually as a function of ability (Hambleton & Cook, 1977). Thus items that have a slope, α, with a high value discriminate over a narrow range of abilities around the item difficulty level, whereas those items with a lower value for α discriminate over a broader ability band. Examples of ICCs for six hypothetical test items are shown in Figure 4-1.

In the figure, each item has a difficulty of 0, the average difficulty for all items. Likewise, the average ability level for all examinees is 0. The probability of an examinee at ability level 0 answering the items with a difficulty of 0 correctly is 50%. Item 6, with a slope value (α) of 1.40, discriminates very well between ability levels $-.70$ to .70 but discriminates little at values lower than $-.70$ or higher than .70. However, Item 1 has an α value of .30; it does not discriminate strongly at any particular point on the scale but discriminates about the same amount across all ability levels.

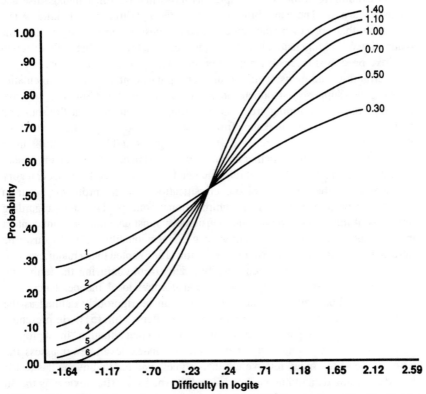

Figure 4-1. Sample item characteristic curves demonstrating the slope effect for discrimination.

Unidimensionality in Reading

Closely linked to the applicability of IRT models to measurement of reading are concerns of "unidimensionality" (see Hattie, 1985). That is, as with all approaches to testing, a critical assumption is that the items on a test or subtest measure only one dominant attribute or trait. However, this assumption is considered stronger for IRT than for traditional approaches. In examining reading skills, researchers naturally face the question of whether or not reading is a unidimensional trait and, consequently, whether IRT can be used to investigate the relative ordering of reading skills. However, there are few, if any, adequate definitions of unidimensionality or explanations of the consequences are of a violation of the unidimensionality assumption. Hambleton and Rovinelli (1986) pointed out that most definitions of unidimensionality are typically abstract and nonoperational. A typical definition, they indicated, is "A set of test items is unidimensional when a single trait can explain or account for examinee test performance" (p. 287). This definition is less than satisfactory from an operational point of view. Clearly, not all differences in dimensionality are the same, particularly in examining abilities as complex as those involved in language use and language learning. There are differences in degree and differences in kind. A test with items that are not of the same difficulty does not necessarily violate the assumption of unidimensionality. However, items that require distinctly different cognitive processes to answer a question may violate the assumptions.

Determining unidimensionality from a conceptual point of view is problematic. For example, suppose our dimension of interest is *birdness*. Suppose we have thrushes, finches, hummingbirds, and penguins. We can see that thrushes and finches are different only in degree from the unidimensional hypothetical bird we picture when we think of birdness, whereas penguins and hummingbirds differ in both degree and kind. Whether hummingbirds and penguins violate unidimensionality and, consequently, would be included in or excluded from the category will depend on the purposes of our classification. Similar problems occur in determining whether reading is a unidimensional concept. Decisions regarding violations of the assumption of unidimensionality must take into account content and descriptive concerns. The notion of unidimensionality must obviously be more than a statistical notion. Moreover, Hattie (1985) noted that a major problem in assessing indices of unidimensionality results from confusing the term with such other terms as reliability, internal consistency, local independence, and homogeneity. For Hattie, "unidimensionality can be rigorously defined as the existence of one latent trait underlying the set of items" (p. 151). He presented 30 approaches to testing unidimensionality and noted that although "most proposers do not offer a rationale for their choice of index, even fewer assess the performance of the index relative to other indices, and hardly anyone has tested the indices using data of known dimensionality" (p. 140). After reviewing the 30 approaches, Hattie concluded that ". . . there are still no known satisfactory indices. None of the attempts to investigate unidimensionality has provided clear decision criteria for determining it" (p. 158).

Given the problems in statistically confirming or disconfirming the unidimensionality of a skill, as well as problems with conceptually establishing whether a language skill is unidimensional or not, we need to have compelling reasons to define reading as multidimensional before generally rejecting the use of IRT. Approaches do exist, however, for addressing specific instances of items that apparently violate unidimensionality in terms of the construct measured by all items on the test. One such approach involves application of a chi-square statistic and an item fit statistic that indicate whether a particular item has a response pattern consistent with the response pattern obtained on all other items given the examinee's ability levels. Items that do not fit the particular model are deleted from the analysis. Thus, although it does not address the overall theoretical issue of whether reading, or indeed any language skill area, is unidimensional or multidimensional, the approach does operationally define unidimensionality in terms of the response patterns of the particular test items used to investigate reading skills.

The Role of IRT in Defining Skills and Skill Levels

An empirical examination of skills should address two concerns. First, skills will have narrow ability band widths, though these ability widths may vary. That is, although skills should be narrowly defined, there is no reason to assume that all skills will be of the same width. For example, consider the following illustrations of hypothetical reading skills.

The skills in Figure 4-2 represent ordered skills with relatively similar widths. The widths are not identical but are similar. In Figure 4-3, on the other hand, not only do the various skills overlap, but many have very wide band widths. The overlapping skills represent compensatory skills; those that do not overlap represent separable skills. Second, the items that represent a skill should have high discrimination indices at their level of difficulty. For example, if items in Figure 4-2 that represent Skills D and E have low item discriminations, then these two skills may indeed not be separate skills. On the other hand, if they have very high item discriminations, we can speak with more assurance about their separateness.

IRT procedures can be useful in determining whether the two conditions above have been met. Carroll (1989) investigated the identification and definition of abilities, and ways to relate abilities to the cognitive strategies involved in performing intellectual tasks. He noted that "the person characteristic function is directly useful in defining an ability, in the sense that variations in ability are indexed by reference to the position parameter β of this function, which in turn is referenced to specifiable variations in a task characteristic" (p. 150). He further

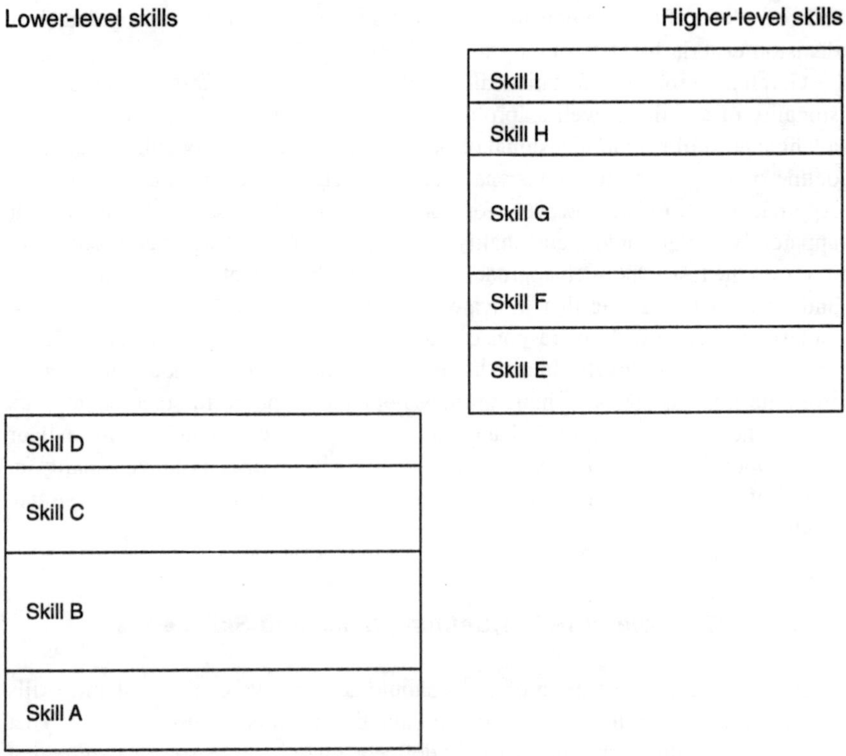

Lower-level skills   Higher-level skills

Skill I
Skill H
Skill G
Skill F
Skill E

Skill D
Skill C
Skill B
Skill A

Figure 4-2.   A distribution of hypothetical reading skills.

speculated about the status of the slope parameter α: "There is a clear possibility that this represents a property of the task variation or difficulty dimension, not a property of individual differences" (p. 150). Similarly, it is proposed here to use item difficulty as an indicator of the band width of skill difficulty and item slope (discrimination) as an indicator of the definability of a skill or prerequisite knowledge source. In examining items that represent differing reading skills in this way, we may be able to determine whether certain skill areas are less prone to compensatory processing than others. The initial hypotheses follow:

1. A skill or subskill will have a narrow band width of difficulty.
2. Skills or subskills may be at different levels depending on whether their general dispersion is at a more difficult or less difficult location on the difficulty continuum.
3. A skill or subskill will have very discriminating items, that is, high slope values.

Note that the relationships that emerge here refer merely to the subject's ability to perform some category of tasks. There is no implication here about acquisition processes or how the particular relationships have developed; that is, no assump-

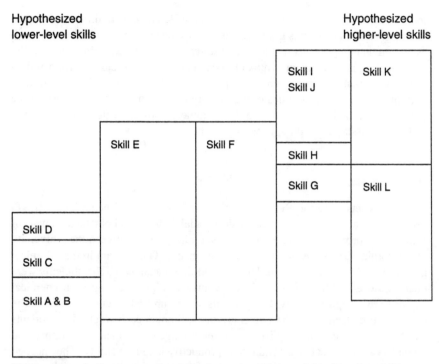

Figure 4-3. A distribution of undefined, overlapping hypothetical reading skills.

tions are made regarding such issues as the role of instruction or whether the mastering of one skill causes the mastering of another skill or is merely incidental.

To examine the existence of skills or subskills as cognitively real, it may be useful to examine a homogeneous group in terms of language background and background knowledge. That is, Barnhardt (n.d.) has criticized studies of second language classrooms because they typically include speakers with several different language backgrounds. We should not assume that the particular skills used, or their relative orders, are the same across languages. Thus research in second language classes may obscure the actual skills used by employing designs that lump speakers of several languages together.

Method

The study described here examined the test results for native Spanish-speaking chemical engineering students who took English for science and technology tests. It used two-parameter β difficulty and α discrimination estimates to examine the relationships among items that test (a) the ability to determine grammar points from context, (b) reading comprehension of specific information and main ideas, and (c) general reading ability as indicated on multiple-choice cloze tests. In looking at these three skill areas, the study considered skills traditionally viewed as low-level skills, such as grammar, as well as those viewed as high level, such as comprehending the gist of a text. The study also investigated interactive skills, such as using knowledge of syntax or vocabulary to understand the propositional information that requires interclausal processing. The test results are examined both in terms of the difficulties of the three types of items and of the slope of the items. Additionally, both one- and two-parameter indices of item fit are used to address the issue of unidimensionality of the data set.

Subjects

The subjects were the Reading English for Science and Technology (REST) Project students at the Universidad de Guadalajara throughout their course of study in the project. The REST Project is a joint project between the University of California, Los Angeles, and the Universidad de Guadalajara in the Chemical Engineering Department of the Universidad de Guadalajara. The students were in their 3rd and 4th years of a 5-year course leading to a degree in chemical engineering. Approximately 150 students were enrolled at any one time. The courses were electives in the university taken 5 hours each week. The students had had 4 or 5 years of English as a foreign language in their preparatory and secondary schools yet had essentially no productive language ability. They needed to be able to read English in order to gain information from journal articles at the University and when they got jobs. The materials in the course were developed around thematic units corresponding to undergraduate course content. Instruction presented grammar and vocabulary only as necessary for comprehension of the texts. Data for the study were collected between September 1987 and November 1989. That is, the students were tested at the beginning of their study, midway through their study, and at the end of their 2-year course.

Materials

The students took three-part reading comprehension tests, each 55 items long with an additional 10 linking items. Each form included a 30-item contextualized grammar test (including the 10 linking items), a 10-item reading comprehension test, and a 25-item general ability multiple-choice cloze test. The grammar subtest contained items like the following:

When a fluid contains abrasive particles, the valve chosen ＿＿＿＿＿＿ have a flow path with a smooth contour to minimize turbulence and impingement.

    (a) which
    (b) should
    (c) therefore
    (d) do

The reading comprehension subtests contained photocopies of texts taken from chemical engineering or technical publications. The passages were preceded by items asking for general comprehension of the purpose of the passage as well as specific information. Samples of the texts, which were not simple, are in Appendix 4A.

The multiple-choice cloze subtest was constructed from a passage selected from a chemical engineering or technical text. The deleted terms included phrases, nouns, adjectives, logical connectors, and so on. This subtest was designed to serve as a measure of general reading ability, not strictly a measure of comprehension of information. The topics for the multiple-choice cloze tests included (a) safety around hazardous materials, (b) methods for meter calibration, and (c) computer set-up in the laboratory.

The three subtests thus examine grammar, reading comprehension, and general reading ability. The results of the items were analyzed using a one- and two-parameter model via PC-BILOG 3 (Mislevy & Bock, 1989). Items deemed misfitting by both analyses were discarded. A two-parameter analysis was considered appropriate, with 200 subjects taking each form of the test, given the homogeneity of the subjects and test content.[1] The tests were linked to one another by the linking items in the following way. Forms A and B were run as two forms of the same test; then Forms A and C were run as two forms of the same test. The common calibrations on these two runs were then linked using Quattro 5.0. There were 14 linking items for Form A to Form B and 7 linking items for Form A to Form C. Descriptive statistics for the test results are presented in Table 4-1. The Kuder-Richardson 20 reliabilities were .83, .89, and .91. On each test form, the multiple-choice cloze was the most difficult, the reading comprehension test was the least difficult, and the grammar test fell in between.

Item Types and Skill Definition

To examine the items as skills or subskills, the items were categorized according to the task or item type they represented. For the reading subtests, the test items were categorized as requiring:

- Specific direct information (SDIN): a fact contained in the passage that can be answered by a single term or number
- Specific restatement (SRST): a phrase or clause taken directly from the text
- Gist (GIST): a question that can be answered by comprehending a section of the text and selecting the appropriate answer that is a paraphrase of the text
- Graph/chart (GRAPH; CHART): a question that directed the students to a chart, illustration, or graph to answer the question.

For the grammar subtests, the items were categorized as requiring:

- Simple verb tense (Vsimp): tenses including simple present (Vspr), copula (Vcop), and simple past (Vspst)
- Connectors (CONN): logical connectors such as *because, thus, therefore,* and *consequently*

Table 4-1

Descriptive Statistics for Tests A, B, and C

Statistic	Total test	Grammar	Reading	Multiple-choice cloze
		Form A		
N	227	—	—	—
K	55	24	10	21
M	31	13.2	6.8	11.0
SD	9.65	4.5	1.9	4.6
KR-20	.89	—	—	—
		Form B		
N	205	—	—	—
K	53	24	10	19
M	30	13.4	6.6	10.0
SD	10.3	5.2	2.5	3.9
KR-20	.91	—	—	—
		Form C		
N	227	—	—	—
K	49	22	10	17
M	30.8	14.0	7.5	9.3
SD	7.03	4.0	1.7	2.7
KR-20	.83	—	—	—

Note. KR-20 = Kuder-Richardson reliability formula 20.

- Passive voice (PASS): the passive voice
- Modal (MODL): modal verbs
- Perfective (Vprf): perfect tenses
- Relative pronouns (RLPRO): pronouns in relative clauses, including reduced relative forms (e.g., both ". . . those features which definitely distinguish . . ." and ". . . of the liquid, caused either by changes in . . ." are included in this category)
- Progressive (PROG): present or past progressive.

The multiple-choice cloze subtests were categorized using the definitions from Hale et al. (1989):

- Reading comprehension/grammar (RC/GR): Understanding propositional information at an interclausal level, but answering a question also emphasizes knowledge of syntax rather than lexicon. (Example: A similar process recycles helium by deep-sea divers; {it/he/then/however} is being tested by Statoil, the Norwegian state-owned oil company.)
- Reading comprehension/vocabulary (RC/VO): The problem is one of long-range (i.e., interclausal) constraints, but a lexical choice is required to solve it. (Example: This change in resistance unbalances the {circuit/tube/equip/convert} causing a meter deflection that indicated the concentration.)
- Grammar/reading comprehension (GR/RC): The source of item difficulty involves relatively short-range grammatical constraints—usually a few

words on either side of the blank or within a single grammatical phrase or clause. The item primarily requires knowledge of surface syntax, and reading comprehension is involved only to the degree that the reader must understand within-clause propositional information. (Example: Development starts with a definition. First, {however/define/predicted/data} the project scope.)

- Vocabulary/reading comprehension (VO/RC): The primary aspect of this category is vocabulary (including idioms and collocations), although it also invokes reading comprehension in that the reader must understand the information presented within clause boundaries. (Example: Their efforts could make it easier to {lung/liquid/invest/deliver} oxygen-enriched air to hospitals.)

Scoring

The ratings were made by three experts in the field of ESL. Items were placed into the category indicated by at least two of the three raters. In two instances, the items were placed into three different categories. In those instances, the items were categorized by whether the first segment they were assigned was clausal or interclausal, and whether they were predominately VO or RC. For example, if an item received the ratings GR/RC, VO/RC, and RC/GR, the item was designated GR/RC because it was determined to be a grammar item by two raters and a noninterclausal item by two raters.

Results

The item distribution (shown in Figure 4-4) generally confirms that Reading is the least difficult test, followed by Grammar and multiple-choice Cloze. The difficulty of Grammar, Reading, or Global Reading ability falls into neither top-down nor bottom-up levels; there is extensive overlap.

Item Difficulty Distribution

The distribution of the items in the three skill areas into subskill areas is presented in Figure 4-5. There are two areas to examine in the figure: the width of the distribution of item difficulties and the location of the distribution on the difficulty continuum. The hypothesis was that the width of the difficulty distribution relates to whether there is a definable skill or not and that the location of the distribution on the difficulty continuum indicates whether there are levels of skills or not.

Within the reading skill, the four skill areas all have about the same width of difficulty distribution, although SRST has a narrower band than the others (SDIN = 2.4, SRST = 1.8, GRAPH = 2.9, GIST = 2.05). However, in the grammar

Subtest

	Reading		Grammar		Cloze	

Item difficulty value

-3.00 SDIN (Reading)
-2.75 SDIN (Reading)
-2.50 SDIN SDIN (Reading)
-2.25 GRAPH SDIN (Reading) ; Vspr (Grammar)
-2.00 CHART (Reading) ; Vspr (Grammar)
-1.75 SRST SRST SDIN (Reading) ; CONN (Grammar) ; VO/RC VO/RC VO/RC (Cloze)
-1.50 SDIN SRST GRAPH SRST (Reading) ; PASS PASS MODL (Grammar) ; RC/VO RC/GR GR/RC (Cloze)
-1.25 GIST (Reading) ; PASS PASS (Grammar) ; RC/VO RC/VO (Cloze)
-1.00 SDIN SRST SDIN SRST SRST (Reading) ; PASS Vspr CONN Vspr (Grammar) ; GR/RC GR/RC (Cloze)
-.75   GIST GIST (Reading) ; Vcop (Grammar) ; RC/VO RC/GR VO/RC (Cloze)
-.50   SRST (Reading) ; PASS MODL Vspr Vsbst PASS MODL Vspr (Grammar) ; VO/RC VO/RC RC/GR RC/VO RC/VO VO/RC GR/RC VO/RC RC/VO (Cloze)
-.25   RLPRO Vcop Vspr RLPRO CONN CONN Vcop (Grammar) ; RCVO RC/VO (Cloze)
 0.00 GR/RC (Grammar) ; RC/GR (Cloze)

(Figure: plot of item difficulty values by subtest and item type across Reading, Grammar, and Cloze.)

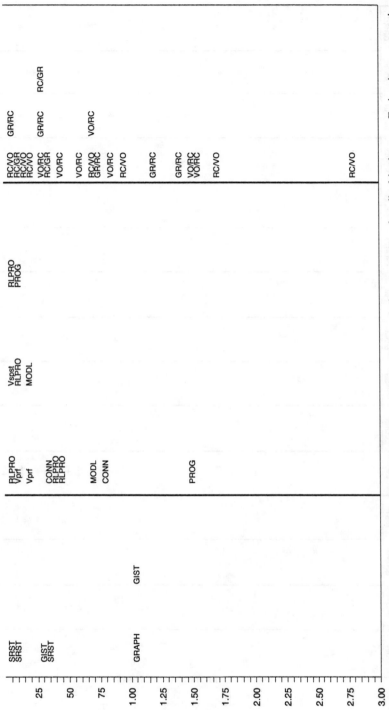

Figure 4-4. Distribution of subtest items by difficulty (two-parameter). Item designators are as described in the text. Easiest items are at the top of the figure; most difficult items are at the bottom.

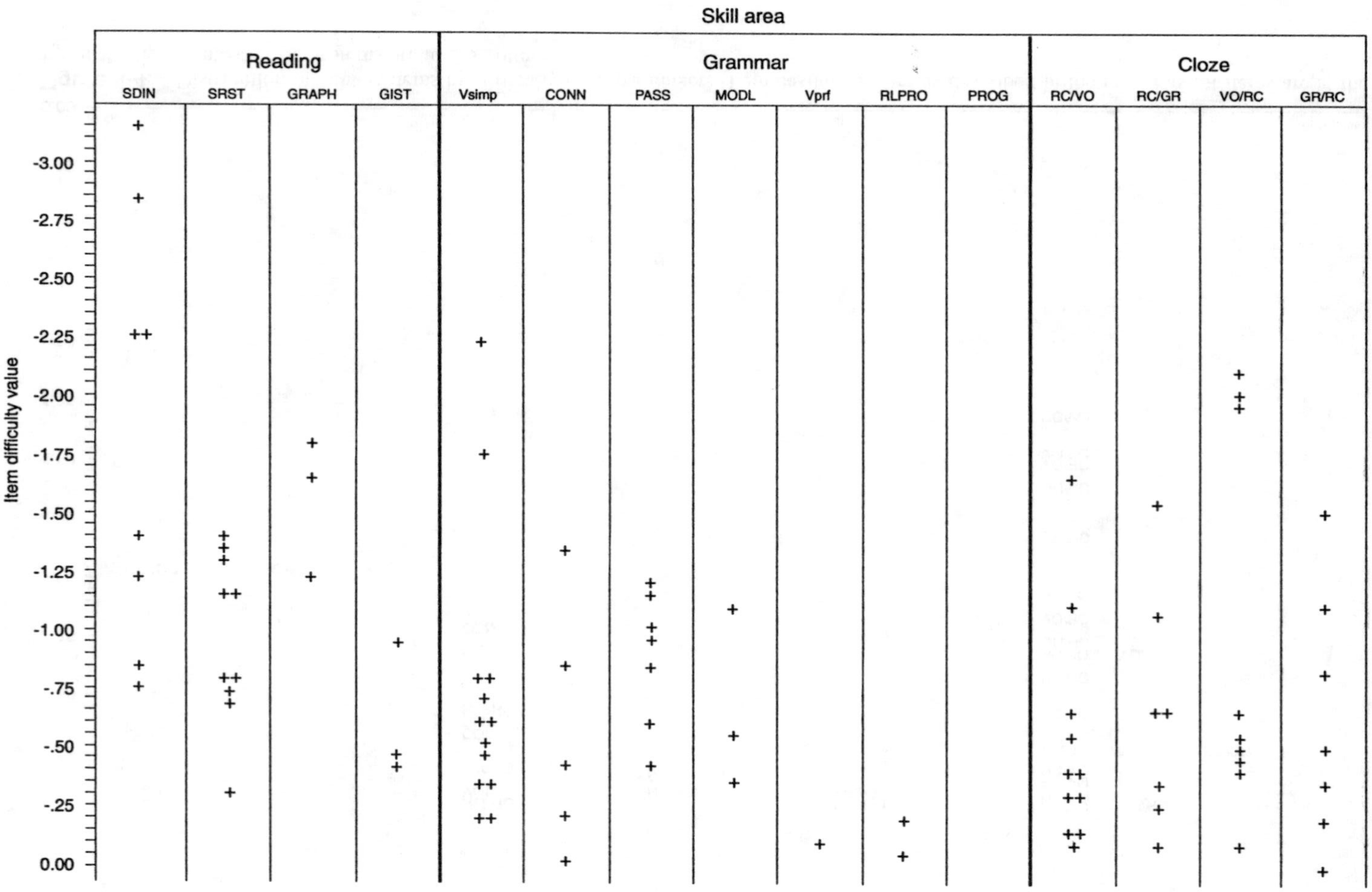
Skill area
Reading
Grammar
Cloze
SDIN
SRST
GRAPH
GIST
Vsimp
CONN
PASS
MODL
Vprf
RLPRO
PROG
RC/VO
RC/GR
VO/RC
GR/RC
Item difficulty value
-3.00
-2.75
-2.50
-2.25
-2.00
-1.75
-1.50
-1.25
-1.00
-.75
-.50
-.25
0.00

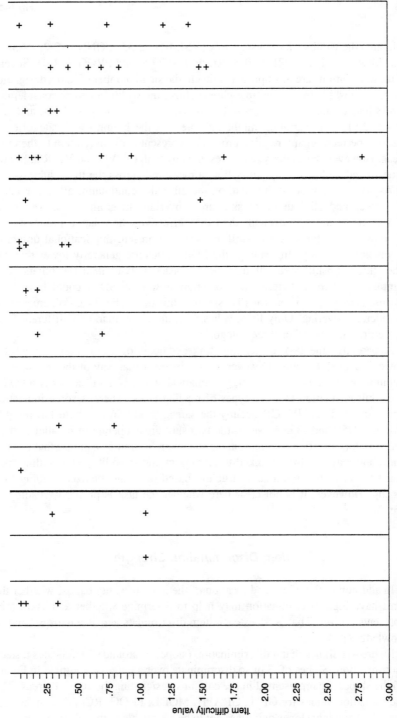

Figure 4-5. Distribution of items in skill areas by difficulty (two-parameter). Skill areas are as described in the text.

skill area the widths vary considerably (VSIMP = 2.35, CONN = 2.2, PASS = 0.8, MODL = 1.8, PERF = 0.3, RLPRO = 0.65, and PROG = 1.4). Several of these variations are most probably due to the small number of items designated for each subskill. In the multiple-choice cloze, the widths are vary considerably across the subskills (RC/VO = 4.45, RC/GR = 1.9, VO/RC = 3.65, and GR/RC = 2.9). This variation might indicate that the grammatical categories of passive, perfective, and relative pronouns represent skills in relation to the other areas. However, vocabulary, as represented by both RC/VO and VO/RC, has the widest band widths of any subskill area measured across the three subtests.

As for the location of the band on the difficulty continuum, all four reading skill areas and all four cloze skill areas overlap. In grammar, however, all passive items are less difficult than the perfective, the relative pronoun, and the progressive items. These skill areas may represent implicational orders of acquisition difficulty. In reading, the SDIN items are generally lower than the other three subskill areas; it may be an easier activity than the others. One complication here is that we do not know how easy SDIN could have been because there were no items at all easier than this skill. The cloze skill areas show considerable overlap. Only RC/GR has a ceiling effect markedly different from the ceilings on the other three categories.

Apparently, the task of reading for specific information may represent a "lower"-level skill. Note, however, that it is lower than any of the measures of grammar or vocabulary. As such, grammatical ability is not necessarily a lower-level skill in relation to some types of reading tasks. There is some indication here that SRST and RC/GR occupy the same "level," in that both fall roughly between -1.50 and .35. As such, the two skill areas operate in parallel in their compensatory functions—a reasonable statement, as finding a phrase that restates a question may be closely linked to reading grammar ability. This finding may indicate a need for grammar instruction based on contextualized reading processing. However, it is not clear here whether the task is primarily reading or grammar.

Item Discrimination Strength

In addition to the width and location of the item difficulty bands, whether the items have high discrimination may help to determine whether a subskill area represents a level. That is, does each item discriminate across a narrow band of knowledge?

Figure 4-1 shows that a discrimination (slope) of around .70 indicates a steep discrimination. Slopes of .3 or so discriminate over a range of abilities. In Figure 4-6 the slopes are represented in the columns designating the subskill areas. The discrimination values for GIST, GRAPH, MODL, PROG, RC/VO, and RC/GR generally have low slopes and seem not to be associable with skill levels because they discriminate over a broad area of abilities. The means for these are GIST =

.54, GRAPH = .61, MODL = .60, PROG = .49, RC/VO = .63, and RC/GR = .63. Again, however, the fact that the numbers of items are small must be considered. As de Jong (personal communication) has pointed out, conclusive evidence for these subskills would require many more items than are represented here.

Difficulty and Discrimination in Skill Definition

Which of the subskills might represent definable skills that could be put in a level within a top-down, bottom-up framework? SDIN, with a mean slope of .81, has a high slope and a definable ceiling lower than that of any other subskill measured by the tests. It may then be a skill, perhaps a "lower-level skill." Likewise, SRST, with a mean slope of .96 and a definable band, may be an "intermediate-level skill." Vsimp, with a mean slope of .74 and a band of scores; CONN, with a mean slope of .71; PASS, with a mean slope of .70; Vprf, with a mean slope of .87; and RLPRO, with a mean slope of .80, may be definable skills on the basis of slope. However, given the wide band widths in the distribution, only SDIN, PASS, Vprf, and perhaps SRST and RLPRO seem to represent discrete "levels" of skills.

Note that, as the difficulty of the items increases, the discrimination values tend to decrease. For example, 63% of the items at a difficulty level of 0 or below have a discrimination value above .70, whereas only 31% of those items above the 0 difficulty level had a discrimination value above .70. Sharply discriminating levels of skills tend to exist primarily, then, to the extent that they exist at all, for readers with lower-level ability.

Conclusions and Implications

Several caveats are necessary in generalizing the results of this study. First, the study included only one language group. Clearly, native speakers of Spanish carry with them a great deal of knowledge about language structure that they can apply to reading in English. Additional studies with native speakers of languages such as Japanese and Arabic may determine the extent to which those readers may possess identifiable levels of skills. Second, it would be useful to examine the results of this study to determine whether the less proficient and the more proficient readers have similar patterns in their relative item difficulties. Third, this study examined reading in English for science and technology. More research needs to be conducted to examine whether these results carry over to four-skills language courses. Fourth, this study used relatively few items for each skill area. Additional studies should include larger numbers of items representing each skill area.

Given the data, the notion of bottom-up and top-down may no longer be

Skill area

Item difficulty value

Item difficulty value	Reading				Grammar							Cloze			
	SDIN	SRST	GRAPH	GIST	Vsimp	CONN	PASS	MODL	Vprf	RLPRO	PROG	RC/VO	RC/GR	VO/RC	GR/RC
-3.00	0.63														
-2.75	0.75														
-2.50															
-2.25	1.09/0.66		0.62		0.53										
-2.00			0.83		0.76										
-1.75	1.28	1.54/0.84/1.77	0.58	0.46										0.75	
-1.50	0.81	0.80/0.54				0.78						0.55	0.53	0.64/0.38	0.71
-1.25						0.72	0.70/0.47	1.04				0.61	0.46		1.19
-1.00	0.66/0.64	1.31/0.65/0.70/1.19		0.76/0.74	0.72/0.88/0.75		0.69/0.46 / 0.92								1.01
-.75					0.55/0.95/0.38 / 1.01/1.15	1.28	0.67	0.48				0.85 / 0.86	0.83/0.43	0.68 / 1.15/1.3/0.95	1.08
-.50		0.70			0.80/0.80	0.52	0.97	0.41					0.77 / 0.51		0.99
-.25						0.81			0.98	1.06		0.91/0.79/0.58/0.40/0.75/0.91/0.89	0.71	0.83	0.50
0.00										1.11					0.78

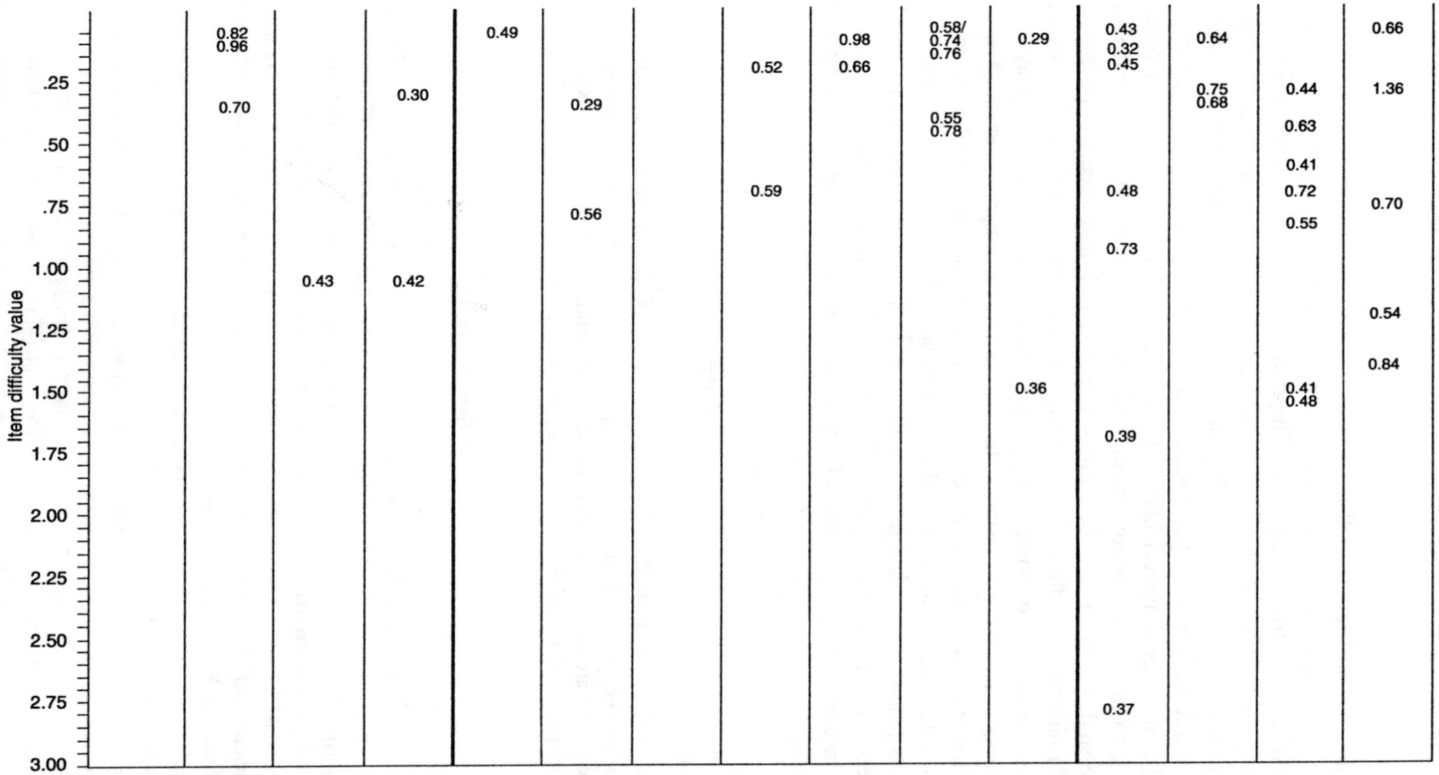

Item difficulty value

.25   .50   .75   1.00   1.25   1.50   1.75   2.00   2.25   2.50   2.75   3.00

Column 1: 0.66   1.36   0.70   0.54   0.84

Column 2: 0.44   0.63   0.41   0.72   0.55   0.41   0.48

Column 3: 0.64   0.75   0.68

Column 4: 0.43   0.32   0.45   0.48   0.73   0.39   0.37

Column 5: 0.29   0.36

Column 6: 0.58/0.74   0.76   0.55   0.78

Column 7: 0.98   0.66

Column 8: 0.52   0.59

Column 9: 0.29   0.56

Column 10: 0.49

Column 11: 0.30   0.42

Column 12: 0.43

Column 13: 0.82   0.96   0.70

Figure 4-6. Distribution of item slopes in skill areas by difficulty (two-parameter). Skill areas are as described in the text.

appropriate analogies for all learners. That is, the skills operate in parallel here, and of the grammar skills, only Vsimp, because of its relatively low ceiling, could be argued to be prerequisite. The ability to process text in fact may correlate with a general knowledge in English of subject-verb-object order, and that grammatical knowledge may be sufficient for much of the reading that ESP students do, particularly native Spanish-speaking learners. The ability to use incomplete and general grammatical knowledge to process complex text would certainly serve to modify the notion, mentioned above, put forth by Eskey and Grabe. The students' goals and the particular reading task may be the most important determinants of reading success. People can process a great deal of text, and extensive control of some unitary component termed "grammar" may not be necessary. Indeed, it is doubtful that such a unitary component exists. The large overlap of performance on the cloze subskill items in relation to the grammatical categories shows clearly that the compensation that takes place is not one of levels in any hierarchical sense. Additionally, given that items tend to have low discriminations at the higher ability levels, the reading process is extremely interactive and not reflective of separable skills at any but the lowest ability levels.

Note

1. The question of which IRT model to use is a clouded one. Hulin, Lissak, and Drasgow (1982) indicate that for the two-parameter model, 30 items with any sample size down to 200 are sufficient for accurate parameter estimation. The use of the two-parameter model here with 65 items and more than 200 subjects is thus justified.

References

Alderson, J. C., & Lukmani, Y. (1989). Cognition and reading: Cognitive levels as embodied in test questions. *Reading in a Foreign Language, 5*, 253–270.

Barnhardt, E. B. (N.d.). *Developments in second language literacy research: Retrospective and prospective views for the classroom.* Unpublished manuscript.

Birnbaum, A. (1968). Some latent trait models and their use in inferring an examinee's ability. In F. M. Lord & M. R. Novick (Eds.), *Statistical theories of mental test scores.* Reading, MA: Addison-Wesley.

Carrell, P. L. (1983). Three components of background knowledge in reading comprehension. *Language Learning, 33*, 183–207.

Carrell, P. L. (1988). Some causes of text-boundedness and schema interference in ESL reading. In P. Carrell, J. Devine, & D. Eskey (Eds.), *Interactive approaches to second language reading* (pp. 101–113). Cambridge: Cambridge University Press.

Carroll, J. B. (1989). Intellectual abilities and aptitudes. In A. Lesgold & R. Glaser (Eds.), *Foundations for a psychology of education* (pp. 137–197). Hillsdale, NJ: Lawrence Erlbaum Associates.

Eskey, D. E., & Grabe, W. (1988). Interactive models for second language reading: Perspectives on instruction. In P. Carrell, J. Devine, & D. Eskey (Eds.), *Interactive approaches to second language reading* (pp. 223–238). Cambridge: Cambridge University Press.

Grabe, W. (1988). Reassessing the term "interactive." In P. Carrell, J. Devine, & D. Eskey (Eds.), *Interactive approaches to second language reading* (pp. 56–70). Cambridge: Cambridge University Press.

Hale, G. A., Stansfield, C. W., Rock, D. A., Hicks, M. M., Butler, F. A., & Oller, J. W. (1989). The relation of multiple-choice items to the Test of English as a Foreign Language. *Language Testing, 6,* 47–76.

Hambleton, R. K. (1979). Latent trait models and their applications. In R. Traub (Ed.), *Methodological developments: New directions for testing and measurement* (no. 4). San Francisco: Jossey-Bass.

Hambleton, R. K., & Cook, L. L. (1977). Latent trait models and their use in the analysis of educational test data. *Journal of Educational Measurement, 14,* 75–96.

Hambleton, R. K., & Rovinelli, R. J. (1986). Assessing the dimensionality of a set of test items. *Applied Psychological Measurement, 10,* 287–302.

Harris, T. L., & Hodges, R. E. (Eds). (1981). *A dictionary of reading and related terms.* Newark, DE: International Reading Association.

Hattie, J. (1985). Methodology review: Assessing unidimensionality of tests and items. *Applied Psychological Measurement, 9,* 139–164.

Hudson, T. (1989). *Measurement approaches in the development of functional ability level language tests: Norm-referenced, criterion-referenced, and item response theory decisions.* Unpublished doctoral dissertation, University of California, Los Angeles.

Hulin, C. L., Lissak, R. I., & Drasgow, F. (1982). Recovery of two- and three-parameter logistic item characteristic curves: A Monte Carlo study. *Applied Psychological Measurement, 6,* 249–260.

Mislevy, R. J., & Bock, R. D. (1989). *PC-Bilog 3: Item analysis and test scoring with binary logistic models.* Mooresville, IN: Scientific Software.

Richards, J., Platt, J., & Weber, H. (1985). *Longman dictionary of applied linguistics.* London: Longman.

Stanovich, K. E. (1980). Toward an interactive-compensatory model of individual differences in the development of reading fluency. *Reading Research Quarterly, 16(1),* 32–71.

Appendix 4A: Selections From Reading Test Texts

Form A

Vast Deposits of Untapped Fuel, *Science Digest*, April 1984

A decade ago, the energy crisis exploded into the public consciousness in the form of long lines at gas stations. It was painful evidence of what geologists already believed: Fossil fuels—the remains of prehistoric plants and animals that have simmered for millennia in the natural pressure cooker of the Earth's upper crust—are running out. There were only so many dinosaurs and rain forests in the first place.

There is an opposing view, however. A small but vocal minority of scientists argue that oil and, more important, natural methane gas come from a different and more plentiful source. These carbon-rich fuels, they claim, have cooked out of materials that lodged deep underground when the Earth was formed. Methane has been flowing slowly upward ever since, sometimes reaching the surface through earthquake faults and sometimes being trapped under subterranean domes of denser rock.

Form B

New Products, *Chemical Engineering*, November 9, 1987

DESIGN SOFTWARE A new computer program, called SWIFT, simulates casting solidification, and allows foundry engineers to determine precisely how the casting must be fed to achieve the required level of soundness. The effects of various feeding methods, and of casting design changes, can be seen readily.—Stainless Foundry & Engineering, Inc., Milwaukee, Wisc.

Circle 301 on Reader Service Card

PROCESS CONTROL ML-4100, a new controller for fermentation and cell culture, is compatible with any size bioreactor. The multiloop system, measuring only 18.5 in. wide and 17.25 in. deep, provides up to 24 control loops to choose from, including temperature, agitation, pressure, level, pH, antifoam, and air and gas flows.—New Brunswick Scientific Co., Inc., Edison, N.J.

Circle 302 on Reader Service Card

Form C

Preventive Maintenance of Electrical Systems
Chemical Engineering, December 3, 1979

The two types of maintenance programs for electrical equipment found in the plants of the chemical process industries may be termed breakdown and preventive. In the event of an electrical failure, plant-maintenance or electric-utility personnel will test the insulation of the electrical components by applying a voltage to all of them. The failed equipment and other components that do not meet the insulation tests will be repaired or replaced. Plants always seem to find money in their budgets to meet such contingencies. However, there are problems with this type of "breakdown" maintenance: Failure time is unpredictable. Protective equipment, designed to remove failed portions of the power system, must function correctly and in proper sequence to minimize damage.

5

A Comparison of Indices for the Identification of Misfitting Items

Kyle Perkins and Sheila R. Brutten
Southern Illinois University

A considerable amount of attention has been devoted to the investigation of item response patterns and to the factors causing people to produce unusual response patterns. Harnisch and Linn (1981) noted that "the same number-right score on a test can disguise the fact that students' incorrect answers may yield important information about student preparation" (p. 133). Harnisch and Linn (1981), Harnisch (1983), and Rudner (1983), among others, have observed that anxiety, carelessness, cheating, cultural bias, different instructional or experiential backgrounds, fumbling, guessing, misunderstanding, and plodding can produce unusual response patterns. The purpose of the indices that have been developed to analyze item response patterns is to identify "misfitting" subjects whose total correct scores call for extra caution in interpretation.

We have listed some reasons why a person or group of people might be considered misfitting. There are also some well-known reasons why an item or an entire test may be invalid and thus considered a misfit. Henning (1987) cited the following as factors that may reduce a test's validity: an invalid application of a test whereby the test is administered for purposes and to students with ability levels for which it was not intended, inappropriate selection of content, imperfect cooperation of the examinees, poor criterion selection, and use of invalid constructs.

Research Questions

The research reported here focuses on the use of group-dependent indices that can be used to identify misfitting items. We are concerned with the issue of whether a standardized proficiency measure is being used invalidly as a placement measure. The use of group-dependent indices to identify misfitting items in this particular context will, we hope, shed light on this important validity issue. The impetus for this study is the practice at the Center for English as a Second Language (CESL), Southern Illinois University, where the research was conducted, of using the Test of English as a Foreign Language (TOEFL) to group students homogeneously by language ability into the appropriate level of full-time English instruction. The TOEFL is a proficiency measure that colleges and universities use in their admissions process to determine which nonnative English-speaking students to accept into academic programs.

Stevenson (1987) described the TOEFL as follows:

> TOEFL seeks to estimate the proficiency of nonnative speakers of English as a second or foreign language with the major purpose of providing impartial compara-tive and current information on the language proficiency of foreign students. TOEFL is administered to individuals from hundreds of language and cultural backgrounds, who seek admission at the undergraduate or graduate levels to some 2,500 universi-ties and colleges in the U.S., Canada, and other countries for study in a wide variety of academic subject areas. (p. 80)

At CESL, as mentioned, the TOEFL is used both as a preinstruction placement measure and as a postinstruction proficiency measure. CESL provides full-time English instruction for students at four proficiency levels, established in 1983: students obtaining scores of 373 or lower are placed into level 1; from 377 to 427, into level 2; from 430 to 467, into level 3; and from 470 to 523, into level 4. In 1983 all students enrolled in CESL sat for the TOEFL and the placement instrument in use at that time. The interval ranges for placement listed above were established on the basis of the means, ranges, and frequencies of scores for all levels on both tests.

The CESL staff are aware that the TOEFL tends to discriminate poorly among students below the effective range of the test (personal communication) and that culture shock and test anxiety can affect test performance. As a result, each new student is afforded the opportunity to take a separate, different retest at the end of the 1st week of classes of each term. The test consists of (a) a 50-item grammar test containing structures taught in the proficiency level out of which the student is trying to test, (b) a 30-minute writing sample on an assigned topic appropriate to the level of the student, and (c) an oral interview with two examiners. The student must obtain a minimum score of 76% on the grammar subtest in order to be eligible to sit for the writing examination and the oral interview. The number of students passing all three parts of the retest is less than 10%, so the staff are comfortable with the TOEFL placement intervals in place.

Because the TOEFL is being used as a placement test, and because it tends to discriminate poorly among students below the effective range of the test, we were concerned that CESL might be using the TOEFL invalidly. We decided to analyze the reading comprehension section of the TOEFL as part of our extensive research program on English as a second language (ESL) reading assessment, using five indices to identify misfitting items. The purposes of this paper, then, are (a) to provide a comparative analysis of the number of misfitting items identified by the indices employed, (b) to determine whether the differences in the number of identified misfitting items and their expected frequencies are large enough to say that they are truly different, and (c) to provide some recommendation on the use of the indices.

The goal of misfitting-item studies is to measure the degree to which the response pattern for an item is unusual. Once having identified the items that contribute least to high values on an index (or a group of indices), test users can then judge the appropriateness of the item content for those placement levels. Violation of a misfit statistic criterion raises doubt about the validity of an item and indicates that caution is called for in interpreting the placement results. For example, a very high scoring examinee might miss a very easy, textually explicit verbatim reading comprehension item. On the other hand, a very low scoring examinee might correctly answer a very difficult item. In both aberrant cases, misfit statistics would signal that item scores and person scores want closer scrutiny and more cautious interpretation. Although the present research has an ESL focus, the results should apply in any context in which a proficiency test is used for placement and proficiency purposes.

Five indices were employed in this research: p-value, or item difficulty; point biserial correlation (r); the modified caution index (MCI); a y' residual; and a Rasch item fit statistic expressed as a t-value. We chose p-value and point biserial correlation because they are employed in traditional item analysis. The MCI and y' residual were chosen because Harnisch and Linn (1981) had used them successfully in non-ESL contexts. We employed the Rasch item fit statistics because we wanted an item response theory (IRT) statistic to compare with non-IRT statistics. Our choice of indices was influenced by the following considerations. First, the non-IRT statistics are known to depend heavily on the range of test scores and the observed ability mean and variances of the calibrating sample, whereas the IRT statistics do not. Second, in a study of this nature it is accepted practice to compare the performance of IRT and non-IRT statistics (cf. Perkins & Miller, 1984).

We are acutely aware that the term *misfit* is used for statistical tests of fit to a measurement model. In this paper, however, we use the term to refer to the observation that the response pattern for an item is unusual.

Method

Subjects

The subjects for this research were 262 Japanese students enrolled in full-time intensive English classes: 80 students from proficiency level 1 (TOEFL 373 or lower), 81 from level 2 (TOEFL 377–429), 80 from level 3 (TOEFL 430–467), and 21 from level 4 (TOEFL 470–523). These students comprised the entire Japanese population enrolled in CESL at the time the data were collected.

For the initial study we collected data from only one native language group because we were examining the behavior of the reading comprehension items.

Reading comprehension research has shown that textually relevant background knowledge (content schemata) and text structure knowledge (formal schemata) can vary widely from one language group to another (Curtis & Glaser, 1983). We chose to control contamination due to cultural background differences, background knowledge differences, and text property differences by studying the item responses from only one native language group.

Instrumentation

The item responses for this study were elicited from the TOEFL, Level I, Form 3HTF3 (Educational Testing Service, 1988) reading comprehension subtest, which contains 30 items. Short reading passages are followed by questions that assess informational or inferential responses (Stevenson, 1987). One of the questions was an experimental item that was not scored; only the item responses from the 29 nonexperimental questions were entered into the analysis.

Indices

Five indices were calculated for each of the 29 reading comprehension items from each of the four proficiency levels: (a) p-value, or item difficulty, (b) point biserial correlation (r), (c) the MCI based on Sato's (1975) caution index and proposed by Harnisch and Linn (1981), (d) a y' residual, and (e) a Rasch item fit statistic expressed as a t-value proposed by Henning (1987).

For each item we calculated the item difficulty as the proportion of correct responses at each of the four proficiency levels. Items with p-values of less than .33 or greater than .67 were considered misfitting for this analysis. We are aware that commercial test developers impose additional constraints that might retain items falling outside the .33 to .67 interval, such as the need to include specific content, the need to provide an easy introduction, the need to shape the information curve, and the availability of items (Henning, 1987, p. 50). John de Jong (personal communication) reckons that the ideal p-value is halfway between chance level and unity; for a four-option item, that value would be .625: $(1.00 - 25)/2 + .25 = .625$. He deduces that a better interval might be from .50 to .75, which affords a maximum avoidance of guessing and ceiling effects. But for this analysis we adhered to the difficulty interval of .33 to .67 for nonmisfitting items because of Tuckman's (1978) advocation to reject items with a proportion of correct answers less than .33 or greater than .67. Tuckman bases his advocation on two reasonable assumptions: that subsequent samples will have similar mean ability levels and that the information curve formed from the .33 to .67 difficulty interval will span the placement decision points.

For an item discriminability index we computed a point biserial correlation for each item; we corrected each point biserial correlation for part-whole overlap because of each item's contribution to the subtest score, thereby removing the spurious inflation of the uncorrected correlation coefficient. For this analysis, we considered items with point biserial correlations of less than .25 to be misfitting. Henning (1987) cited .25 as a minimum point biserial correlation for items with acceptable discriminability.

We used Harnisch and Linn's modified form of Sato's caution index but reversed the roles of i and j in the equation because our focus was the item index. To calculate the MCI we had to permute the data matrices so that the examinees (columns) were arranged from left to right in ascending order of person ability and the items (rows) were arranged from top to bottom in increasing order of item difficulty.

Harnisch and Linn scaled the index to yield a lower bound of 0 and an upper bound of 1 to eliminate the extreme scores sometimes obtained with Sato's original formulation. An item with an MCI of .30 or greater was considered to be a misfit. The MCI is defined below.

$$MCI = \frac{\sum\limits_{j=1}^{n_{i.}} (1 - u_{ij})\, n_{.j} - \sum\limits_{j=n_{i.}+1}^{J} u_{ij} n_{.j}}{\sum\limits_{j=1}^{n_{i.}} n_{.j} - \sum\limits_{j=J+1-n_{i.}}^{J} n_{.j}}$$

where

$i = 1, 2, \ldots I$, indexes the examinee,

$j = 1, 2, \ldots J$, indexes the item;

$u_{ij} = 1$ if examinee i answers item j correctly,

   0 if examinee i answers item j incorrectly;

$n_{i.}$ = total correct for the ith examinee; and

$n_{.j}$ = total number of correct responses to the jth item.

(Harnisch & Linn, 1981, p. 135)

A more conceptual definition of the MCI statistic entails the notion that an item with an unusual response pattern is associated with a large value. A large MCI value implies that caution is needed in interpreting the item score and, by extension, the examinees' total correct scores. Harnisch and Linn (1981), Harnisch (1983), Henning (1987), Rudner (1983), and Wright and Stone (1979), among others, have discussed the potential sources for these unusual response patterns.

Following Harnisch and Linn (1981), we calculated the y' residual by first determining the p-value for each item based on the proportion of the 262 students who answered the item correctly. Then we performed a linear regression on the p-values for each proficiency level with the p-values from the entire sample. We used the regression equation to compute the expected proportion correct on each item for each proficiency level. We calculated the y' residual for each item by subtracting the expected proportion correct from the observed proportion correct for each proficiency level. We did not standardize p before the regression analysis but probably should have, because p is not equal-interval data.

We used the following fit criterion for the y' residual. Scores were considered misfitting when the residual exceeded ± 1.96 times the standard error of estimate; in other words, misfit was identified as occurring whenever the residual fell outside of the 95% confidence interval. We used a mean standard error to standardize cross-group comparisons.

To calculate the Rasch item fit statistics, we first estimated the person abilities and item difficulties by the PROX method described in Wright and Stone (1979). The person measures were adjusted for test width expansion, and the item difficulties were adjusted for sample spread expansion. We did not use the iterative process of rejecting items and persons, for we wanted to subject all the responses from all the persons to all the indices. We are aware of the standard practice of eliminating misfitting persons and misfitting items and then recalibrating the estimates for person ability and item difficulty, but we did not do so for the reason stated above.

Rasch analysis assumes unidimensional data, and the TOEFL reading comprehension subtest data meet that assumption. Perkins, Parish, and Pohlmann (1990) used factor analysis to examine the latent structure of the subtest by subjecting the interitem correlation matrix to a principal components analysis. The number of factors present in the test was estimated using a scree test and a parallel analysis (Horn, 1965). The scree test suggested a one-factor structure.

We used the formula below from Henning (1987), which uses the sum of squared standardized residuals for any item, to indicate the degree of misfit to the model, which is expressed as a t-value.

$$t = [Ln\frac{\Sigma z^2}{d.f.} + \frac{\Sigma z^2}{d.f.} - 1]\frac{(d.f.)^{\frac{1}{2}}}{8}$$

We considered any item with a t-value of $+2.00$ or above to be a misfit following Henning (1987):

> The establishment of a critical value of t for the rejection of persons or items as misfitting is somewhat arbitrary. Commonly the t-value of positive 2.00 is set as the critical value, so the items or persons with t-values of 2.00 or above are considered misfits to the model, lacking response validity. A negative t-value of -2.00 or below reflects overfit to the model and usually does not constitute grounds for the rejection of items or persons. There is some suspicion, however, that overfitting items or persons may exhibit less stable difficulty or ability estimates on recalibration. (p. 123)

As noted, the CESL staff are comfortable with the current TOEFL placement intervals because less than 10% of the students pass all three parts of the retest. For this reason our criterion for evaluating misfit statistics in this context is the one that indicates the fewest misfitting items.

Table 5-1

Means and Standard Deviations of the Correct Responses and the Item Indices

Proficiency level (TOEFL score)		Correct responses (N = 29)	p	r	MCI	y' residual	Rasch t
1. 373	M	7.40	.26	.02	.38	−.00	−7.15
and below	SD	2.45	.09	.14	.10	.05	4.93
2. 377	M	9.17	.31	.01	.37	.00	−4.36
to 427	SD	2.63	.12	.13	.07	.05	5.60
3. 430	M	11.79	.41	.04	.33	.01	−2.23
to 467	SD	2.60	.17	.14	.09	.16	6.86
4. 470	M	16.00	.55	.11	.30	.00	3.87
to 523	SD	3.48	.19	.15	.13	.13	6.19

Results

Table 5-1 presents the means and standard deviations of the correct responses, and the indices. The means found in Table 5-1 do not lend themselves to the use of analysis of variance (ANOVA) for comparison because the variables are not normally and independently distributed. For example, misfit for p and y' occurs at both ends of the continua whereas MCI, r, and Rasch misfit are more unidirectional.

We counted misfitting items at each level by each method and then compared the methods using chi-square analysis to test for the independence of the categorical variables. A two-way chi-square analysis was performed on the 5 x 4 contingency table of misfitting items identified by index by proficiency level (Table 5-2). Because the number in four cells was less than 5, we applied Yates' Correction for Continuity throughout. The results indicated that the choice of the index does influence the number of misfitting items identified: chi-square = 41.439, $df = 12$, $p < .001$.

We then conducted one-way chi-square analyses for each level to compare the observed frequencies of misfitting items identified by the five indices with the

Table 5-2

Number of Misfitting Items Identified, by Index and by Proficiency Level

Proficiency level[a]	p	r	MCI	y' residual	Rasch t
1	22	27	22	0	0
2	17	28	25	0	0
3	11	27	21	6	6
4	11	22	13	3	15

Note. MCI = modified caution index.
[a]Proficiency levels are as defined in Table 5-1.

frequencies that would be expected by chance if the choice of indices had no relationship to the distribution. The differences in numbers of misfitting items and the expected frequencies were large enough to say that they were truly different:

- Level 1: chi-square = 45.233, df 4, $p<.01$
- Level 2: chi-square = 47.375, df 4, $p<.01$
- Level 3: chi-square = 22.661, df 4, $p<.01$
- Level 4: chi-square = 13.519, df 4, $p<.01$.

Appendixes 5A, 5B, 5C, and 5D contain the misfitting item data in levels 1–4, respectively.

Discussion

An inspection of the contingency table (Table 5-2) indicates that p, r, and MCI identified far more items as misfitting than y' residual and Rasch t did. The chi-square analysis and the contingency table data suggest that departures from expectation are greatest for y' residual and Rasch t and that few or no distinctions exist for proficiency levels. The implication is that y' residual and Rasch t function independently of the other misfit statistics.

For two sets of reasons, we are far more comfortable with the y' residual and Rasch t results than with the p, r, and MCI results. First, as mentioned, each new student at CESL may take a separate, different (from the TOEFL) retest at the end of the 1st week of classes of each term, and fewer than 10% of the students pass all three parts of the retest. The second set of reasons involve psychometric considerations, the thesis of which is that y' residual and Rasch t function independently of the other misfit statistics because y' residual and Rasch t are not adversely affected by the observed ability mean and variance of the calibrating sample; the other misfit statistics—p, r, and MCI—are.

Item difficulty presents sufficient problems for us not to recommend it as a misfit statistic for the following reasons. P-values, as a statistic, reflect group differences—as they should, because the items are measures of the same ability used to stratify the groups. The p-values do not "fit" within groups, however, because they are too difficult for most of the groups according to our criterion range of difficulty for the item to "fit" the group. In addition, the item p-value is not linear in the implied variable and is affected by the observed ability mean and variance of the calibrating sample—problems precluded by Rasch analysis (Wright & Stone, 1979).

Our difficulties with p-values are clearly delineated in Roid and Haladyna (1982), in a discussion of criterion-referenced testing, in which item difficulty is a relative matter:

> The major problem with item difficulty is the nature of the sample on which the item difficulty estimate is based. If the item is given to students following instruction,

the item appears to be easy in most instances. A p-value might be .75 or higher, indicating an easy item. On the other hand, if one gave that same item to students before instruction, the p-value might be lower than .40. Which p-value is appropriate? Or is it better to take the mean of these two p-values? The problem of sampling in the estimation of difficulty has led to dissatisfaction with the traditional notion of "difficulty." Difficulty, as you can see, is a relative matter. (p. 216)

The point biserial correlation did not discriminate well within groups because the range of the ability measure used as the criterion in the computation of the point biserial was severely restricted when the groups were formed. The issue here is that the point biserial discrimination index is influenced by the range of test scores. Compressing the range of test scores attenuates the correlation between the item and the total test; consequently, all the point biserial correlations are low (Haladyna, 1974). For these reasons, Popham and Husek (1969) have criticized the wholesale removal of nondiscriminating items. We do not recommend the use of the point biserial discrimination index as a misfit statistic for the following reasons, cited by Wright & Stone (1979):

The item point-biserial has two characteristics which interfere with its usefulness as an index of how well an item fits in with the set of items in which it appears. First, there is no clear basis for determining what magnitude item point-biserial establishes item acceptability. Rejecting the statistical hypothesis that an item point-biserial is zero does not produce a satisfactory statistical criterion for validating an item. The second interfering characteristic is that the magnitude of the point-biserial is substantially influenced by the score distribution of the calibrating sample. A given item's point-biserial is largest when the persons in the sample are spread out in scores and centered on that item. Conversely as the variance in person scores decreases or the sample level moves away from the item level, so that the p-value approaches zero or one, the point-biserial decreases to zero regardless of the quality of the item. (p. 26)

According to Harnisch (1983), "high MCI's [for items] indicate an unusual set of responses by students of varying ability, and thus these items should be examined closely by the test constructors and the classroom teacher" (p. 199). A large value of the caution index is supposed to raise doubts about the validity of the item. The contingency table of misfitting items (Table 5-2) shows a degree of relatedness between item difficulty and point biserial discrimination, which is not at all surprising because the MCI formula has, as part of its input, correct person scores and correct item scores. The MCI is affected by the observed ability mean and variance of the calibrating sample and by the range of test scores as item difficulty and point biserial were; consequently, we do not recommend the MCI as a misfit statistic.

Although the y' residual is ultimately based on item difficulty, the criterion weight of ± 1.96 times the standard error of estimate apparently leavens the effect of observed ability mean. Consequently, the y' residual did not identify as many misfitting items as p, r, and MCI. The use of a smaller weight would probably lead to the identification of more misfitting items. The y' residual's behavior is more in line with our qualitative observation that few students pass the retest; therefore, the TOEFL as a placement measure is doing a fairly respectable job. At this juncture in our research, we need more experience with the y' residual before we make a recommendation on its use.

Of the five misfit statistics employed in this research, we have the highest confidence in the Rasch fit validity statistic, which is a "measure of the unlikelihood of the pattern of responses obtained assuming that the item conforms to the conditions and assumptions of the model" (Henning, 1984, p. 129). Rasch item difficulties and person abilities are estimated without being affected by or referring to the sample of the students responding to the items, that is, sample-free item calibration and test-free person measurement. Once the item difficulty and person ability estimates are placed on the same difficulty-ability continuum, one can then analyze item and person fit to the model. Rasch analysis frees one from two problems: that the observed ability mean and variance of the calibrating sample affect the p-value, and that a compressed range of test scores attenuates the point biserial correlation. As a result, we can recommend the Rasch fit validity statistic for item misfit studies.

Future Research

We intend to continue our research on misfit statistics by enlarging the numbers of subjects and native languages represented in the sample. The next phase of the research will also examine the entire subtest, including the Vocabulary, Listening Comprehension, and Structure and Written Expression sections of the TOEFL. To establish a benchmark for the psychometric behavior of these items, our future research will include subjects from the high end of the proficiency continuum, with TOEFL scores of 527 to 600 and higher.

We also need to develop a criterion dichotomous classification of accurate/ inaccurate assessment so we can determine the proportion of examinees correctly classified by each index. With such a classification, we will be able to hold the probability of a Type I error constant across indices.

Acknowledgments

We express appreciation to Grant H. Henning, Educational Testing Service, and John de Jong, Centraal Instituut voor Toetsontwikkeling, for their careful review of the manuscript and for their thoughtful suggestions. We owe a debt of gratitude to Pavlos Pavlou for coding the data. Any errors or misconceptions in the paper are solely our responsibility.

References

Curtis, M. E., & Glaser, R. (1983). Reading theory and the assessment of reading achievement. *Journal of Educational Measurement, 20*, 133–147.

Educational Testing Service. (1988). *Test of English as a Foreign Language*. Level I, Form 3HTF3. Princeton, NJ: Author.

Haladyna, T. M. (1974). Effects of different samples on item and test characteristics of criterion-referenced tests. *Journal of Educational Measurement, 11*, 93–100.

Harnisch, D. L. (1983). Item response patterns: Applications for educational practice. *Journal of Educational Measurement, 20*, 191–206.

Harnisch, D. L., & Linn, R. L. (1981). Analysis of item response patterns: Questionable test data and dissimilar curriculum practices. *Journal of Educational Measurement, 18*, 133–146.

Henning, G. H. (1984). Advantages of latent trait measurement in language testing. *Language Testing, 1*, 123–133.

Henning, G. H. (1987). *A guide to language testing: Development, evaluation, research*. Cambridge, MA: Newbury House.

Horn, J. L. (1965). A rationale and test for the number of factors in factor analysis. *Psychometrika, 30*, 179–185.

Perkins, K., & Miller, L. D. (1984). Comparative analyses of English as a second language reading comprehension data: Classical test theory and latent trait measurement. *Language Testing, 1*, 21–32.

Perkins, K., Parish, C., & Pohlmann, J. T. (1990). *The determination of hierarchies among TOEFL vocabulary and reading comprehension items*. (ERIC Document Reproduction Service No. ED 311 054)

Popham, W. J., & Husek, T. R. (1969). Implications of criterion-referenced measurement. *Journal of Educational Measurement, 6*, 1–9.

Roid, G. H. & Haladyna, T. M. (1982). *A technology for test-item writing*. New York: Academic Press.

Rudner, L. M. (1983). Individual assessment accuracy. *Journal of Educational Measurement, 20*, 207–219.

Sato, T. (1975). *The construction and interpretation of S-P tables*. Tokyo: Meiji Tosho.

Stevenson, D. K. (1987). Test of English as a Foreign Language. In J. C. Alderson, K. J. Krahnke, & C. W. Stansfield (Eds.), *Reviews of English language proficiency tests* (pp. 79–81). Washington, DC: Teachers of English to Speakers of Other Languages.

Tuckman, B. W. (1978). *Conducting educational research* (2nd ed.). New York: Harcourt Brace Jovanovich.

Wright, B. D., & Stone, M. H. (1979). *Best test design: Rasch measurement*. Chicago: MESA Press.

Appendix 5A

Item Misfit Statistics for Proficiency Level 1

Item	p	r	MCI	y′ residual	Rasch t
31	.38	−.18*	.48*	.06	−2.48
32	.12*	.24*	.25	.01	0.00
33	.24*	.26	.21	−.13	−10.02
34	.39	−.04*	.36*	.01	−3.12
35	.18*	−.04*	.46*	.01	−14.06
36	.23*	−.06*	.45*	.00	−10.02
37	.18*	.00*	.38*	−.09	−14.64
38	.21*	−.05*	.51*	−.03	−12.39
39	.38	−.11*	.44*	.05	−2.48
40	.25*	.18*	.27	.06	−9.60
41	.31*	.04*	.28	−.06	−5.29
42	.19*	.17*	.32*	.00	−14.64
43	.29*	−.03*	.41*	.02	−5.29
44	.41	.19*	.26	.05	−1.81
45	.25*	.03*	.37*	−.10	−10.02
46	.36	.29	.21	.06	−4.05
47	.32*	−.02*	.40*	.02	−4.05
48	.34	−.11*	.45*	.01	−3.93
49	.16*	.17*	.27	−.02	−16.74
50	.19*	.12*	.54*	−.02	−5.29
51	.16*	−.12*	.51*	.01	−16.74
52	.46	.09*	.33*	.10	−2.79
53	.30*	.04*	.36*	.03	−5.29
54	.14*	−.10*	.51*	−.07	0.00
55	.11*	.17*	.30*	−.04	0.00
56	.24*	−.05*	.43*	.04	−10.02
57	.28*	−.26*	.57*	.04	−8.02
58	.14*	−.06	.48*	−.02	0.00
59	.20*	.05*	.35*	−.01	−14.64

Note. MCI = modified caution index.
*Does not meet fit criterion.

Appendix 5B

Item Misfit Statistics for Proficiency Level 2

Item	p	r	MCI	y' residual	Rasch t
31	.51	−.21	.46*	.11	0.99
32	.12*	.00*	.40*	.01	0.00
33	.42	.09	.33*	−.05	−1.61
34	.42	−.01*	.39*	.00	1.99
35	.17*	.00*	.39*	−.03	0.00
36	.22*	−.14*	.54*	−.06	−12.46
37	.36	−.08*	.37*	.02	−3.09
38	.26*	−.02*	.38*	−.03	−5.53
39	.44	.25	.31*	.03	−0.57
40	.21*	−.08*	.46*	−.02	−12.46
41	.51	−.25*	.43*	.04	0.99
42	.30*	.05*	.36*	.08	−5.53
43	.32*	.14*	.29	−.02	−4.39
44	.48	.23*	.26	.02	1.99
45	.48	.13*	.32*	.03	1.99
46	.42	.23*	.23	.05	−1.61
47	.33	−.20*	.53*	−.04	−4.39
48	.33	.14*	.34*	−.08	−4.39
49	.19*	−.07	.44*	−.01	−16.96
50	.19*	−.02*	.39*	−.07	−16.96
51	.27*	−.02*	.41*	.10	−6.95
52	.46	.10*	.32*	.00	−0.32
53	.30*	.05*	.36*	.03	−5.53
54	.27*	.08*	.30*	.02	−6.95
55	.17*	−.09*	.42*	.00	0.00
56	.25*	−.04*	.39*	.01	−6.95
57	.26*	.11*	.33*	−.03	−5.53
58	.16*	.11*	.29	−.01	0.00
59	.22*	−.12*	.36*	−.03	−12.46

Note. MCI = modified caution index.
*Does not meet fit criterion.

Appendix 5C
Item Misfit Statistics for Proficiency Level 3

Item	p	r	MCI	y' residual	Rasch t
31	.56	−.03*	.45*	.15	2.53*
32	.10*	.06*	.30*	−.27*	0.00
33	.76*	−.12*	.32*	.35*	11.39*
34	.64	−.17*	.45*	.22*	5.76*
35	.24*	−.02*	.37*	−.14	−10.58
36	.40	−.20*	.45*	.01	−1.98
37	.50	.14*	.09	.10	0.47
38	.40	−.04*	.33*	.01	1.98
39	.46	.11*	.40*	.05	−0.32
40	.26*	.05*	.33*	−.13	−8.99
41	.66	.05*	.39*	.25*	5.76*
42	.24*	−.07*	.42*	−.14	−10.58
43	.49	−.02*	.37*	.09	0.47
44	.54	.39	.25	.13	1.42
45	.66	.24*	.23	.25*	5.76*
46	.45	.05*	.26	.05	−0.92
47	.54	.04*	.39*	.14	1.42
48	.56	.07*	.35*	.15	2.53*
49	.23*	.25	.21	−.15	−10.58
50	.35	.14*	.32*	−.04	−3.42
51	.15*	.00*	.45*	−.23*	0.00
52	.54	.21*	.25	.13	1.42
53	.44	.01*	.38*	.04	−1.42
54	.35	.10*	.28	−.04	−3.42
55	.20*	.08*	.31*	−.18	−16.96
56	.25*	−.14*	.42*	−.14	−8.99
57	.38	.20*	.24	−.01	−1.98
58	.20*	−.06*	.39*	−.18	−16.96
59	.31*	−.08*	.38*	−.08	−4.52

Note. MCI = modified caution index.
*Does not meet fit criterion.

Appendix 5D
Item Misfit Statistics for Proficiency Level 4

Item	p	r	MCI	y' residual	Rasch t
31	.76*	−.06*	.27	.09	8.58*
32	.19*	.06*	.47*	−.09	−5.06
33	.90*	−.04*	.32*	.15	26.57*
34	.67	.10*	.27	−.11	5.21*
35	.48	.31	.18	.08	1.43
36	.62	.37	.08	.11	3.37*
37	.62	.24*	.18	.04	3.37*
38	.62	−.02*	.38*	.10	3.37*
39	.71*	.15*	.22	.03	6.63*
40	.38	.36	.20	−.06	−1.23
41	.76*	.24*	.11	.00	8.58*
42	.29*	.12*	.40*	−.14	−2.69
43	.48	.28	.22	−.10	1.43
44	.71*	.24*	.16	−.03	6.63*
45	.76*	.35	.05	.03	8.58*
46	.38	.03*	.42*	−.25*	−1.23
47	.57	−.19*	.57*	−.11	2.44*
48	.86*	−.40	.63*	.18	17.77*
49	.57	.05*	.33*	.17	2.44*
50	.71*	.15*	.22	.24*	6.63*
51	.05*	−.13*	.64*	−.30*	0.00
52	.62	−.11*	.44*	−.12	3.37*
53	.52	.31	.14	−.05	1.69
54	.43	.29	.27	−.03	0.46
55	.38	.00*	.44*	.03	−1.23
56	.43	.14*	.33*	−.02	0.46
57	.48	.32	.20	−.04	1.43
58	.52	−.12*	.36*	.16	1.69
59	.52	.22*	.18	.06	1.69

Note. MCI = modified caution index.
*Does not meet fit criterion.

6

The Effect of Prompt in Essay Examinations

Mary Spaan
The University of Michigan

The past decade has seen a trend toward the use of direct measures in large-scale writing assessment. In the field of English as a second language (ESL), the trend may be due to the influence of teaching and testing for "communicative competence," in which writing competence is seen as integral to effective communication; it reflects an interest in task-based learning and performance testing. ESL professionals prefer direct measures of writing, employing actual writing samples that more nearly approximate real discourse and real communication, over indirect, multiple-choice measures that often seem to require only editing skills.

With the increased use of direct measures of writing ability has come the need to demonstrate the construct validity of the measures, that is, to find evidence that the test measures what it purports to measure—namely, *writing ability*. The concept of writing ability, which is complex and difficult to define, includes the ability to use written language to convey an intended message clearly and effectively. Students may achieve this ability through a combination of sociocultural competence, involving appropriate conventions, register, and (rhetorical) style; discourse competence, involving ideas and their structuring, coherence, and cohesion with an intended audience in mind; and linguistic competence, involving appropriate and broad lexis, fluent and accurate syntax, and accurate mechanics (cf. Canale & Swain, 1980).

A writing measure, then, ideally requires the examinee to produce an effective written communication representative of the type of writing found in a particular setting. Writing tasks, however, like tasks on any ESL proficiency test, of necessity result in only a limited sampling of what the writer can produce. Constraints on testing mean that the tasks are often impromptu; furthermore, the task is a single type, such as a 30-minute expository essay. Other types of writing tasks, such as take-home final examinations, research papers, and summaries, are not evaluated. Moreover, the prompts (topics) assigned may be too general or too specific to the writer.

In spite of these shortcomings, in large-scale ESL writing assessment in the United States only one writing sample is collected from each examinee, and in most cases only one assigned prompt (topic) is offered. Generally, the task is the same: "Write a 30- to 60-minute impromptu essay on (this) assigned topic." Examinees are not invited to take the essay home and edit and revise it, nor are they prepared for its general content area as they would be if they were taking a course in a specific subject. These problems arise because of test constraints, which stipulate that the test topic must be kept secure—the examinees must not have prior knowledge of it—and that the test situation be controlled and uniform— all writing must be accomplished within the specified time period, and all examinees must have the same access (or in this case, lack thereof) to experts: dictionaries, thesauri, native-speaker writers, and so on.

Background

The differences between authentic writing contexts and the writing test situation bring into question the validity of a single writing sample as a predictor of future writing performance in authentic situations. Breland (1983) suggests that limited sampling causes greater errors than unreliability problems due to readers' disagreement or inconsistency: "When only one writing sample has been scored, it is not possible to estimate accurately anything but reading reliability." Carlson, Bridgeman, Camp, and Waanders (1985) echo this idea in stating that a single writing sample is essentially a one-item test.

Research has shown that different types of writing topics (prompts) make different cognitive demands on writers and may elicit different types of responses, which may not be assigned equivalent scores. There is no consensus on what constitutes a "difficult" or "easy" writing topic in terms of either rhetorical mode of discourse or of content or subject matter. The relationships between these prompt variables are unclear and may in fact change in evaluations of native versus nonnative writing, persons with high versus low language proficiency, and secondary school students versus graduate students. Certain rhetorical modes and certain subject or content areas may be more or less difficult to write on in an impromptu situation.

Quellmalz, Capell, and Chou (1982), in a study of native English-speaking high school students writing in the expository and narrative modes, found that all narrative essays were graded lower than expository essays on overall impression, focus, and organization, but not on support and mechanics. However, Mohan and Lo (1985) found that the Hong Kong ESL writers in their survey perceived the narrative mode as the easiest, descriptive as middling in difficulty, and expository and argumentative modes as the most difficult.

The Educational Testing Service revealed another kind of problem with the rhetorical mode when it developed the Test of Written English (TWE) option for the Test of English as a Foreign Language (TOEFL) (Bridgeman & Carlson, 1983). Initially the TWE used two types of prompts recommended by faculty in an initial survey: a pro-con argumentative- or discussion-type prompt and a graph or chart used as a content base or jumping-off point for the writer to summarize. The mean scores of a group of native and nonnative speakers given two of each type of topic to write on did not vary much (Carlson et al., 1985), but cross-topic correlations among holistic scores were not high enough to indicate close reliability. Indeed, as Carlson and Bridgeman later wrote, "Readers reported that overall writing performance of candidates on the chart or graph topics was not as high in quality as performance on the compare/contrast topic" (1986).

Witte (1987), dealing with native-speaking writers in a comparison of argumentative and expository writing prompts, found that the argumentative prompt provided more specific background information, suggested discourse schema and usable ideational content, and offered a clear choice. Expository or descriptive prompts were more unfocused and open-ended, thus demanding more of the writers' organizational and decision-making abilities.

In addition to rhetorical mode, a second variable to consider when designing prompts is subject matter, or content or point of view. Freedman and Pringle (1980) observed that the skills of native-speaking writers deteriorate when they take on a more complex, intellectually taxing subject. "Intellectually taxing" to them involves not only cognitive difficulty in terms of rhetorical specification, but also difficult subject matter or content in terms of world knowledge and vocabulary. Hoetker and Brossell (1986), in discussing the development of prompts for native-speaking college students, declared their confidence in methods of controlling for language and phrasing but stated that the area of content or subject matter still presents problems; they offered ideas for semispecific topics in which the prompt suggests a general content area and the writer-examinee determines a more specific aspect of the subject. Tedick (1988, 1990), however, argued that reducing content specification to an "Everyman" level penalizes those with specific knowledge and that writers should be allowed to perform at their optimal rather than at their minimal level. She found that non-native-speaking graduate students with prior knowledge of the subject matter achieved higher holistic scores on field-specific topics than on general topics.

When dealing with a population that may include both graduate and undergraduate writers, it is difficult to accommodate the graduates without doing so at the expense of the undergraduates. Ruth and Murphy (1984) indicated that different background knowledge results in different interpretations of the task (prompt) and suggested that a writing assessment model should accommodate a range of responses. They postulated, however, that no prompt can be free of bias with regard to content or subject matter. In their opinion, providing prompt options will only invite confusion, as topics are not equally difficult and students may not be wise in choosing their optimal prompt; the students may select complex prompts and write complex but poor essays. Swinford (1964) noted this phenomenon in an earlier study in which native-speaking students appeared unable to select prompts on which they would exhibit their best writing: the better students tended to select the more difficult topics, and in consequence received lower scores because of the difficulty level. This study is problematic in that "difficulty" was not fully specified and that the judges apparently did not adjust their scoring to the selected prompt.

Spaan (1989), investigating writers' choices of prompts when given an option, studied two prompt sets, each of which employed one prompt that appeared more challenging than the other:

1A. There are many different energy sources (for example, sun, wind, oil, water, natural gas, coal, nuclear fission, etc.). Pick one such source and discuss the situation for which it is best suited. (You might consider availability, safety, geographical features, etc.)

1B. What is your favorite time of day? Why?

2A. When you go to a party, do you usually talk a lot, or do you prefer to listen? What does this show about your personality?

2B. What is your opinion of mercenary soldiers (those who are hired to fight for a country other than their own)? Discuss.

The writers were assigned Set 1 or Set 2 and could choose one of the two prompts in the set. The more challenging prompts (1A, 2B) appeared to have more sophisticated content and more structured rhetorical specification than the less challenging prompts (1B, 2A). For both groups, a larger percentage chose the seemingly less challenging prompt. Spaan found significant differences in writing scores and overall ESL test scores for both prompt sets, though in different directions. For one group, those who chose the apparently less challenging prompt (1B) scored higher, but in the other group those who chose the seemingly more challenging prompt (2B) scored significantly higher.

Research Questions

The purpose of the study described here was to investigate possible differences in performance on an essay examination when one variable, the prompt, is manipulated. In addition to providing evidence on the validity of essay examinations, the question of prompt is of interest to test constructors who must use different prompts but who wish the different forms of their writing tests to be equivalent. This study, then, focused on the following questions:

1. Does performance differ when prompts differ?
2. If so, how can the differences be measured—through holistic scores, text analysis, or both?
3. If so, do the differences occur at different ESL proficiency levels, different academic levels, or both?
4. If performance differs in writing tasks in which students may select a topic, do they choose their optimal topic (the prompt on which they write better)?

Method

Subjects

The subjects who participated in the study were 88 nonnative speakers of English who took an English language proficiency examination in the United States between August 1988 and January 1989 (see Table 6-1): 49 males and 39 females, 27 graduate level students and 61 undergraduates representing 25 native languages and 36 countries of origin.

Table 6-1

Description of Sample Population

	Scholastic level	Mean age
Graduate	27	28.1
Undergraduate	61	20.5
Total	88	22.9

	Sex
Male	49
Female	39

Native language					
Arabic	30	French	1	Nepali	1
Japanese	17	Guajarati	1	Portuguese	1
Spanish	7	Ibo	1	Romanian	1
Chinese	6	Korean	1	Russian	1
German	3	Krahn	1	Somali	1
Tagalog	3	Luganda	1	Telegu	1
Tigre	3	Marathi	1	Turkish	1
Farsi	2	Mina	1	Urdu	1
Amharic	1				

Country of origin					
Japan	17	Iran	2	Nicaragua	1
Lebanon	8	Israel	2	Nigeria	1
Ethiopia	4	Syria	2	Pakistan	1
Jordan	4	Uganda	2	PRC	1
Kuwait	4	Brazil	1	Romania	1
Saudi Arabia	4	Cameroon	1	Somalia	1
Taiwan	4	Ecuador	1	Spain	1
India	3	Egypt	1	Togo	1
Iraq	3	France	1	Turkey	1
Mexico	3	Hong Kong	1	USSR	1
Philippines	3	Liberia	1	Venezuela	1
Germany	2	Morocco	1	Yeman	1

Materials

The Michigan English Language Assessment Battery (MELAB), a testing service available throughout the world, has a purpose similar to that of the TOEFL: to assess the English language proficiency of nonnative speakers of English before academic work at a North American university or work-study in medical, banking, or engineering management. The MELAB includes three compulsory components: (a) a 30-minute impromptu writing sample, written on one of two assigned topics and holistically scored; (b) a 25-minute, 50-item tape-recorded multiple-choice listening test that includes both short utterance items and questions based on longer discourse (a lecture and a conversation); and (c) a 75-minute multiple-choice test containing 30 grammar items in a conversational format, 20 cloze items based on a single passage, 30 vocabulary items for which examinees are to select a synonym or the word that best completes a sentence, and 20 reading comprehension questions based on four to five reading selections. The final MELAB score is the mathematical average of these three components.

In the MELAB composition section, examinees may normally choose from two prompts. Rhetorical specification for the prompts may be expository, descriptive, or argumentative/persuasive, and often a prompt calling for content coming from personal experience is paired with one for which content must come from the external world. The MELAB composition is a 30-minute impromptu essay, written without prior knowledge of the prompt and without a dictionary or other aids. Appendix 6A shows the standard MELAB composition form and instructions.

The compositions are scored holistically on a 10-point scale and converted to scores equivalent to, or scaled to scores on, the other sections of the test battery. Appendix 6B contains a description of the writing at each level on the scale. Note that a MELAB composition score of 73 is at the midpoint of the 10-point scale. Two raters independently evaluate each essay, and the average score is taken. The scoring scale contains 10 ranks, but because some scores are averaged, 19 scores are actually possible: 97, 95, 93, 90, 87, and so on. For instance, a composition rated 77 and 73 will be reported as a 75. If the two raters' scores are more than one ranking apart (e.g., 87 and 77), a third rater adjudicates. Average interrater correlations (product-moment correlation coefficients), unenhanced by Spearman-Brown correction, range between .84 and .92, with about 4% of the papers requiring adjudication. Intrarater correlations range from .88 to .92.[1]

Prompt Selection and Analysis

Four MELAB prompts were selected because they differed in two features: rhetorical mode and content or subject matter. (The same prompt sets were analyzed in Spaan [1989].) Prompt 1A ("Energy") was paired with 1B ("Time"), and 2B ("Soldiers") with 2A ("Talk").

The prompts were analyzed in terms of cognitive demand, purpose, role, audience, content, and rhetorical specification. The analytical scheme for describing composition assignments was developed by Vahapassi (1982) and Purves, Soter, Takala, and Vahapassi (1984) in their work for the International Association for the Evaluation of Educational Achievement (IEA) Study of Written Composition. This particular analytical scheme was chosen because it is part of the most comprehensive comparative research project known to date on the writing achievement of school children. In the IEA study, thousands of writing samples employing a variety of writing tasks were collected from secondary school students in 14 countries.

The first part of the prompt analysis involved cognitive demands. In some cases the writer has both the material and structure(s) of the discourse and needs only to reproduce. In others, the writer has the material but not the structure so must organize or reorganize the material. In yet other cases, the writer must generate both the material and the structure. Generally, for both the "Energy" and "Soldiers" prompts the writer must invent or generate facts and ideas and evaluate them. The material comes from the writer's world knowledge and intellect rather than personal experience, and "Soldiers" is especially demanding in that it requires specialized knowledge. For the "Time" and "Talk" prompts the writer must organize and reorganize visual images and events with material from the writer's own personal experience. "Energy" suggests some organizing principles, whereas neither "Time" nor "Talk" provides much structure.

Second, in terms of intention or purpose, "Time" and "Talk" require writers to convey feelings and emotions (emotive), whereas "Energy" and "Soldiers" require writers to convince or persuade (connotative).

Third, as for the role of the writer, audience, and point of view, "Time" and "Talk" both ask writers to write as themselves in a personal autobiographical sketch; the audience is both self and others. On the other hand, both "Energy" and "Soldiers" ask the writer to write as the "other," a detached observer; the audience is others, and the writer writes as the detached self.

Fourth, as for the demands of the content, some of the content categories Vahapassi and Purves presented were self; family and friends; school; leisure activities; social, economic, or political issues; science; and philosophy. For the "Talk" and "Time" prompts, content appears limited to the self and leisure activities, whereas for "Energy" the content is that of science. For "Soldiers" the writer must deal with a sociopolitical issue. Finally, turning to rhetorical specification, both "Time" and "Talk" require a quick analysis followed by a narrative or descriptive exposition. "Energy" requires exposition, analysis, definition, classification, and evaluation, whereas "Soldiers" asks for argument with evaluation and comment.

For the purposes of this study, the four prompts were classified under two major headings, one addressing rhetorical specification and the other involving content or subject matter. "Time" and "Talk" were classified as Narrative/Personal (NP) because they both call for a narrative/descriptive rhetorical mode and because the subject matter or content comes from the writer's personal experience. The "Energy" and "Soldiers" prompts were classified as Argumentative/Impersonal (AI) as they both call for a persuasive exposition, with content derived from the world outside the writer.

Procedures and Design

Data were collected during five separate MELAB administrations in Michigan. Normally, the MELAB consists of Part 1 (writing), Part 2 (listening), and Part 3 (grammar, cloze, vocabulary, reading), administered in that order. Part 1 normally offers a choice of two prompts, but in the MELAB administrations for this study two writing samples were collected from each subject, with no choice of prompts offered. The order of administration was Part 1, Part 2, Part 3, Part 1. As mentioned, the prompts were paired. Thirty-six of the subjects wrote on topic Set 1 (Energy/Time), and 52 wrote on Set 2 (Talk/Soldiers). In the test administrations, the order of the prompts was rotated so that half of the subjects wrote on prompt choice A first and half on choice B first. This rotation was an attempt to offset any differences in performance that might be due to practice effect, either positive (warm-up) or negative (fatigue). The examinees were told that their final composition scores would be based on their best performance on the two writing tasks. The usual holistic method of scoring MELAB essays, as described, was used for these subjects' essays. Each subject had two Part 1 scores; if they differed, the higher of the two was reported on the official score report.

Following administration of the entire test battery, the examinees completed a questionnaire (see Appendix 6C) dealing with the availability of a choice of prompts, prompt preference, a self-assessment of performance, and the preferred order of administration of component tests. Rather than using a Likert scale format, the questions were open ended to yield a variety of responses. The responses were subsequently categorized and coded. Information about each subject's age, native language, national origin, and scholastic level was gathered as part of the normal MELAB identification procedures. The questionnaire did not ask about academic field of specialization, duration of residence in the United States, or duration and location of previous English language study.

To discover if any differences in performance could be related to academic achievement or to English language proficiency level, subjects were classified as either graduate or undergraduate students and by English language proficiency level. Language proficiency classification—beginning, intermediate, or advanced—was determined by the final MELAB scores. The score ranges for such assignment are based on official MELAB norms[2] and are interpreted according to the academic load an examinee may carry without being overly disadvantaged because of an English language deficiency. Generally, an examinee with a beginning-level score (49–69) is regarded as not yet ready for any academic work; intermediate (70–79), restricted to a reduced academic load plus supplemental English study; and advanced (80–100), probably capable of carrying a full-time academic load, with supplemental English possible for the 80–85 range depending on the examinee's field and level of study.

Performance was measured by holistic composition score and compared with the independent measures (Parts 2 and 3 of the battery). In addition, the performance of a selected group, those scoring inconsistently, who were matched with consistent scorers, was also measured for sentence-level features (fluency/length, syntax, lexis) and for rhetorical features.

Results

Reliability of Holistic Scoring

The composition raters' scores were used to determine the reliability of the final composition scores. Initial interrater correlations ranged from .85 to .88, and following third rater adjudication interrater correlations rose to .92 to .94 (see Table 6-2). For this group, 13, or 7% of the 176 essays, required adjudication by a third rater because the first two raters' scores were more than one score level apart. Reliability of composition scoring, then, appears to have maintained normal standards in this study.

Comparability of Subjects to Norms

Descriptive statistics were collected for performance on the entire test battery and for the age of the sample. Table 6-3 gives the figures for the total sample as

Table 6-2

Interrater Reliability

Prompt	n	Interrater correlation	Adjudicated interrater correlation[a]	Spearman-Brown correction
Talk	52	.8487	.9441	.9712
Time	36	.8765	.9333	.9655
Soldiers	52	.8544	.9222	.9595
Energy	36	.8647	.9362	.9670
NP prompt	88	.8607	.9369	.9674
AI prompt	88	.8560	.9225	.9597

Note. NP = narrative/personal; AI = argumentative/impersonal.
[a]For this group, 13 of the 176 total essays, or 7.4%, required adjudication by a third rater because the scores given by the first two raters were more than one score level apart.

Table 6-3

Descriptive Statistics, by Proficiency and Scholastic Levels

Group	Essay topic[a]		MELAB[b]				Age
	NP	AI	Part 1	Part 2	Part 3	Final	
Beginning (n = 34)							
M	67.88	66.17	67.74	66.97	51.41	62.00	22.00
SD	3.57	4.88	3.65	9.18	9.86	5.05	4.9
Range	63–75	53–75	63–75	42–82	31–70	49–69	16–37
Intermediate (n = 27)							
M	72.67	71.89	73.26	77.82	72.48	74.56	22.11
SD	3.36	3.63	2.85	6.33	5.79	2.59	4.3
Range	67–77	65–77	67–77	62–90	59–85	70–79	17–31
Advanced (n = 27)							
M	82.30	82.33	83.74	85.89	87.70	85.63	24.67
SD	5.97	6.03	5.38	4.92	5.29	3.78	5.9
Range	75–93	75–93	75–93	73–96	79–99	80–92	17–41
Graduate (n = 27)[c]							
M	76.04	75.15	77.04	75.82	76.00	76.22	28.15
SD	7.59	8.41	7.61	12.95	15.95	11.05	5.2
Range	63–93	55–93	63–93	42–96	37–95	49–92	20–41
Undergraduate (n = 61)							
M	72.77	71.89	73.15	76.23	65.92	71.72	20.51
SD	7.21	8.17	7.65	9.65	16.62	10.26	3.0
Range	63–93	53–93	63–93	52–92	31–99	52–92	16–34
Whole sample (n = 88)							
M	73.77	72.89	74.34	76.10	69.01	73.10	22.85
SD	7.44	8.33	7.81	10.70	16.98	10.65	5.2
Range	63–93	53–93	63–93	42–96	31–99	49–92	16–41

[a]NP = rhetorically narrative, personal content topic 1B (Time) or 2A (Talk); AI = rhetorically argumentative, impersonal content topic 1A (Energy) or 2B (Soldiers). [b]Part 1 = writing test score (whichever was the higher of the two composition scores); Part 2 = listening test score; Part 3 = score on grammar, cloze, vocabulary, and reading test. [c]There were significant differences between graduates' and undergraduates' mean scores on Part 3 ($p < .01$) and on Part 1 on Prompt 1A ($p < .05$). There were no significant differences in mean scores on any measure for the two groups who wrote on the two different prompt sets.

well as for the proficiency-level and scholastic-level subgroups. Means for the total sample appear comparable to usual MELAB norms, though the Part 3 mean is somewhat lower than normal.

Performance of Proficiency Level and Academic Level Subgroups

T-tests were conducted for differences in means for the subgroups. For the different language proficiency levels, the scores on the three measures progress steadily higher and, as expected, all means differ significantly. For the scholastic level subgroups, graduates scored a full score level higher (77 is one ranking higher than 73) on Part 1 ($p<.05$) and on Part 3 (grammar, cloze, vocabulary, reading) ($p<.01$).

Comparability of Performance on Two Different Prompt Types

Correlation coefficients for the two composition topics for all the subjects, as well as for the proficiency-level and scholastic-level subgroups, are found in Table 6-4. For the whole sample the correlation between NP and AI scores is .89; for Prompt Set 1 (Energy/Time), .89; and for Prompt Set 2 (Soldiers/Talk), .90. Correlations are high for the scholastic-level subgroups but are lower for the more homogeneous proficiency-level subgroups.

To assess the consistency of scores on the NP and AI prompts, the mean difference in scores was computed at the .95 confidence level for the entire sample as well as for the proficiency-level and scholastic-level subgroups (Table 6-5). The mean difference is the NP score minus the AI score; thus a positive number indicates better performance on the NP prompt whereas a negative number shows better performance on the AI prompt.

As seen in Tables 6-3 and 6-5, the mean scores on the two prompt types were very close. The difference in means was only .886 for the total sample and ranged from .037 to 1.71 for the subgroups. The whole sample and most subgroups performed only slightly better on the NP prompt. One, the advanced proficiency-level subgroup, performed slightly better on the AI prompt. All .95 confidence intervals are small, indicating fairly certainly that 95% of the time the difference in scores will be small, within the range shown for each group. For example, for the total sample the mean difference in scores was .886, and for 95% of cases differences in scores will range from .069 to 1.70. The largest confidence interval occurred for the advanced proficiency-level subgroup, where the range was from

Table 6-4

Correlations Between NP and AI Prompts for the Whole Sample and for Subgroups

Prompt	Whole sample	Graduate	Under-graduate	Beginning	Intermediate	Advanced
1A/1B	.89	.79	.90	.53	.78	.52
n	36	9	27	12	13	11
2A/2B	.90	.91	.91	.82	.39	.77
n	52	18	34	22	14	16
NP/AI	.89	.87	.89	.75	.60	.65
n	88	27	61	34	27	27

Note. For abbreviations, see note to Table 6-3.

Table 6-5

Consistency of Scores on NP and AI Topics for Whole Sample and for Scholastic-Level and Proficiency Level Subgroups

Difference in scores	n	Mean difference	SD	Range	.95 confidence interval
Whole sample	88	.886	3.86	−10–12	.0696, 1.703
Undergraduate	61	.885	3.78	−10–12	.0834, 1.854
Graduate	27	.889	4.09	−10–8	−.7286, 2.506
Beginning	34	1.706	3.21	−6–10	.584, 2.828
Intermediate	27	.778	3.14	−6–8	−.465, 2.021
Advanced	27	−.037	4.99	−10–12	−2.013, 1.939

−2.01 to 1.94. This group had the smallest difference in means but showed the greatest variation in individual performance on the two prompt types. The variation is close to the standard error of measurement (SEM) for Part 1 of the MELAB battery and, in fact, is smaller than the normal MELAB SEM for the whole sample.

Responses to Questionnaire

An analysis of the responses to the questionnaire indicated that 85% of the subjects wished to have a choice of prompts, 11% did not want a choice, and 4% had no preference. As in the earlier study, the majority of those who had written on Prompt Set 2 preferred "Talk" to "Soldiers," whereas for Prompt Set 1 preferences were evenly split between "Time" and "Energy." Table 6-6 shows the subjects' preferred prompts and the self-evaluation of their performance on the two essays they wrote.

In evaluating their own performance, the subjects were evenly divided on which of their essays, the NP or AI, was better. Their reasons for their answers included not only the prompts but other factors, such as "warming up to the task" or, contrarily, "fatigue." There were no significant differences in any questionnaire responses between the two prompt set groups (those writing on Set 2 and those writing on Set 1) or between those who preferred a choice of prompts and those who did not.

Matching of Inconsistent Scorers With Consistent Scorers and Text Analysis

Although Tables 6-3, 6-4, and 6-5 provide evidence that, as a group, the subjects scored the same on the two essay samples and that any differences can be attributed to chance, 9 of the 88 subjects, or 10%, received scores more than

Table 6-6

Responses to Questionnaire

Which essay did you think was better?

Topic	n preferring topic
Soldiers (2B, AI)	27
Talk (2A, NP)	22
Energy (1A, AI)	15
Time (1B, NP)	14

Which topic did you like the best?

Topic	n preferring topic
Talk (2A, NP)	31
Time (1B, NP)	18
Energy (1A, AI)	17
Soldiers (2B, AI)	14
No preference	8

Preferred topic by Proficiency-Level Subgroup

Level	NP	AI	None
Beginning	18	13	3
Intermediate	15	9	3
Advanced	16	9	2
Total	49	31	8

Note. For abbreviations, see note to Table 6-3.

one ranking apart (8 or more points on the 19-point reporting scale) on their two essays. These scores would have required adjudication if they had represented two raters' scores on a single essay. No significant differences in means were found on any measure between this small group of inconsistently scoring writers and the 79 "consistent" writers.

The 9 "inconsistent" writers fell into each of the proficiency levels: 3 beginning, 1 intermediate, and 5 advanced. All 4 beginning- and intermediate-level "inconsistent" writers scored higher on the NP prompt. Of the 5 advanced-level "inconsistent" writers, 2 scored higher on the NP prompt and 3 scored higher on the AI prompt. All but 1 did better on their preferred prompt. One advanced-level writer scored higher on the AI prompt but gave the NP prompt as her preference; another advanced-level "inconsistent" scorer said he would have chosen the NP prompt but believed his AI essay was better, giving as his reason that he had budgeted his time better on the AI essay, which he wrote second.

The 9 "inconsistent" scorers were then matched with 12 "consistent" scorers according to proficiency level, part scores, and, where possible, language and native country. Three of the 9 were double-matched with 2 "consistent" writers because of difficulty in matching part scores and language background. The 42 essays of these 21 subjects were then analyzed for a number of linguistic and rhetorical features. The linguistic features were chosen to represent fluency, syntactic sophistication and accuracy, and lexical range and sophistication. For fluency, I counted the number of words, number of sentences, and number of T-units[3] were counted; for syntax, I counted the number of error-free T-units (spelling and punctuation errors were not considered errors in this measure in this study), mean length of T-units, and mean length of error-free T-units. These measures were selected because they have been shown to be significant in measuring ESL writing proficiency (Arthur, 1980; Larson-Freeman & Strom, 1977; Homburg, 1984; Tedick, 1988). For lexis, I counted the type/token[4] ratio, the number of occurrences of words with three or more syllables, the percent of occurrences of words with three or more syllables, the number of types of three-syllable words, and the percent of three-syllable word types. Biber (1986) demonstrated that longer word types are more representative of formal written than of informal oral discourse and that longer words convey more explicit meanings, resulting in high informational content in a condensed text. Thus longer words and a smaller type/token ratio would be connected to more sophisticated written discourse.

One measure, employing three features, was used to assess rhetoric. Connor and Lauer (Connor, 1988) constructed a scoring scale for three features seen in argumentative writing—Claims, Data, and Warrants—based on the work of the philosopher Stephen Toulmin. (See Appendix 6D for a description of the scale and examples.)

Table 6-7 shows descriptive statistics for the linguistic and rhetorical measures analyzed in the 42 compositions of the 12 consistent and 9 inconsistent writers. No significant differences in mean scores were found on any measure for these two groups of writers.

Length tends to decrease and lexis to become more sophisticated (as shown by the increase in the number of three-syllable words) in the AI prompts, whereas the syntactic and rhetorical features appear similar in both prompt types. Data scores are slightly lower for the AI prompts, perhaps in part because of the shorter length. It is difficult, however, to interpret these findings or to determine if there are any trends because the sample size is so small, a by-product of the low number of "inconsistent" writers.

Though the inconsistent writers appear to have used fewer three-syllable words on their NP essays than the consistent writers did, the differences were not significant. Syntax measures indicate slightly fewer error-free T-units on the AI prompts, but mean length of T-unit and error-free T-unit appear not to change from one prompt type to the other. Again, the sample is too small to hypothesize from this.

Of interest was the relative contribution of each of these linguistic and rhetorical features to the holistic score, especially in the proficiency-level subgroups for

Table 6-7

Descriptive Statistics for Linguistic and Rhetorical Features

Feature	Whole sample (n = 21) Prompt		Consistent writers (n = 12) Prompt		Inconsistent writers (n = 9) Prompt	
	NP	AI	NP	AI	NP	AI
Holistic						
score	75.10	73.86	75.25	75.33	74.89	71.89
SD	(9.1)	(11.3)	(10.1)	(10.1)	(8.2)	(13.2)
Fluency						
N words	253.38	207.86	272.33	229.08	228.11	179.56
SD	(88.8)	(100.7)	(86.7)	(83.4)	(90.2)	(119.2)
N sentences	15.86	13.62	17.50	15.00	13.67	11.78
SD	(6.3)	(7.7)	(7.1)	(6.1)	(4.5)	(9.5)
Syntax						
N T-units	20.71	15.95	22.92	17.67	17.78	13.67
SD	(8.4)	(8.3)	(8.6)	(6.6)	(7.6)	(10.1)
N EFTUs	11.62	9.10	13.17	10.50	9.56	7.22
SD	(7.1)	(7.6)	(6.7)	(7.4)	(7.6)	(8.1)
Mean LTU	12.45	12.56	12.41	13.18	12.50	11.7
SD	(3.1)	(4.5)	(3.3)	(4.1)	(2.9)	(5.1)
Mean LEFTU	10.50	10.39	11.28	11.35	9.57	9.11
SD	(3.5)	(4.6)	(3.8)	(3.9)	(3.1)	(5.4)
Lexis						
TT ratio	.475	.494	.468	.498	.483	.489
SD	(.07)	(.14)	(.07)	(.06)	(.07)	(.21)
N Oc3Syl	17.33	24.24	17.50	28.50	17.11	18.56
SD	(10.5)	(17.1)	(10.7)	(17.7)	(10.9)	(15.5)
% Oc3Syl	6.56	10.57	6.05	12.17	7.24	8.4
SD	(2.9)	(5.3)	(2.5)	(4.8)	(3.5)	(5.5)
N Ty3Syl	12.86	16.29	12.67	18.75	13.11	13.00
SD	(7.6)	(11.3)	(7.1)	(12.2)	(8.7)	(9.7)
% Ty3Syl	10.47	13.90	9.73	15.69	11.44	11.51
SD	(4.3)	(6.5)	(3.9)	(6.0)	(4.9)	(6.7)
Rhetoric						
Claim	1.93	1.90	1.92	2.04	1.94	1.72
SD	(.76)	(.93)	(.79)	(.86)	(.85)	(1.03)
Data	2.12	1.81	2.13	1.92	2.11	1.67
SD	(.61)	(.78)	(.61)	(.76)	(.65)	(.83)
Warrant	1.81	1.98	1.71	2.21	1.94	1.67
SD	(.73)	(.93)	(.66)	(.72)	(.85)	(1.11)

Note. NP = narrative personal prompt (Talk/Time); AI = argumentative impersonal prompt (Energy/Soldiers); N EFTUs = number of error-free T-units; mean LTU = mean length of T-units; mean LEFTU = mean length of error-free T-units; TT ratio = type/token ratio; N Oc3Syl = number of occurrences of words with three or more syllables; % Oc3Syl = percentage of occurrences of words with three or more syllables; N TySyl = number of word types with three or more sylllables; % Ty3Syl = percentage of word types with three or more syllables.

consistent and inconsistent writers. However, multiple regression analysis was not carried out because the sample size of inconsistent writers was so small. Instead, correlations of linguistic and rhetorical features with overall holistic scores are shown in Table 6-8; significant correlations are marked. Most of the correlations were only moderate; however, those features that had both relatively strong and significant correlations (.70 and over, significant at .05, .01, or .001) may be worth noting.

Of the fluency measures, length appeared strongly and significantly related to the overall holistic score for both consistent and inconsistent writers for both prompt types, NP and AI. Of the syntax measures, the number of T-units for inconsistent writers on the NP prompt and the mean length of error-free T-units for all writers on the AI prompt were strongly related to the overall holistic score. Of the lexical measures, the number of occurrences of three-syllable words and the number of types of three-syllable words appeared related to the holistic score for all writers on the AI prompt and for consistent writers on the NP prompt. The percentage of occurrences of three-syllable words was related for inconsistent writers on the AI prompt, and the percentage of word types with three or more syllables was related for consistent writers on the NP prompt and for inconsistent writers on the AI prompt. The rhetorical features all appeared closely related to the overall holistic score, especially for inconsistent writers on both prompt types. Consistent writers had high significant correlations for Claim on both prompt types and for Data on the AI prompts.

Discussion

The subjects in this study were a normally scoring MELAB group, but caution is necessary in generalizing about the findings reported here. The subjects were all tested in the United States, and no information is available about the duration of their residence there; also lacking is information about the duration and nature of their ESL study and their academic field. Furthermore, their background knowledge of the subject matter in the two AI prompts was not assessed.

In this study, most subjects performed the same, as measured by holistic score, on the two prompt types given them. Of the few who did not, all but two scored better on their preferred prompt. Most of the subjects preferred to have a choice of prompts, but if they had been offered prompts more similar in rhetorical specification or content, they might not have expressed such a clear preference. Judging by the small subgroup whose essays were analyzed, writers appear to perform consistently as far as linguistic features are concerned. Indeed, in an initial reading of the inconsistent writers' essays, one is struck by the linguistic similarity of each writer's two essays.

The second AI prompt, "Soldiers," appeared to have caused content difficulties for the beginning- and intermediate-level inconsistent writers, all but one of whom produced markedly shorter essays on this prompt than on the NP prompt

Table 6-8

Correlations of Holistic Scores With Linguistic and Rhetorical Features

Feature	Group	Prompt NP	Prompt AI
Fluency			
N words	Consistent[a]	.75**	.92***
	Inconsistent[b]	.81**	.76**
	Total[c]	.74***	.83***
N sent	Consistent	.20	.43
	Inconsistent	.64	.43
	Total	.31	.45*
Syntax			
N T-units	Consistent	.12	.48
	Inconsistent	.78**	.58
	Total	.33	.55**
N EFTUs	Consistent	.49	.69**
	Inconsistent	.67*	.62
	Total	.54**	.66***
Mean LTU	Consistent	.68**	.67*
	Inconsistent	.29	.68*
	Total	.55**	.68***
Mean LEFTU	Consistent	.44	.80**
	Inconsistent	.57	.80**
	Total	.47*	.80***
Lexis			
TT Ratio	Consistent	−.25	−.40
	Inconsistent	−.27	.11
	Total	−.26	−.00
N Oc3Syl	Consistent	.83***	.78**
	Inconsistent	.65	.83**
	Total	.76***	.79***
%Oc3Syl	Consistent	.71**	.39
	Inconsistent	.23	.84**
	Total	.46*	.63**
N Ty3Syl	Consistent	.9i***	.82***
	Inconsistent	.66*	.85**
	Total	.79***	.81***
% Ty3Syl	Consistent	.76**	.63*
	Inconsistent	.48	.89**
	Total	.61**	.76***
Rhetoric			
Claim	Consistent	.91***	.82***
	Inconsistent	.76*	.87**
	Total	.85***	.85***
Data	Consistent	.68*	.91***
	Inconsistent	.96***	.80**
	Total	.78***	.85***
Warrant	Consistent	.59*	.66*
	Inconsistent	.87**	.92***
	Total	.68***	.81***

Note. For abbreviations, see note to Table 6-7. [a]Consistent writers; *n* = 12. [b]Inconsistent writers; *n* = 9. [c]Total whose compositions were analyzed; *n* = 21.
* $p<.05$. ** $p<.01$. *** $p<.001$.

and were consequently penalized for brevity by the holistic raters. This result indicates that prompt developers should take particular care to make the subject content accessible or universal. Pairing "Soldiers" with "Energy" may have flawed the study in that "Energy" did appear content accessible to these subjects. The advanced-proficiency-level writers did not all perform better on one prompt type or the other. Their inconsistencies appeared more closely related to rhetorical features of their essays, and the nature of their difficulties with one prompt type or the other took on a more idiosyncratic nature.

Length bore a strong relation to the holistic score for the 42 essays analyzed, but the AI essays tended to be briefer than the NP ones and contained longer, perhaps more explicit words. The raters may have adjusted their expectations regarding length and lexis for each prompt type. In addition, some of the longer lexical items in the AI essays may have come from the prompts themselves. A more accurate lexical analysis might deduct the lexical items that appear in the prompts. The rhetorical features measured in this study bore the strongest relation to the overall holistic score for the inconsistent writers.

Although prompt type did not make a difference in the holistic scores of the total sample, it may be noteworthy that the largest percentage of "inconsistent" scorers came from the advanced-proficiency-level group. The advanced-level writers did not show a clear superiority in either the NP or the AI prompt, as the beginning- and intermediate-level inconsistent writers did. The responses of additional advanced-level writers to prompts of various types, such as NP, AI, NI, and AP, may be worth investigating.

Advanced-proficiency-level writers did not prefer the seemingly more challenging AI prompt more frequently than the less advanced writers did. When they did, the preference did not appear to be to their detriment. Providing a prompt choice, both safe and challenging, may accommodate a broad proficiency range, keeping in mind that what is difficult for one person may not be for another. The choice may prove beneficial from an affective standpoint but remain neutral from the standpoint of performance or scoring.

The writing task in this study, a 30-minute impromptu essay written without a dictionary or other aid, may not provide a writing sample that is representative of all writers' work. A comparison of performance on other task types, such as summary writing, research papers, and editing tasks, was outside the scope of the study, which focused instead on prompts in one kind of writing task. The results therefore cannot be applied to other task types or to the writing construct without further research in those areas.

Conclusions

The purposes of the study were to determine the validity of collecting a single writing sample and to determine if performance would vary when one element, the prompt, was manipulated. Although the study was limited to a certain task type, performance on the two prompt types generally did not differ as measured by holistic ratings. Text analysis revealed some possible relations between holistic score and length, lexis, and rhetorical features. Offering a choice of prompts appears not to be detrimental to test takers.

Acknowledgments

An earlier version of this paper was presented at the TESOL convention in San Antonio, Texas, in March 1989. I thank Ulla Connor and Sarah Briggs for their generous support, suggestions, and criticisms of earlier versions of the paper; and Dan Douglas and Carol Chapelle for their helpful editorial suggestions.

Notes

1. The English Language Institute Testing Office at the University of Michigan provided me with MELAB statistics.

2. These norms are based on 10,447 MELAB examinees tested between May 1985 and March 1989 (Michigan English Language Institute internal records).

3. Hunt (1965, 1970) developed the T-unit to measure developing maturation or sophistication in the writing of native speakers. A T-unit is defined as an independent clause and all its subordinate clauses. Usually a simple sentence or a complex sentence will contain one T-unit; a compound sentence contains two T-units. Long T-units are associated with complex sentences.

4. A word type is a particular word, counted just once, regardless of how many times it occurs; a token is any of the individual occurrences of the type. Usually the type/token ratio decreases as the length of the document increases.

References

Arthur, B. (1980). Short-term changes in EFL composition skills. In C. Yorio, K. Perkins, & J. Schachter (Eds.), *On TESOL '79* (pp. 330–342). Washington, DC: Teachers of English to Speakers of Other Languages.

Biber, D. (1986). Spoken and written textual dimensions in English: Resolving the contradictory findings. *Language, 62*, 384–414.

Breland, H. (1983). *The direct assessment of writing skill: A measurement review* (College Board Report 83-6, ETS RR No. 83-82). New York: College Entrance Examination Board.

Bridgeman, B., & Carlson, S. (1983). *A survey of academic writing tasks required of graduate and undergraduate foreign students* (TOEFL Research Report No. 15). Princeton, NJ: Educational Testing Service.

Canale, M., & Swain, M. (1980). Theoretical bases of communicative approaches to second language teaching and testing. *Applied Linguistics, 1*, 1–47.

Carlson, S., & Bridgeman, B. (1986). Testing ESL student writers. In K. Greenburg, H. S. Wiener, & R. A. Donovan (Eds.), *Writing assessment: Issues and strategies* (pp. 126–152). New York: Longman.

Carlson, S., Bridgeman, B., Camp, R., & Waanders, J. (1985). *Relationship of admission test scores to writing performance of native and nonnative speakers of English* (TOEFL Research Report 19). Princeton, NJ: Educational Testing Service.

Connor, U. M. (1988). Linguistic/rhetorical measures for International Persuasive Student Writing. *Research in the Teaching of English, 24* (1), 67–87.

Freedman, A., & Pringle, I. (1980). Writing in the college years: Some indices of growth. *College Composition and Communication, 31*, 311–324.

Hoetker, J., & Brossell, G. (1986). A procedure for writing content-fair essay examination topics for large-scale writing assignments. *College Composition and Communication, 37*, 328–335.

Homburg, T. (1984). Holistic evaluation of ESL composition: Can it be validated objectively? *TESOL Quarterly, 18*, 87–107.

Hunt, K. W. (1965). *Grammatical structures written at three grade levels*. Champaign, IL: National Council of Teachers of English.

Hunt, K. W. (1970). Syntactic maturity in school children and adults. *Monographs of the Society for Research in Child Development, 53*(1).

Larson-Freeman, D., & Strom, V. (1977). The construction of a second-language acquisition index of development. *Language Learning, 27*, 123–134.

Mohan, B., & Lo, W. A. Y. (1985). Academic writing and Chinese students: Transfer and developmental factors. *TESOL Quarterly, 19*, 515–534.

Purves, Alan C., Soter, A., Takala, S., & Vahapassi, A. (1984). Towards a domain-referenced system for classifying composition assignments. *Research in the Teaching of English, 18*, 385–416.

Quellmalz, E., Capell, F. J., & Chou, C. P. (1982). Effects of discourse and response made on the measurement of writing competence. *Journal of Educational Measurement, 19*, 241–258.

Ruth, L., Murphy, S. (1984). Designing topics for writing assessment: Problems of meaning. *College Composition and Communication, 35*, 410–422.

Spaan, M. (1989, March). Essay tests: What's in a prompt? Paper presented at the TESOL convention, San Antonio, TX.

Swinford, F. (1964). *Test analysis, advanced placement examination in American history, form MBP* (ETS SR No. 53). Princeton, NJ: Educational Testing Service.

Tedick, D. J. (1988). *The effects of topic familiarity on the written compositions of international graduate students*. Ohio State University Research and Scholarly Activities Forum. Columbus, OH: Ohio State University Council of Graduate Students.

Tedick, D. J. (1990). ESL writing assessment: Subject-matter knowledge and its impact on performance. *English for Specific Purposes, 9*, 123–143.

Toulmin, S. E. (1958). *The uses of argument*. Cambridge: Cambridge University Press.

Toulmin, S. E., Rieke, R., & Janik, J. (1979). *An introduction to reasoning*. New York: Macmillan.

Vahapassi, A. (1982). On the specification of the domain of written composition. In A. Purves & S. Takala (Eds.), *An international perspective on the evaluation of written composition: Evaluation in education: An international review series* (pp. 265–290). Oxford: Pergamon Press.

Witte, S. P. (1987). Pre-text and composing. *College Composition and Communication, 38*, 397–425.

Appendix 6A:
Topics and Standard Instructions From Michigan English Language Assessment Battery

Part 1: Composition

Name _____ DATE _____
      (family/last/surname)   (given/first name)
INSTRUCTIONS:

1. You will have 30 minutes to write on one of the two topics printed below. If you do not write on one of these two topics, your paper will not be graded. If you do not understand the topics, ask the examiner to explain or to translate them.

TOPICS. SET _____ (CIRCLE THE LETTER OF THE TOPIC YOU CHOOSE)
         A. _____
         B. _____

2. You may make an outline if you wish, but your outline will not be used to determine your grade.
3. Write about 1 to 2 pages. You will lose credit if your paper is extremely short. Write on both sides of the paper. Ask the examiner for more paper if you need it.
4. You may make any changes or corrections in the body of the composition. You will not be graded on the appearance of your paper, but be sure your handwriting is legible. Do not waste time copying your composition over.
5. Your essay will be graded on the clarity of your writing and the linguistic range and accuracy you show.

PLEASE SIGN YOUR NAME BELOW WHEN YOU HAVE UNDERSTOOD THESE INSTRUCTIONS.
NAME (SIGNATURE) _____
START HERE:

Appendix 6B:
Descriptions of Score Levels for MELAB Compositions

97 Topic is richly and fully developed. Flexible use of a wide range of syntactic (sentence level) structures, and accurate morphological (word forms) control. There is a wide range of appropriately used vocabulary. Organization is appropriate and effective, and there is excellent control of connection. Spelling and punctuation appear error free.

93 Topic is fully and complexly developed. Flexible use of a wide range of syntactic structures. Morphological control is nearly always accurate. Vocabulary is broad and appropriately used. Organization is well controlled and appropriate to the material, and the writing is well connected. Spelling and punctuation errors are not distracting.

87 Topic is well developed, with acknowledgment of its complexity. Varied syntactic structures are used with some flexibility, and there is good morphological control. Vocabulary is broad and usually used appropriately. Organization is controlled and generally appropriate to the material, and there are few problems with connection. Spelling and punctuation errors are not distracting.

83 Topic is generally clearly and completely developed, with at least some acknowledgment of its complexity. Both simple and complex syntactic structures are generally adequately used; there is adequate morphological control. Vocabulary use shows some flexibility, and is usually appropriate. Organization is controlled and shows some appropriacy to the material, and connection is usually adequate. Spelling and punctuation errors are sometimes distracting.

77 Topic is developed clearly but not completely and without acknowledging its complexity. Both simple and complex syntactic structures are present; in some "77" essays these are cautiously and accurately used while in others there is more fluency and less accuracy. Morphological control is inconsistent. Vocabulary is adequate, but may sometimes be inappropriately used. Organization is generally controlled, while connection is sometimes absent or unsuccessful. Spelling and punctuation errors are sometimes distracting.

73 Topic development is present, although limited by incompleteness, lack of clarity, or lack of focus. The topic may be treated as though it has only one dimension, or only one point of view is possible. In some "73" essays both simple and complex syntactic structures are present, but with many errors; others have accurate syntax but are very restricted in the range of language attempted. Morphological control is inconsistent. Vocabulary is sometimes inadequate, and sometimes inappropriately used. Organization is partially controlled, while connection is often absent or unsuccessful. Spelling and punctuation errors are sometimes distracting.

67 Topic development is present but restricted, and often incomplete or unclear. Simple syntactic structures dominate, with many errors; complex syntactic structures, if present, are not controlled. Lacks morphological control. Narrow and simple vocabulary usually approximates meaning but is often inappropriately used. Organization, when apparent, is poorly controlled, and little or no connection is apparent. Spelling and punctuation errors are often distracting.

63 Contains little sign of topic development. Simple syntactic structures are present, but with many errors; lacks morphological control. Narrow and

simple vocabulary inhibits communication. There is little or no organization, and no connection apparent. Spelling and punctuation errors often cause serious interference.

57 Often extremely short; contains only fragmentary communication about the topic. There is little syntactic or morphological control. Vocabulary is highly restricted and inaccurately used. No organization or connection are apparent. Spelling is often indecipherable and punctuation is missing or appears random.

53 Extremely short, usually about 40 words or less. Communicates nothing, and is often copied directly from the prompt. There is little sign of syntactic or morphological control. Vocabulary is extremely restricted and repetitively used. There is no apparent organization or connection. Spelling is often indecipherable and punctuation is missing or appears random.

Appendix 6C:
Questionnaire

(Note: More writing space was provided to examinees.)
Name _____ DATE _____
This morning, you wrote two compositions.

1. If you had only one composition to write, would you want a choice of topics? Why or why not?
2. If you had a choice of topics, which one would you have chosen to write on today?

_____ Energy sources   _____ Party talk
_____ Time of day   _____ Mercenary soldiers
Why?

3. Which of your two compositions do you think was better? Why?
4. Usually for MELAB tests, only one composition is given.

There are three parts to the regular MELAB:

Composition,
Listening, and
Objective (Grammar, Cloze, Vocabulary, Reading).

In what order would you like to take these three tests?

First:
Second:
Third:

Why?

Appendix 6D:
Toulmin/Connor-Lauer Evaluation Scheme for Persuasive Essays

Definitions and Examples

Claim

"Conclusions whose merits we are seeking to establish" (Toulmin, 1958, p. 97) and "assertions put forward publicly for general acceptance" (Toulmin, Rieke, & Janik, 1979, p. 29).
Example: *There's a fire.*

Data

Support for the claim in the form of experience, facts, statistics, or occurrences.
Example: *I smell smoke.*

Warrant

Bridges from data to claim, a logical step or connection. "Rules, principles, inference—licences or what you will instead of additional items of information . . . to show the step to the original claim or conclusion is an appropriate or legitimate one. . . . general hypothetical statements which act as bridges" (Toulmin, 1958, p. 98) and authorize the step from the data to the original claim.
Example: *Where there's smoke, there's fire.*

Connor-Lauer Criteria (scale 1-3) for Judging Quality of Claim, Data, and Warrant

Claim

1 No specific problem stated and/or no consistent point of view. May have one subclaim. No solution offered, or if offered non-feasible, unoriginal, and inconsistent with claim.
2 Specific, explicitly stated problem. Somewhat consistent point of view. Relevant to the task. Has two or more subclaims that have been developed. Solution offered with some feasibility with major claim.
3 Specific, explicitly stated problem with consistent point of view. Several well developed subclaims, explicitly tied to the major claim. Highly relevant to the task. Solution offered that is feasible, original, and consistent with major claim.

Data

1 Minimal use of data. Data of the "everyone one knows" type, with little reliance on personal experience or authority. Not directly related to major claim.

2 Some use of data with reliance on personal experience or authority. Some variety in use of data. Data generally related to major claim.
3 Extensive use of specific, well-developed data of a variety of types. Data explicitly connected to major claim.

Warrant
1 Minimal use of warrants. Warrants only minimally reliable and relevant to the case. Warrants may include logical fallacies.
2 Some use of warrants. Though warrants allow the writer to make the bridge between data and claim, some distortion and informal fallacies are evident.
3 Extensive use of warrants. Reliable and trustworthy, allowing rater to accept the bridge from data to claim. Relevant. Evidence of some backing. Tries to deal with some counterargument.

7

Computer-Assisted Testing of Reading Comprehension: Comparisons Among Multiple-Choice and Open-Ended Scoring Methods

Grant Henning
Educational Testing Service

Michael Anbar
The State University of New York at Buffalo

Carl E. Helm
R. W. Johnson Medical School

Sen J. D'Arcy
The State University of New York at Buffalo

Much has been written about the potential advantages of computerized teaching and testing of language abilities in general and of reading comprehension in particular (Canale, 1986; Henning, 1987; Hicks, 1986; Jung, 1988; Stansfield, 1986). Many computerized reading tests proposed to date, however, have employed only multiple-choice-type items, and in this way have failed to harness computer capabilities by (a) using more open-ended item formats, (b) scoring degrees of correctness and incorrectness, or (c) engaging in interactive communication with the examinee. Furthermore, the quest for suitable alternatives to the multiple-choice format has not always been productive, although testing specialists have extensively investigated open-ended test item formats that might allow for more productive and creative response behaviors than the recognition and option-selection response behaviors usually associated with multiple-choice items (Breland & Gaynor, 1979; Bridgeman, 1989; Ward, 1982). Among the problems commonly posed by alternative, open-ended item formats are (a) the increased time and cost of scoring, (b) the decreased reliability of scores obtained, and (c) the lack of consistent empirical validity evidence in support of particular open-ended approaches over multiple-choice approaches.

The pilot study reported here is an attempt to investigate approaches to the open-ended testing of reading comprehension via computer that may be economically scored, enhance test reliability, and yield advantages in comparative item statistics over multiple-choice approaches. The CASIP (Computer-Assisted Socratic Instruction Procedure) employed in the study has been used successfully elsewhere in the testing of medical students and residents (Anbar, 1987, 1988; Anbar & Loonsk, 1988; Anbar, D'Arcy, & Loonsk, 1989). In one case, in which CASIP provided an authoring environment for training and assessing medical case management, trainees were requested to query a computer-simulated patient for information leading to a successful diagnosis of illness. Evaluation was based on the appropriateness of both queries and diagnoses. In the study described here the authoring environment was used to present and evaluate responses to multiple-choice and constructed-response items for assessing English as a second language (ESL) reading comprehension.

Method

Subjects

To compare different item formats and scoring techniques, the study relied on the responses of 44 nonnative speakers of English who were students at the State University of New York at Buffalo. These students represented about eight language backgrounds; approximately two-thirds were Japanese. Drawn from both graduate and undergraduate levels, the sample consisted of both males and females in proportions representative of ESL students at that institution (approximately 60% male and 40% female).

Instrumentation

The computer-assisted reading test consisted of eight reading passages selected from the August 1985 and the July 1986 disclosed forms of the Test of English as a Foreign Language (TOEFL) and their associated 40 four-option multiple-choice items. In addition, 40 open-ended items requested response information identical to that requested by corresponding multiple-choice items. Typical examples of multiple-choice and corresponding open-ended items follow. The items accompanied reading passages that varied in length from about 100 to 250 words. The number of each of the three general types of items per passage varied from about four to eight, depending on the length of the passage. The reading passages are not reproduced here to conserve space.

Multiple-Choice
According to the passage, mistletoe seeds travel from place to place by: (1) clinging to birds' beaks; (2) sticking to berries; (3) spreading over loose bark; (4) blowing to nearby branches.

Corresponding Open-Ended
How do mistletoe plants spread from tree to tree?

Multiple-Choice
The main topic of this passage is: (1) an explanation of marine biology; (2) new locations for oyster beds; (3) improvements in the oyster industry; (4) the shellfish industry before 1950.

Corresponding Open-Ended
What is the main topic of this passage?

In addition to these item types, approximately 40 experimental open-ended questions were devised to investigate item function when a greater variety of response type is encouraged. An example of an open-ended item of the experimental type follows.

Experimental Open-Ended
What was the role of the government in the economic growth of the 1950's?

The computerized version of the present ESL reading test employed the Computer Assisted Socratic Instruction Program developed by Anbar (1986). The program was originally developed to author interactive programs for training physicians in medical case management. CASIP also lent certain advantages to the test development process:

1. The test versions could be scored instantaneously by machine, which was especially helpful for scoring open-ended, free-response items.
2. An automatic log was made of response time for each individual responding to each item in each format.
3. The open-ended responses could be scored not only as correct or incorrect but also according to degrees of correctness and incorrectness. In practice, this resulted in four separate scoring methods for the open-ended items: (a) binary, 0-1, correct/incorrect; (b) three-step negative, 0-2, incorrect irrelevant/incorrect relevant/correct; (c) three-step positive, 0-2, incorrect/correct/preferred correct; (d) four-step balanced, 0-3, incorrect irrelevant/incorrect relevant/correct/preferred correct.
4. All examinee responses were stored by computer and could be retrieved on demand to verify and debug computer scoring procedures. Frequent debugging was necessary at the pilot stage because the computer had to be programmed to recognize all acceptable answers. This recognition entailed use of a spelling algorithm added to allow recognition of some misspelled words.
5. We planned, but did not fully implement, a procedure by which the computer would interact further with the examinee, for example, by asking why a particular incorrect relevant answer was given and by highlighting portions of text where specific answers might be found.

Procedures

Because all subjects answered the same items in both the multiple-choice and the open-ended formats, we thought it necessary to balance the design of the presentation to prevent practice and sequence effects, even though we did not provide feedback on performance in this version of the test. Half the subjects received all the multiple-choice items for each passage before receiving the open-ended items, and the other half encountered the items in the opposite sequence. Also, because the same 90-minute time limit had to be imposed on all subjects, no subject was able to complete all 120 items based on all eight passages. It subsequently became apparent that the problem of insufficient time resulted primarily from certain of the 40 experimental questions that purposely requested information not available in the passage. We had intended the examinees to respond quickly by indicating that the information was not available in the passage, but in practice they spent excessive amounts of time searching for the information. For purposes of comparative analysis, then, the study was restricted to the 27 subjects who were able to respond to all items associated with only the first three reading passages (38 items, consisting of 19 multiple-choice and 19 corresponding open-ended items). The 40 experimental open-ended items designed to encourage greater variety of response, for reasons already indicated, did not function in the manner intended. For these reasons, the subsequent analyses and reporting of results considered neither passages 4 through 8 nor the experimental-type open-ended questions.

The multiple-choice and binary open-ended items were scored by computer and later checked manually. The open-ended items initially were scored by degree of correctness manually from the computer record of stored responses, and the scores were incorporated into the computerized scoring system later. Thus, with regard to the data analyzed in this preliminary study, human and computer judgments of correctness corresponded perfectly because only the computer judgments that agreed with human judgments were eventually allowed and were programmed into the CASIP system.

Results

Means, standard deviations, and Kuder-Richardson Formula 20 (KR-20) reliabilities for the 19-item reading comprehension test, both for multiple-choice and open-ended item format, and for four open-ended scoring variations, are reported in Table 7-1. Also in the table are Spearman-Brown projected reliability estimates for a hypothetical test of 50 items assuming the same level of homogeneity of item variance present in the 19-item experimental test.

When the open-ended items were scored as correct or incorrect in the same binary mode as the multiple-choice items, the multiple-choice version of the test

Table 7-1

Means, Standard Deviations, and Reliability Estimates for Variations of a 10-Item ESL Reading Comprehension Test ($N = 27$)

Format	Scoring method	M	SD	KR-20	SB-50[a]
Multiple choice	Binary	13.07	3.562	0.738	0.881
Open ended	Binary	13.15	3.266	0.691	0.855
Open ended	3-step negative	29.56	5.515	0.750	0.888
Open ended	3-step positive	18.22	6.465	0.804	0.915
Open ended	4-step balanced	34.74	8.799	0.831	0.928

[a]Expected reliability estimate when test length is adjusted to 50 items by means of the Spearman-Brown Prophecy Formula.

had a slight reliability advantage (KR-20 = 0.738 versus 0.691 for 19 items). However, as the open-ended scoring techniques increasingly took into account degrees of correctness, the reliability advantage turned in favor of the open-ended version of the test (KR-20 = 0.750, 0.804, and 0.831, versus 0.738 for the multiple-choice version). Presumably, the increase in reliability associated with the open-ended item format resulted from an increase in item information and discrimination when degrees of correctness and incorrectness were taken into account.

Table 7-2 reports individual and mean item-total point biserial correlation coefficients for the 19 reading items as an indication of item discriminability. Discrimination at the item level was greater for the open-ended than for the multiple-choice item formats when degrees of correctness and incorrectness were considered in the scoring of the open-ended items. The mean adjusted item-total point biserial correlation for multiple-choice items was only 0.445, whereas the same mean correlation for open-ended items in the balanced scoring condition increased to 0.539. No doubt these higher item discriminations accounted in large measure for the superior estimates of internal consistency reliability reported in Table 7-1. The pattern of test reliability advantage by test method shown in Table 7-1 was identical to the pattern of advantage observed in the mean adjusted item discrimination coefficients (Table 7-2).

A final question of interest concerns the extent to which the multiple-choice and open-ended tests with the same content were measuring the same abilities in the examinee. A sufficiently high correlation between multiple-choice and open-ended formats might suggest that employing an open-ended rather than a multiple-choice item format would add little new information. Pearson product-moment correlations among all tests by format and scoring method are reported in Table 7-3. The correlations between multiple-choice and open-ended tests ranged from 0.686 to 0.722, depending on the scoring method. More important, the higher, disattenuated coefficients in parentheses, ranging from 0.890 to 0.993, show that only when degree of correctness was considered in scoring of the open-ended tests did a trend appear suggestive of those tests possibly adding new information.

Table 7-2

Item-Total Point Biserial Correlations for 19 Reading Comprehension Items in Various
Experimental Conditions ($N = 27$)

Item	Binary multiple choice	Binary open ended	Negative open ended	Positive open ended	Balanced open ended
1	0.327	0.302	0.308	0.328	0.338
2	0.128	0.435	0.413	0.394	0.423
3	0.424	0.485	0.567	0.664	0.672
4	0.474	0.494	0.494	0.515	0.569
5	0.593	0.498	0.542	0.564	0.568
6	0.375	−0.013	0.156	0.163	0.232
7	0.190	−0.083	0.107	−0.033	0.101
8	0.277	0.553	0.443	0.685	0.600
9	0.487	0.646	0.678	0.817	0.811
10	0.784	0.347	0.355	0.528	0.517
11	0.328	0.090	0.102	0.127	0.165
12	0.516	0.312	0.228	0.387	0.290
13	0.404	0.608	0.498	0.526	0.505
14	0.262	0.562	0.633	0.577	0.629
15	0.546	0.476	0.430	0.716	0.649
16	0.266	0.441	0.545	0.355	0.431
17	0.496	0.479	0.609	0.560	0.654
18	0.595	0.410	0.498	0.432	0.482
19	0.653	0.260	0.225	0.403	0.282
M^a	0.428	0.384	0.412	0.458	0.469
	(0.445)	(0.423)	(0.457)	(0.530)	(0.539)
SD^a	0.169	0.201	0.179	0.213	0.192
	(0.224)	(0.231)	(0.217)	(0.285)	(0.259)

[a]Estimates in parentheses were made from Fisher z transformations and are thus more accurate.

Discussion

The primary purpose of the study was to compare test results obtained from
varying the format and scoring for a computer-administered test of ESL reading
comprehension. Both internal consistency reliability estimates and mean item
discriminations were higher for the open-ended version than for the multiple-
choice version of the test, but only when the open-ended items were scored for
degree of correctness or incorrectness. The same results for simple binary correct/
incorrect scoring of open-ended items were less satisfactory than the scores
obtained for multiple-choice items on the same passage content. Also, the disattenuated correlations between multiple-choice and open-ended tests of the same
content approached unity unless open-ended tests were scored according to degree
of correctness. The latter phenomenon suggests that the open-ended item format
may hold little informational advantage over the multiple-choice item formats of

Table 7-3

Pearson Product-Moment Correlations Among 19-Item Multiple-Choice and Open-Ended Tests of the Same Content, By Scoring Method ($N = 27$)[a]

	MC	OE1	OE2	OE3	OE4
MC	1.000	—	—	—	—
OE1	0.709	1.000	—	—	—
	(0.993)				
OE2	0.722	0.962	1.000	—	—
	(0.970)				
OE3	0.686	0.985	0.926	1.000	—
	(0.891)				
OE4	0.697	0.923	0.963	0.927	1.000
	(0.890)				

Note. MC = multiple choice, binary; OE1 = open ended, binary; OE2 = open ended, negative; OE3 = open ended, positive; OE4 = open ended, balanced.
[a]Coefficients in parentheses have been disattenuated to hold reliability constant.

the kinds used in this study unless open-ended items are scored according to degree of correctness or incorrectness.

The study suggests several possible advantages of the CASIP authoring system over more traditional approaches to the development and administration of reading comprehension tests:

1. Subjects can be allowed to proceed at their own pace while the system maintains a log of the actual time expended with each item encounter.
2. The same items can be scored by multiple methods while the system maintains a record of all examinee responses.
3. Text that contains the tested information can be highlighted, on behalf of subjects in particular responding categories, and the system can record the amount of reliance placed on such help techniques.
4. Other relevant aids can be assigned or presented to subjects experiencing difficulty with particular items, and the effect of such aid on the pattern of responding can be analyzed.
5. Examinees in particular responding categories (e.g., incorrect relevant response) can be asked why they gave a particular response.

Several limitations of the piloted methodology also surfaced:

1. Programming the computer to recognize all correct open-ended responses according to degree of correctness is a nontrivial task involving frequent piloting and debugging. Even when the task is approaching completion, random subsets of examinee responses should be checked manually to ensure that possible unanticipated correct answers are not scored as incorrect.
2. The extent to which unfamiliarity or anxiety associated with computer use may have affected the pattern of responses of some of these ESL learners is not yet known.

3. Owing to hardware and facility constraints, it is frequently not so easy to gather large sample data sets via computer as it is to gather data from paper-and-pencil tests. The sample of students and test items in our study, though large enough to permit analysis and statistical generalization, was understandably small. Intended future applications will involve larger samples, greater reliance on open-ended item types, and implementation of other aforementioned advantages of CASIP.

Acknowledgments

We thank the Cognitive and Assessment Research Division of Educational Testing Service for encouragement and support of this project. We also acknowledge Professor Stephen C. Dunnet, Director, Intensive English Institute, Faculty of Educational Studies, State University of New York at Buffalo, for his cooperation in arranging access to test subjects.

References

Anbar, M. (1986). CASIP—A novel authoring tool for open-ended natural language CAI. *Proceedings of the 28th International Conference of the Association for the Development of Computer-Based Instructional Systems* (pp. 1–4). Bellingham, WA: Association for the Development of Computer-Based Instructional Systems.

Anbar, M. (1987). CAI—A way to avoid the pitfalls of multiple-choice behavior in medical practice. *Medical Electronics, 18*, 118–124.

Anbar, M. (1988). Cue free computerized interactive tests—Computer emulation of oral exams. In W. E. Hammond (Ed.), *Proceedings of the AAMSI Congress* (pp. 11–15). Washington, DC: American Association for Medical Systems and Informatics.

Anbar, M., D'Arcy, S. J., & Loonsk, J. W. (1989). Insights into students' medical knowledge and decision making skills using tests with unrestricted natural language input. In W. E. Hammond (Ed.), *Proceedings of the AAMSI Congress* (pp. 190–194). Washington, DC: American Association for Medical Systems and Informatics.

Anbar, M., & Loonsk, J. W. (1988). Computer emulated oral exams—Rationale and implementation of cue-free interactive computerized tests. *Medical Teacher, 10*, 175–180.

Breland, H. M., & Gaynor, J. L. (1979). A comparison of direct and indirect assessments of writing skill. *Journal of Educational Measurement, 16*, 119–128.

Bridgeman, B. (1989). *Comparative validity of multiple-choice and free-response items on the advanced placement examination in biology.* New York: College Entrance Examination Board.

Canale, M. (1986). The promise and threat of computerized adaptive assessment of reading comprehension. In C. W. Stansfield (Ed.), *Technology and language testing* (pp. 29–45). Washington, DC: Teachers of English to Speakers of Other Languages.

Henning, G. (1987). *A guide to language testing: Development, evaluation, research.* New York: Newbury House/Harper & Row.

Hicks, M. (1986). Computerized multilevel ESL testing, a rapid screening methodology. In C. W. Stansfield (Ed.), *Technology and language testing* (pp. 79–90). Washington, DC: Teachers of English to Speakers of Other Languages.

Jung, U. O. H. (Ed.) (1988). *Computers in applied linguistics and language teaching: A CALL handbook.* Frankfurt am Main: Peter Lang.

Stansfield, C. W. (Ed.) (1986). *Technology and language testing.* Washington, DC: Teachers of English to Speakers of Other Languages.

Ward, W. C. (1982). A comparison of free-response and multiple-choice forms of verbal aptitude tests. *Applied Psychological Measurement, 6*(1), 1–11.

8

The Role of Instructions in Testing Summarizing Ability

Andrew D. Cohen
University of Minnesota

Summarizing tasks on reading comprehension tests have a natural appeal as "authentic" tests in this era of communicative language testing, given that they attempt to simulate real-world tasks in which nonnative readers are called on to read a text and write a summary of its main ideas. To summarize successfully, respondents need both reading and writing skills. First, they must select and use effectively those reading strategies that are appropriate for summarizing the source text—that is, identifying topical information, distinguishing superordinate from subordinate material, and identifying redundant as well as trivial information. Then they must perform the appropriate writing tasks to produce a coherent text summary—that is, selecting topical information or generating it if none appears explicitly in the text, deleting trivial and redundant material, substituting superordinate terms for lists of terms or sequences of events, and, finally, restating the text so that it sounds coherent and polishing it so that it reads smoothly (Kintsch & van Dijk, 1978; van Dijk, 1980; Brown, Campione, & Day, 1981; Brown & Day, 1983; Chou Hare & Borchardt, 1984; Basham & Rounds, 1986; Davies & Whitney, 1984).

Background

The results of a summarizing test are intended to reflect how the respondents might perform on such a task in an authentic setting. In fact, a real-world summary is often quite different from a test summary. Real summaries are usually prepared for others who have not read the text and simply want to know what it is about. Such readers would probably not be concerned about the form in which the summary appears. Test summaries, on the other hand, usually have restrictions as to length, format, and style and are prepared for an assessor who has already decided what the text is about and wants to see to what extent the respondents approximate those decisions.

The test summary may thus result in a mismatch whereby respondents use one set of criteria in preparing their summaries whereas the raters use another in assessing them. For example, perceptions undoubtedly differ regarding what a "main idea" consists of and the appropriate way to write it up (e.g., precisely how telegraphically). Views may also differ as to the acceptability of introducing commentary into the summary. In research by Basham (1987) with Alaska Native students, respondents used their own world view as a filter in the summaries they wrote, personalizing them. If such differences are not eliminated through prior training, careful instructions on the test, or both, the result could be a misfit between the way the summary task is executed and the criteria the raters use to evaluate it.

Along with possible cultural differences, there are other potential causes of discrepancy between the way respondents are "supposed" to prepare summaries and the way they actually do it. For example, a study of 40 Hebrew-speaking university students writing English as a foreign language (EFL) summaries (Kozminsky & Gratz, 1986) found that, whereas the notes the students took on the text were of a word-level, "bottom-up" nature, their summaries were constructed top-down—that is, based on general knowledge. The researchers concluded that the reading was fragmented rather than reflecting ongoing interaction with the text that would combine top-down and bottom-up analysis. Likewise, a recent survey of Brazilian studies of reading processes (Cohen, 1987) indicated that the respondents involved were often not executing summarizing tasks in a way consistent with the model of what summarizing should entail, as presented above. A study by Holmes (1986), for example, found that six EFL graduate students did little monitoring of their summaries. They read in a linear and compartmentalized manner, rather than globally so as to extract the main ideas.

Consistent with Holmes' study, a study by Gimenez (1984) with five EFL graduate students revealed the major summarizing strategy to be word-level processing as opposed to syntactic analysis or text-level analysis. Often the summaries reflected a focus on only part of the text, with the interpretation of the text based on both the words the subject had learned (however effectively) and collected in reading the text and on previous knowledge.

In a study comparing a group of high-proficiency college-level EFL students with a low-proficiency group, Johns and Mayes (1990) found neither group to be using macropropositions[1] in their summaries. Furthermore, the low-proficiency students were doing a considerable amount of direct copying of material from the source text into their summaries, as the summaries were required to be written in the second language as well. In an earlier study, Johns (1985) found that underprepared natives were likewise more prone to use reproductions (copying and paraphrase) in their summaries than macropropositions. In a case study, Sarig (1988) helped explain the propensity to lift material directly out of the text for use in summaries. She found conceptual transformation or reconceptualization at the macro level to be a skill that did not come naturally to a competent college student either in native- or foreign-language summarizing and concluded that it had to be taught explicitly. Nonetheless, the explicit teaching of such reconceptualization may not yield such positive results either. Bensoussan and Kreindler

(1990), for example, found that EFL students with a semester's training in summary writing were able to see summaries as an important tool for grasping the gist of a text but still expressed frustration at their inability to distinguish macro- from micropropositions.

A previous study (Cohen, in press) had as its main purpose to investigate the ways in which respondents at different proficiency levels carry out summarizing tasks on a reading comprehension test. The respondents for that study were five native Portuguese speakers who had all recently completed a course in English for academic purposes (EAP) (at the Pontifícia Universidade Católica de São Paulo, Brazil) with an emphasis on reading strategies, including summarizing. They represented three proficiency levels. The respondents had little difficulty identifying topical information, yet they had difficulty in distinguishing superordinate, nonredundant material from the rest, in large part because of an insufficient grasp of foreign-language vocabulary. For their written summaries, they did not need to generate topic information because all the texts provided it. They did not, however, have a good sense of balance with respect to how much information to delete. Either the summaries were too vague and general or too detailed. Although they showed some concern for coherence, the respondents appeared to pay relatively little attention to producing thoroughly coherent and polished summaries. In essence, the respondents appeared more concerned about their interpretation of the source text than about their production of a summary.

Aside from problems that the respondents have in preparing summaries of texts on tests, a further problem is the reliability of the ratings of the summaries. In addition, the statistical results from summarizing tasks are not always consistent with results from other types of tests (e.g., multiple-choice, short-answer, and cloze). Shohamy, for example, set out to compare tests of summarizing EFL texts to tests with a multiple-choice and an open-ended response format—with responses either in the native or the foreign language, depending on the test version. She found the results from the summarizing data so inconsistent with the results on the other subtests that she eliminated the findings from the published study (Shohamy, personal communication; Shohamy, 1984).[2]

My previous study (Cohen, in press) also investigated how raters dealt with the responses of the five participating students. Two EAP course instructors who typically rated the EAP examinations in summarizing skill at that institution also participated in the study as raters. Some inconsistencies were found in the raters' behaviors, underscoring the importance of developing rigorous rating keys with main ideas and connecting schemata for each text.

Research Questions

One main purpose of the study described here was to determine the effects of specific guidelines for taking tests of summarizing ability. Tests of summarizing do not usually include specific, guided instructions for the respondents on how to construct their summary. Previous research on test-taking strategies suggests that examinees may not even read instructions on tests, if they noticed them at all (e.g., Cohen, 1984). The intention in this study was to build into the test a set of instructions that would serve as a genuine guide for the respondent. My colleagues and I had found that test instructions were often notoriously vague and presupposed an understanding of how to do the task—especially in the case of an activity as complex as summarizing. Although one might think that respondents would draw upon previous knowledge (e.g., from classroom instruction) on how to summarize, they appear not necessarily to exercise this knowledge in a testing situation.

The other purpose of the study was to investigate the rating of such tests of summarizing with a rigorous, empirically derived scoring key, as the absence of such guidelines was seen as contributing to a lack of reliability in the ratings of summaries. The study looked at the consistency across raters idea by idea to determine causes for disagreement in ratings.

The study addressed the following questions:

1. In what ways do guided instructions affect performance on a summary task?
2. How consistent are the ratings of the summaries across raters?

Method

Subjects

Respondents
The respondents for this study were 63 native Hebrew-speaking students from the Seminar Hakibbutzim Teacher Training College in Tel Aviv. Twenty-six were from two high-proficiency EFL classes, and 37 were from two intermediate EFL classes.

Raters
Four raters assessed the students' summaries in the study. The two who rated the Hebrew summaries of the Hebrew texts were both native Hebrew-speaking undergraduates in their last year at the Hebrew University. Of the two rating the Hebrew summaries of the EFL texts, one was a native Hebrew-speaking freshman at the Hebrew University and the other, an English speaker doing a graduate degree at Tel Aviv University. The latter was highly proficient in Hebrew, as she had received 12 years of schooling at a Hebrew day school in the United States, was married to an Israeli, and had lived in Israel for 5 years.

Instruments

Texts

Five texts were selected for the study (Appendix 8A), two in Hebrew and three in English. The two Hebrew texts were intended to reflect two levels of difficulty both in terms of content, complexity of language, and summarizability (i.e., how easy to summarize they appeared). The first Hebrew text (800 words), entitled "Movies—From a Form of Magic to an Art Form," was divided into five sections, each containing a subtitle, thus making it "summarizer friendly." The second text (1,200 words), entitled "Problems With New Israeli Prose: Between Isolation and Integration," was written in a more problematic style, and writing a successful summary of the text required a certain degree of background knowledge about the topic. Three EFL texts were selected to represent three levels of difficulty. The easiest (1,000 words), entitled "How to Avoid Foolish Opinions," presented a series of procedures for avoiding such opinions. Its clear organization facilitated summarizing. The second text (1,200 words), entitled "Modern Constitutions," was more complex both in language and conceptual organization. The third article (850 words), entitled "Specialization," was intended to be the most difficult article but turned out to have a relatively easy structure for the purposes of summarizing.

Instructions for Summarizing

Two sets of instructions were developed. One version was "guided," with specific instructions on how to read the texts and how to write the summaries. The other version had the typical "minimal" instructions. The guided instructions told the respondents to read each text in order to identify the most important points—those that contained the key sentences in each paragraph or those that would make the summary interesting to read. The respondents were then instructed to write the summary such that the content would be reduced to only the essential points and that less important details or those detracting from the main points would be eliminated. They were also requested to write briefly—e.g., 80–120 words per summary.[3] Their text was to comprise one paragraph with all the ideas linked by connecting words. They were requested to write the summaries in their own words and, in the case of the Hebrew summaries of EFL texts, not to translate word for word. They were also asked to write a draft first and then to copy it over legibly (see Appendix 8B).

The more traditional, nonguided instructions simply told the respondents to read each text so as to be able to write a summary of it. They were asked to be brief—80- to 120-word summaries—and to write their summary first in draft form and then to copy it over legibly.

Construction of Rating Keys

Nine Hebrew speakers, all experts in the areas of reading and writing, read and summarized the two Hebrew texts. Three were university lecturers specializing in

Table 8-1

Number of Raters Agreeing on Points Selected for Key (of Nine Raters)

| | Point on Key | | | | | | | |
	1	2	3	4	5	6	7	8
Hebrew texts								
"Movies—From a Form of Magic to an Art Form"	9	6	7	6	5	6	8	7
"Problems With Modern Israeli Prose—Between Isolation and Integration"	8	7	7	6	9	9	8	—
EFL Texts								
"How to Avoid Foolish Opinions"	8	8	7	9	9	8	8	—
"Modern Constitutions"	8	9	6	8	7	5	8	—
"Specialization"	7	5	9	9	—	—	—	—

discourse. The rest were university students of language arts and teachers in their own right. Nine native English speakers, most of whom were university instructors of EFL, read and summarized the three EFL texts. The summaries of these experts were analyzed, and a key was constructed to include only the main ideas and linking ideas that a majority (i.e., five or more) of the experts had included in their summaries (after Sarig, 1989). In this study, no effort was made to distinguish the macro- from the micropropositions in the scoring key. (See Appendix 8A for the scoring keys.)

One of the two raters produced the key for the Hebrew texts. I produced the key for the EFL texts, and the Hebrew-speaking rater of the EFL texts, whose English skills were also quite advanced, translated it into Hebrew. The EFL key was translated into Hebrew. The keys appeared in the form of a list of numbered ideas, each in sentence form. Table 8-1 shows the level of agreement on each point selected per passage.

The summaries of the Hebrew experts reflected an 80% average agreement on which main ideas and connecting ideas should be included in the summary; the summaries of the EFL experts reflected an 85% average agreement. Thus even the experts did not fully agree on which ideas were essential to the construction of a meaningful summary.

Procedures

Data Collection

The students were requested to write the summaries in two meetings of their EFL course—the first one for the Hebrew texts, the second one for the English

Table 8-2

Number of Respondents for Text Summaries, by Level and Version

Text	Guided version			Unguided version			
	Inter-mediate	Ad-vanced	Total	Inter-mediate	Ad-vanced	Total	Overall
Hebrew texts							
"Movies"	19	13	32	18	13	31	63
"New Israeli Prose"	16	11	27	17	9	26	53
EFL texts							
"Foolish Opinions"	12	—	12	5	—	5	17
"Modern Constitutions"	8	3	11	4	7	11	22
"Specialization"	—	3	3	—	4	7	10

texts. The sessions took place in December 1988, 1 week apart. Each lasted approximately 1.5 hours. The task with guided instructions was administered to every other student according to how the students were seated in a given classroom. The other students received the unguided version. In the second sitting, all students received the same type of instructions as they had in the first, as this time their name was written on the instruction sheet in advance. The tasks were not presented as obligatory and were not to count toward the students' grade in the course.

All 63 respondents summarized the first Hebrew text, 32 receiving guided instructions and 31 not. Fifty-three respondents summarized the second Hebrew text, 27 receiving instructions and 26 not. On average, only a little more than a third of the students wrote summaries for the EFL texts. A breakdown of the numbers of respondents for each text according to version (guided versus unguided) and the respondents' level of proficiency (intermediate versus advanced) appears in Table 8-2. The 15% of the students who chose not to summarize the second Hebrew text and the 65% who chose not to summarize the EFL texts did so primarily because they found them too difficult to summarize.

Although the instructions for both the guided and unguided versions specified that the students were to write a draft summary and then copy it over neatly, only 7 of the 67 students did so for the Hebrew summaries, 4 intermediate students and 3 advanced ones. As for the summaries of the EFL texts, only one advanced student wrote a draft, as that student had done for the Hebrew texts as well. This element in the instructions was thus not followed in either of the two versions.

Data Analysis

I trained the raters briefly in rating the summaries, and they rated several in my presence to resolve problems of immediate concern. The raters were also asked to note problems to be resolved in consultation with the investigator after completing the ratings. Each main idea and linking idea received 1 point in the rating process. No effort was made to have the pairs of raters of the Hebrew and EFL texts "conference" while learning how to do the ratings. However, the ratings of the two pairs of raters for the Hebrew and EFL texts were correlated to determine interrater reliability, and discrepancies were identified point by point to determine the types of ideas for which raters had difficulty reaching consensus.

Cross tabulations were run using the SPSS-PC program to check for differences in success at summarizing between the respondents given the guided and unguided versions. The Correlations program was run to determine interrater reliability.

Results

The Effect of Guided Instructions on Summarizing

Summaries of Hebrew Texts

Guided instructions seemed to have a mixed or even negative effect on the summarizing of native-language texts. On the first Hebrew text, on movies, the second rater rated the unguided group significantly better overall than the group with guided instructions. Yet when behavior was examined idea by idea, some interesting differences emerged, suggesting that the provision of guided instructions has a differential effect on summarizing, perhaps helping in some instances and interfering in others. In examining the main ideas within that text, both raters rated the unguided group significantly better on idea 5 (see Table 8-3), which involved giving details as to why movies are an art form (e.g., they deal with shape, color, movement, words, and music). Those receiving the instructions warning them not to include unnecessary details were likely reluctant to provide this level of detail for fear that it would be rated as extraneous.

Summaries of the second Hebrew text revealed two significant differences by version, one favoring the guided and one favoring the unguided instructions. In the first instance, the guided group, which was told to identify all the main ideas in the key sentences, included idea 6 more than the unguided group did. This idea consisted of the second of two examples of "separatism and then reintegration in Israeli prose." In other words, the guided group was more sensitive to including both of the examples. In the second instance, the unguided group was more likely to include in their summaries a linking statement to the effect that new Israeli prose is characterized by continuity in the midst of apparent separatism (see Table 8-3). In this case, the guided group was reminded of the importance of linking ideas, but the unguided group practiced it more successfully.

Summaries of EFL Texts

According to the first rater, the EFL text summaries differed significantly by version in two instances, both in favor of the guided group. Members of the guided group were more likely to include the first idea in the summary of the Modern Constitutions text—namely, the idea that provides a historical perspective

Table 8-3

Ratings of Summaries of Hebrew Texts, by Version

Rater	Idea	Points	Version Guided	Version Unguided	chi-square	df
			"Movies" text (N = 32 guided, 31 unguided)			
2	Total	0	—	—	15.19**	5
	performance	2	4	1		
		3	13	2		
		4	8	18		
		5	4	7		
		6	2	1		
		7	1	2		
1	5 (Details)	0	26	15	7.48**	1
		1	6	16		
2	5 (Details)	0	28	18	6.92**	1
		1	4	13		
			"New Israeli Prose" text (N = 27 guided, 26 unguided)			
1	6 (Second	0	7	14	4.32*	1
	example)	1	20	12		
2	7 (Linking	0	15	7	4.47*	1
	idea)	1	12	19		

*$p<.05$. **$p<.01$.

for the passage. They were also more likely to include the detail that countries differ in the number of special checks and balances stipulated by their constitution (see Table 8-4).

Hence, with respect to native language summaries of foreign language texts, the group given the fuller instructions seemed more sensitive to inclusion of the

Table 8-4

Ratings of Summaries of "Modern Constitutions" EFL Text, by Version (n = 11)

Rater	Idea	Points	Version Guided	Version Unguided	chi-square	df
1	1 (Per-	0	0	5	6.47**	1
	spective)	1	11	6		
1	6 (Detail)	0	6	10	3.67*	1
		1	5	1		

*$p<.05$. **$p<.01$.

introductory idea as well as detail that might not be deemed central to the summary.

Consistency of Ratings Across Raters

Raters of the Hebrew Texts

The average correlation of the ratings of the two Hebrew native speakers across the two texts they rated was significant but relatively low as a reliability coefficient ($r = .73, p < .001$). On the Movies text, raters agreed significantly on five of the points, four involving basic description and one involving basic exemplification (i.e., what makes movies an art form). Raters were inconsistent on three points, two involving contrast (both involving the contrast between then and now) and one involving detailed exemplification (i.e., regarding modern technology in movie making).

On the New Israeli Prose text, raters agreed considerably on the opening contrastive idea (i.e., separatism and integration), two examples of this, and a linking idea (i.e., dealing with the continuity in Israeli prose) (see Table 8-5). Raters agreed somewhat on a descriptive point regarding the origins of separatism

Table 8-5

Interrater Agreement on Summaries of the Hebrew Texts

Idea	*Correlation*
"Movies" text (n = 63)	
1. Description	.55***
2. Description	.84***
3. Contrast	.23
4. Description	.59***
5. Basic exemplification	.83***
6. Description	.57***
7. Detailed exemplification	.10
8. Contrast	.20
Overall	.34*
"New Israeli Prose" text (n = 53)	
1. Contrast	.60**
2. Description	.45**
3. Description	.04
4. Description	.06
5. Exemplification	.89***
6. Exemplification	.88***
7. Linking	.65***
Overall	.81***

Note. Average correlation of ratings across both texts = $.73^{***}$ ($N = 53$).
*$p < .05$. **$p < .01$. ***$p < .001$.

and agreed less on two other descriptive points—one about continuity and one introducing the two examples of separatism and integration.

Raters of the EFL Texts

The average correlation of the two raters across the three EFL texts was high ($r = .85$, $p<.001$), especially considering that the first was a native Hebrew speaker and the second, a native English speaker. Yet the level of consistency from idea to idea within the three EFL texts showed marked differences (see Table 8-6). On the Opinions text, the raters agreed on their ratings of the fifth and sixth ideas, and more or less so on the third idea, but not for the first or opening statement (i.e., the article suggests procedures for avoiding foolish opinions), the second, or the fourth (an extension of the second suggestion).

On the second text, the raters agreed on the opening statement, which gives a historical perspective, and on three of the basic points (a justification for constitutions being above law, protection of special communities, constitutions of countries differ), but disagreed on the topic sentence linking the passage

Table 8-6

Interrater Agreement on Summaries of the EFL Texts

Idea	Correlation
"Foolish Opinions" text (n = 16)	
1. Purpose of article	.19
2. First suggestion	.04
3. Second suggestion	.45
4. Extension of suggestion	−.09
5. Third suggestion	.54*
6. Fourth suggestion	.75***
Overall	.56*
"Modern Constitutions" text (n = 22)	
1. Perspective	.59**
2. Description	—
3. Justification	.47
4. Details	.20
5. Description	.91**
6. Description	.46
7. Linking	−.05
Overall	.62**
"Specialization" text (n = 7)	
1. Opener	.17
2. General ignorance	1.00**
3. Ignorance in field	.47
4. Result of mechanization	.73
5. Overall	.94***

Note. Average correlation of ratings across both texts = .85*** ($N = 27$).
*$p<.05$. **$p<.01$. ***$p<.001$.

together cohesively (in terms of the constitution as a fresh start) and on an item dealing with details of what rights a constitution includes. On the third text, the raters agreed on all but the opening idea (that by the end of the 19th century the intellectual generalists had given way to specialists) (Table 8-6).

The raters were thus inconsistent in their ratings of several of the more global, linking ideas and of ideas involving details in the EFL texts. These discrepancies do not appear to result from native language differences. Instead, those ideas may be the ones that lend themselves to the most controversy in rating, even when a precise key is provided. This study did not attempt to investigate why raters disagreed on their assessments of respondents' answers, as a previous study did (Cohen, in press), but the findings indicate that certain ideas on a rating key are problematic for scoring and others are not, and that the language of the rater may not be as important here as other factors.

Discussion and Conclusions

In the study described here, guided instructions had a mixed effect on the summarizing of native-language texts but a somewhat positive effect on the summarizing of foreign-language texts. An item-by-item analysis of summaries revealed that, in reality, the guided instructions appeared to be both helpful and detrimental. In some cases they assisted respondents in finding the key elements to summarize, and in others they probably dissuaded the respondent from including details that in fact proved to be essential in the eyes of the experts on whose judgments the rating key was based.

Because all the students were admonished to read the instructions carefully, it is likely that they did so and that the results do reflect the two conditions for test taking—with and without guided instructions. The results, then, suggest that the nature of the instructions may be more important in foreign-language testing than in native-language testing. In other words, test constructors may wish to give more explicit guidance to nonnatives concerning recommended means for carrying out the given task than they would give to natives. With regard to native-language testing tasks, the respondents may either pay less attention to the instructions altogether or may simply exercise appropriate test-taking strategies without needing a reminder how to do so.

With respect to interrater consistency, the raters differed in their ratings, both on several of the more macrolevel, global, linking ideas and of microlevel ideas involving details in the EFL texts. Certain ideas at these two disparate levels appear to lend themselves to controversy in rating, even when a precise key is provided.

Limitations in the current study lead to recommendations for future research. Although the intention was to indicate for each summary for whom the text was being summarized, this information was inadvertently left out of the instructions for both groups. In the EFL text on Specialization, for example, the respondents were to be told, say, that they worked for a company that makes documentary movies and that their boss had asked them to read an article on the dangers of overspecialization and to summarize it for him so that they might get some ideas for the preparation of the script for the documentary. Perhaps the addition of this modicum of functionality would have prompted more of the students to do the task in a context where participation was not obligatory.

It may have been beneficial to the research to have the summaries count for course credit; then perhaps more of the students would have made an effort to summarize the second Hebrew text and the two EFL texts they were assigned. In fact, the respondents probably did not behave on these tasks as they would on a genuine test.

Regarding the scoring key, the first rater of the Hebrew texts felt that using a key based on the judgment of "experts" skewed the assessment away from the level of the students being assessed. She observed that the experts wrote a different type of summary than the seminar students did—i.e., they used a more logical sequence in the presentation of their ideas, demonstrated a tighter use of words, and displayed greater overall quality in their writing. Besides these observations, she noted that, although the experts did not agree on some points, which were thus left out of the key, students nonetheless felt these points to be important enough to include. A compromise would be to build a rating key based both on the suggestions of the respondents as to key ideas and the insights of the examiners, as Bensoussan and Kreindler did (1990).

In the work by Bensoussan and Kreindler, as soon as the respondents finished summarizing the given texts, they were asked as a group to react to the two teachers' set of main ideas for the summary, arrived at through conferencing. If they disagreed with any of the teachers' points, they had to convince the teachers that a change in the scoring key was in order. Apparently the students became more proficient at this task the more they performed it. At the beginning of the course the teachers dictated the correct summaries, but by the end of the semester the students had learned how to suggest changes (Bensoussan, personal communication).

No test-taking data were collected in this study using verbal report techniques, as had been collected in studies reported on elsewhere (e.g., Cohen, 1984; in press). Hence, there was no assurance, for example, that the students taking the guided version had paid full attention to the elaborated instructions they received. It was impossible to read those instructions aloud, as half the students received the unguided instructions. Perhaps a future study will collect data regarding the processing of the instructions.

The raters did not conference with each other on the appropriate ratings for each summary. A follow-up study would include rater conferencing with other raters, say, in pairs, to allow for potentially greater consistency across raters. Such conferencing could also be studied at the process level through analysis of verbal reports to determine what such conferencing entails.

More global ideas were not given more credit in the summaries than more local ideas were. Future work could distinguish main ideas at the level of micro- and macropropositions to see the extent to which the level of abstraction of the proposition influences the behavior of the rater.

Acknowledgments

I acknowledge Elana Shohamy for her assistance in the design of this study and Rachel Segev for her help in collecting the data. I also acknowledge Don Porter, Gissi Sarig, and Iris Geva for their constructive comments regarding the study. In addition, I thank the 18 informants who graciously consented to provide expert summaries of the texts.

Notes

1. Higher-level or superordinate idea units or statements.

2. It is also possible that Shohamy's summarization subtest was measuring some aspects of reading that the other subtests were not—e.g., a more overall view of the text. But it was also probably measuring writing skill, as well as reflecting possible lack of reliability in the ratings.

3. The stipulation of the number of words is based on common practice in the United States. In Israel, students are used to being told to write a paragraph or a page (a less precise measure).

References

Basham, C. S. (1987). *Summary writing as cultural artifact*. Fairbanks, AK: Cross-Cultural Communications, University of Alaska.

Basham, C. S., & Rounds, P. L. (1986). A discourse analysis approach to summary writing. *Papers in Applied Linguistics—Michigan, 1*(2), 88–104.

Bensoussan, M., & Kreindler, I. (1990). Improving advanced reading comprehension in a foreign language: Summaries vs. short-answer questions. *Journal of Research in Reading, 13*(1), 55–68.

Brown, A. L., Campione, J. C., & Day, J.D. (1981). Learning to learn: On training students to learn from text. *Educational Researcher, 10*, 14–21.

Brown, A. L., & Day, J. D. (1983). Macrorules for summarizing texts: The development of expertise. *Journal of Verbal Learning and Verbal Behavior, 22*, 1–14.

Chou Hare, V., & Borchardt, K. M. (1984). Direct instruction of summarization skills. *Reading Research Quarterly, 20*(1), 62–78.

Cohen, A. D. (1984). On taking language tests: What the students report. *Language Testing, 1*, 70–81.

Cohen, A. D. (1987). Research on cognitive processing in reading in Brazil. *D.E.L.T.A.* [Depto. de Linguística, Pontifícia Universidade Católica de Sao Páulo] *3*(2), 215–235.

Cohen, A. D. (In press). English testing in Brazil: Problems in using summary tasks. In C. Hill & K. Parry (Eds.), *Testing and assessment: International perspectives on English literacy*. London: Longman.

Davies, E., & Whitney, N. (1984). Study skill 11: Writing summaries. In *Study Skills for Reading: Students' Book* (pp. 56–58). London: Heinemann.

van Dijk, R. A. (1980). *Macrostructures*. Hillsdale, NJ: Lawrence Erlbaum Associates.

Gimenez, R. N. (1984). *Legibilidade de textos acadêmicos em inglés da area de serviço social*. Unpublished master's thesis, Pontifícia Universidade Católica de São Paulo, Brazil.

Holmes, J. L. (1986). Snarks, quarks and cognates: An elusive fundamental particle in reading comprehension. *The ESPecialist* [Centro de Pesquisas, Recursos e Informação em Leitura, Pontifícia Universidade Católica de São Paulo], *15*, 13–40.

Johns, A. M. (1985). Summary protocols of "underprepared" and "adept" university students: Replications and distortions of the original. *Language Learning, 35*, 495–517.

Johns, A. M., & Mayes, P. (1990). An analysis of summary protocols of university ESL students. *Applied Linguistics, 11*, 253–271.

Kintsch, W., & van Dijk, T. A. (1978). Toward a model of text comprehension and production. *Psychological Review, 85*, 363–394.

Kozminsky, E., & Graetz, N. (1986). First vs. second language comprehension: Some evidence from text summarizing. *Journal of Reading Research, 9*, 3–21.

Sarig, G. (1987). High-level reading tasks in the first and in a foreign language: Some comparative process data. In J. Devine, P. L. Carrell, & D. E. Eskey (Eds.), *Research in reading in English as a second language* (pp. 105–120). Washington, DC: Teachers of English to Speakers of Other Languages.

Sarig, G. (1988). *Composing a study-summary: A reading-writing encounter*. Unpublished manuscript, Open University, Ramat Aviv, Israel.

Sarig, G. (1989). Testing meaning construction: Can we do it fairly? *Language Testing, 6*, 77–94.

Sarig, G., & Folman, S. (1987). *Metacognitive awareness and theoretical knowledge in coherence prediction*. Unpublished manuscript, Everyman's University, Ramat-Aviv, Israel.

Shohamy, E. (1984). Does the testing method make a difference? The case of reading comprehension. *Language Testing, 1*, 147–170.

Appendix 8A: Texts and Scoring Keys

English Translation of Hebrew Texts and Scoring Keys

Movies—From a Form of Magic to an Art Form, by Lea Dovev-Rosenbaum

Films as a Form of Magic. The first movie makers and viewers did not see movies as an art form, but rather as amusing trickery. The first creations were the property of eccentrics and fanatics. They claimed that just as it was possible to film something at rest, so it was possible to film motion by combining a series of single shots and then projecting them rapidly one after another. The idea seemed amusing at the time, and this is what the audience thought when they came to see the first film shows. The spectators were common people: the unemployed and the illiterate. This audience was not at all familiar with works of art, were not educated to appreciate art, and were preoccupied with the daily concerns of making a living. They simply wanted to be entertained, and the new amusing form of trickery served their needs. They thoroughly enjoyed the hocus-pocus of the films. The first films startled and marveled the viewers. They did not understand how it was possible for a train to travel on a stretched out cloth and how people were able to walk on that same cloth. Their understanding was that films were an illusion of reality that through a miracle were transferred onto the screen. It was as much a marvel to them as a magician's pulling rabbits and doves out of a hat.

Films at Present.   Although films were not originally created to be an art form, they have become the principal form of art that we come in contact with in our daily lives. Films were not created as an art form—to say that seems strange today, as millions of people are not interested in art of any kind except for movies and TV. Furthermore, it is difficult to imagine how painting and sculpture, literature and music of today would appear if movies had not changed our concept of art so greatly. Artists of today paint, sculpt, write literature, stage theatrical productions, or create any other works under the influence of films, which make use of special perceptual senses.

From a Form of Magic to an Art Form.   Technological advances and sophisticated equipment changed the film industry from an amusing form of magic to an art form. The new techniques were able to let the film industry overcome obstacles that constrained other forms of art, to such a degree that they saw in the film industry possibilities greater than those in any other art form. Every art form has its limits. If you are a painter, you cannot use words. If you are a sculptor, you can not expect the sculpture to dance. Painters have their paint and a canvas, which is a lot but also limiting. The gap between reality and art is always there because artistic means are limited, while reality is infinite. The invention of movies was a challenging step towards closing the gap between art and life. Movie making is the art of all art forms. It contains everything: shape, color, movement, words, and music. It is no wonder that movies appear so complete, rich and full of opportunities, more than any other art form. Through the use of the movie camera, films can show wide-open spaces, and can realistically recreate the different scenes that people see walking along the streets, driving in their cars, etc. Unlike the human eye that sees everything from the same angle, movie makers can change the angle of filming and the distance of the camera. They can decide the amount of light and sharpness of focus. All of these can bring about amazing changes and reveal new scenes for the viewers.

Are Movies an Art Form? The fact that movies can create an illusion of reality better than any other art form brought up the question: are movies an art form? The issue facing the spectators at the turn of the century was: is it good that filmmaking has greater means for creating an illusion of reality? How can films be thought of as art if they are so similar to reality? If the filmmaker does not in any way process the pictures that are caught by the eye but just films the scenes—then this is just a simple, mechanical craft, and for this you do not need any talent. The filmmakers' reply was that just like any other art form, movies have possibilities and boundaries of their own. The film industry can be similar to reality, more than any other field, but it can also depart from reality. Film in the hands of the filmmaker is like clay in the hands of sculpture. Photographers decide what to film, how to film, what to add, and what to delete. They can edit the film in a way that will create a new reality, that is not just a carbon copy of existing reality. They can create a reality that is worked, sophisticated, complex, pretty, and even more interesting than reality. Filmmakers, the pioneers of filmmaking, wanted to create films that would not just be a substitution for reality, but which would create an artistic experience.

Artistic Means for Movie Making. For filmmakers there are technical means whereby they can change reality. What can the filmmaker do to create films in the modern world, different from reality, deeper, and more interesting? One of the principal means of design that stand before the filmmaker is related to the special possibilities of the camera and its limits. The constraint of the camera is that its range of focus is more limited than that of the human eye. The camera can film just what fits within a given frame. This frame is rectangular and its measurements are standard. But this constraint can also be a great advantage. The filmmaker can decide which details from the enormous range of data will be included inside the frame and which will not. They decide upon a certain portion of reality and the one that is chosen is not accidental. The limited range of vision of the camera gives filmmakers the ability to focus the viewers' attention on certain pretty or meaningful details. They may have an event happen beyond the limits of the frame and may select the most important event at that moment in order to heighten suspense. (For example, the filmmakers may decide not to let us see a love scene in a room but instead have us look at a view that the lovers see from the window.) Another advantage that the camera has unlike the human eye is that it can give different perspectives from different distances, different viewpoints, at with different intensity of lighting, at different degrees of focus, etc.

Another interesting aspect that without it, filmmaking would be a boring copy of reality, is editing. Editing a movie, i.e., cutting out parts of the film and reconnecting them elsewhere in a different order, is where the most important difference is between the human eye and the perspective of the movie maker. The human vision is always continuous in time and space, and there are no "jumps": we see just what is in our field of vision. The view of the filmmaker is different. Using editing, the filmmaker can decide which scenes we will see and which we will not, and in which order. The possibilities standing in front of the editor are different and manifold.

Scoring Key for "Movies: From a Form of Magic to an Art Form"

1. Movies started as entertainment, a circus act, amusement.
2. The spectators that came to the movies were simple folks, from a low socioeconomic level, without an art background.
3. Movies today have turned into the principal art form, the art form of all art forms.
4. This art form modifies or influences all other art forms.
5. It includes the following components: shape, color, movement, words, and music.
6. Thanks to modern technology, the film industry as changed from simple amusement into an art form.
7. Through the artistic channels of movie making, i.e., choice of subject matter, focus, and editing, reality is fashioned into a new creative art form.
8. The contrast between the notion of early films as simple entertainment and current films as an art form.

Problems With New Israeli Prose: Between Isolation and Integration, by Benjamin Yitzhak Michaeli

In the new Hebrew prose originating in Israel, two markedly different trends emerged that were not simultaneous but appeared one after the other: separatism from literary heritage at the start, during its period of fermentation and propagation, and later on in its maturation, an effort to overcome this separatism, out of a recognition of the power of continuity. The nature of this new prose, whose first buds were seen during the struggle with an occupying power, and whose fruits ripened during the years of the State, is perceived retrospectively not as a foreign implant, whereby its winds brought its seed from a foreign land, but rather as a Hebrew "tree of creation" from whose roots it emerged and from whose juices it was saturated. Its buds, and probably its unripe fruit, emphasized its difference and individuality. Here comes its ripe fruit and indicates to us the similar and closeness, the fundamental unity it preserved even as its appearance changed. And the question that arises: could this separatism over which so much clamor was made be but an imaginary one? No, this could not be. But an inspection of its uniqueness, its goals, and its results is likely to prove that it was not an separatism brought on from the outside, a total irremedial separatism, but one that was caused by pressure from the inside and it is like a chain with broken links that are constantly being reunited.

   In its essence it was an unconscious separatism and not a conscious one, and there is a crucial distinction to be drawn here between the two. The former originated in a given existing reality, the latter in the attempt to overthrow it. The generation growing up in Israel did not revolt against the cultural heritage of the

Diaspora and did not abandon its moral values. It simply did not know of their existence. The revolts and abandonment of the heritage that took place were consciously made by their forefathers. However, these forefathers, the pioneers, did not mean to separate themselves from the nation and from its culture. On the contrary, they wanted to save them and bring them from the Diaspora to their own country. However, in the height of the revolt, they could not properly distinguish between the important and the secondary. Not only did they break open the old wine barrel, but they also let all its exquisite wine spill out. But the object of their revolt did not stimulate their children to revolt in a similar fashion. They accepted its results at face value, for what they were. They said: the Diaspora spoiled everything good in us; it is the source of all our afflictions and maladies. The homeland was expected to solve problems and cure maladies. At the same time, a strange phenomenon appeared in the field of literature that could have been accounted for in terms of the dominance of a period of formalism. The sons never rejected the contents that their fathers wrote about, but they kept their distance from what they considered to be the older forms of literature, and in distancing themselves from these forms, did not notice the values that had been preserved in those contents and forms. However, when the period of formalism ended, they became aware that their fathers and forefathers had in fact left them great riches in their writings and that they themselves were but the continuants of these writing, and that they had a long way to go until they would be as good as their predecessors. Thus, they never really made a conscious separation from the larger world of their culture and their people. Conscious separatism occurred for a brief period only in the limited sphere of literature, but the separatism was only with respect to the outward trimmings and not with respect to the deeper content.

For our purposes, I will use two examples in order to be more concrete. The first: the example of the Yevreyskaya in the Soviet Union. In this instance, the separatism was twofold: not only complete separatism from the people's past, from its historic homeland, from its ancient culture, from its dreams and hopes, but also separatism from the people at present, scattered in the Diaspora, and a commensurate reduction of the Jewish entity in its Russian branch. This meant separation not only from the national language and literature but from the language of the people, Yiddish, and from its pre-revolutionary literature. Just as the history of the Jewish community in Russia started in the first year of the Revolution, so did the "genesis" of Yiddish literature, according to their perception, start in the Days of October or during the period of the struggle that led to it—that is to say, a brief chronological affinity or a brief thematic affinity. Nevertheless, the conscious separatism, militant in nature and abominably cruel, was to no avail. Underneath the conscious stand, however, latent, irrational factors were operating, and at the first opportunity, these surfaced. Whatever the Revolution did not accomplish in bringing about ideological division along class lines within the Jewish collective, was brought about by the massive destruction that erased class distinctions and brought together all the different divisions of the Jewish people under the tyranny of the Nazis. A brotherly hand was extended to groups of Jews outside the country of the Revolution. According to Bergson, the ancient cry could be heard, as in his play, "I won't die for I will live!" Poets and storytellers who were formerly content to praise Stalin and events taking place in the Soviet Union, were reminded of their Jewish past and gave expression to their excitement in literature, revolving around ancient figures such as Rachel, King Solomon, Isaiah, the Maccabees, Bar Kochba, Rabbi Akiva, and Yehuda Halevy. Suddenly with the destruction of the Jews in the Holocaust, separatism vanished. There was a continual undercurrent of forces seeking a way of breaking through the man-made barriers. In other words, as long as it had not been accomplished through assimilation—which takes many generations—conscious separatism was eliminated by reality itself.

The second example: the "Canaanite" group. Certainly this group and the Yevreyskaya were not on one plane and did not aspire to the same goals. The latter group denied its heritage, seeking to eliminate any traces of identification with the Jewish people, and preserving what was merely subsidiary, the Yiddish language that was spoken by the Jewish community at large in the Soviet Union; whereas the former group adhered to its historic homeland declaring its desire to extend its borders, at the same time that it was planning to reduce the geographic borders of the Jewish nation. That is, their view was that Jews of the Diaspora were second-rate and should not have a stake in Eretz Israel and in its people. Their use of historical roots produced a strange schism: the "Canaanites" acknowledged their historical homeland, but they denied the reality of the historical people, its generations, and its dispersion. Moreover, this inconsistency with regard to facts of Jewish history does not just concern the Diaspora, but also applies to the homeland as well. Not for naught were they drawn to the long lost period of their ancestry: before we became a people, before the Lord gave us the Torah and the Ten Commandments, before the appearance of the prophets, whereas the later period was perceived for all that primordial reminiscing as memories of the Molech, Baal, and Astarte. It was not that those ancient times were enlivened to ensure a foothold in later times, but that they, and they only, were considered to be the be-all and end-all of everything. In this way the "Canaanites" transformed the Israeli nation from an organic being, within which unity operates in spite of the multitude of changes, into a mechanical being, which is like clay in the potter's hands. But such a change is sure to be undone. Just as a living tree does not exist only as roots at the bottom and leaves at the top, but rather also as a trunk and the ever increasing network of branches, so too a change does not consist solely of a beginning and an end with a void between them.

But is not this Canaanitism but an anomalous phenomenon? Was it only an arbitrary occurrence? Whoever does not feel content with its public declarations but rather looks for a hidden motive will not rush to such a conclusion. When looking for traces of the Canaanites, one will find evidence of their predecessors and then will discover that the younger generation of authors was not that different, in fact, from the older. This did not imply departing for ancient regions, as did the authors of the Enlightenment Movement, but to a faithfulness to their intentions. Michal was fascinated by the love of Solomon and the wisdom of Ecclesiastes while perceiving what was tragic in the extinction of beauty and grandeur; Mappu envisioned an ancient period when the Jewish people were still rooted in their homeland, in contrast to their current detachment—as an expression of their hope of restoration; Yalag employed the clashes between King Zedekiah and Jeremiah as a means of indicating his preference for statehood and the need for heeding the words of the prophets. What these authors had in common was a nostalgia for the period of independence of the people of Israel while prospering in their homeland and subordinated to the regime of the high priests, judges, and kings. Their followers differed in that they aimed for an earlier period—that of the pagans, before these impulses were restrained and subjected to the Bible, the Ten Commandments, and public governmental structures. This was the case with Frishman in his "desert" tales (referring to the Book of Numbers) and Berdichevsky exploring the manifestations of the rule of blood and impulse; the same was true of Tchernichovsky in his psalms to Astarte, Baal, and Shneor in the hidden tablets (of the decalogue). Of course, there were differences among these later authors, but what they had in common was their fascination with the primitive, a fascination to account for their repulsion of the symptoms of decadence exhibited by the Jewish people oppressed in their exile. These authors were united by a wish to cure the Jewish people through reigniting their impulses that were suppressed, and transfusing healthy blood into its stricken body—to bring life into the nation. Apparently, the major difference between them and the Canaanite sons was how they dealt with a change of circumstances for the Jewish people. The former were content in a nostalgic visionary form, matching the diasporic detachment in exile and the yearning to overcome it. The latter group, on the other hand, aspired for political-social concretization, that would match the reality of the homeland. Still wasn't there a hidden inclination for a reunion in the claim for separatism? Was it not a meritorious continuity achieved through a wrongful separation? That is to say, it was an intermittent continuity, whose advocates clung to an ancient and unknown stratum, because they believed that thence precisely would flow the healing serum of the nation that was to immunize it and help it to survive in times of change and crisis, as was taking place at the present time.

These two examples, extreme in their essence, illustrate the internal struggles among the literary groups. While for the first group separation had been a conscious act, latent trends toward continuity operated within the latter group, marking its Zionistic-pioneering nature. From the beginning this was a separation for the sake of continuity. This distancing themselves from the national heritage was not planned purposely, but was the result of major changes in the life of the Jewish people—of the descent of one way of life and cultural patterns on the one hand, and the rise of another on the other hand. In any case, the goal of continuity was latent during the period of uprootedness, and conscious separation, which the pioneering ancestors had bequeathed their sons, did not characterize the atrophic and spoiled patterns of existence in exile.

Scoring Key for "Problems with New Israeli Prose: Between Isolation and Integration"

1. There are two trends in modern Hebrew prose: first, separatism from the literary heritage and later on return to this heritage.
2. Separatism from the literary heritage was not created purposely and consciously but rather was a temporary and unavoidable result of ignorance of the heritage.
3. Despite attempts at separatism of modern Hebrew prose from its heritage, the younger generation started to recognize the value of the literary heritage and its spiritual richness.
4. The author gives two extreme examples of the separatism that lead ultimately to a coming to terms with this heritage.
5. First example: the Yevreyskaya in the Soviet Union.
6. Second example: the "Canaanite" group in Israel.
7. The concluding sentence concerning the trends of continuity within the separatism and/or the continuity as a need within separatism in new Israeli prose.

EFL Texts and Scoring Keys

How to Avoid Foolish Opinions, by Bertrand Russell

To avoid the various foolish opinions to which mankind is prone, no superhuman genius is required. A few simple rules will keep you, not from all error, but from silly error.

If the matter is one that can be settled by observation, make the observation yourself. Aristotle could have avoided the mistake of thinking that women have fewer teeth than men, by the simple device of asking Mrs. Aristotle to keep her mouth open while he counted. He did not do so because he thought he knew. Thinking that you know when in fact you don't is a fatal mistake, to which we are all prone. I believe myself that hedgehogs eat black beetles, because I have been told that they do; but if I were writing a book on the habits of hedgehogs, I should not commit myself until I had seen one enjoying this unappetizing diet. Aristotle, however, was less cautious. Ancient and medieval authors know all about unicorns and salamanders; not one of them thought it necessary to avoid dogmatic statements about them because he had never seen one of them.

Many matters, however, are less easily brought to the test of experience. If, like most of mankind, you have passionate convictions of many such matters, there are ways in which you can make yourself aware of your own bias. If an opinion contrary to your own makes you angry, that is a sign that you are subconsciously aware of having no good reason for thinking as you do. If someone maintains that two and two are five, or that Iceland is on the Equator, you feel pity rather than anger, unless you know so little of arithmetic or geography that his opinion shakes your own contrary conviction. The most savage controversies are those about matters as to which there is no good evidence either way. Persecution is used in theology, not in arithmetic, because in arithmetic there is knowledge, but in theology there is only opinion. So whenever you find yourself getting angry about a difference of opinion, be on your guard; you will probably find, on examination, that your belief is going beyond what the evidence warrants.

A good way of ridding yourself of certain kinds of dogmatism is to become aware of opinions held in social circles different from your own. When I was young, I lived much outside my own country—in France, Germany, Italy, and the United States. I found this very profitable in diminishing the intensity of insular prejudice. If you cannot travel, seek out people with whom you disagree, and read a newspaper belonging to a party that is not yours. If the people and the newspaper seem mad, perverse, and wicked, remind yourself that you seem so to them. In this opinion both parties may be right, but they cannot both be wrong. This reflection should generate a certain caution.

For those who have enough psychological imagination, it is a good plan to imagine an argument with a person having a different bias. This has one advantage, and only one, as compared with actual conversation with opponents; this one advantage is that the method is not subject to the same limitations of time and space. Mahatma Gandhi deplored railways and steamboats and machinery; he would have liked to undo the whole of the industrial revolution. You may never have an opportunity of actually meeting anyone who holds this opinion, because in Western countries most people take the advantages of modern technique for granted. But if you want to make sure that you are right in agreeing with the prevailing opinion, you will find it a good plan to test the arguments that occur to you by considering what Gandhi might have said in refutation of them. I have sometimes been led actually to change my mind as a result of this kind of imaginary dialogue, and, short of this, I have frequently found myself growing less dogmatic and cocksure through realizing the possible reasonableness of a hypothetical opponent.

Be very wary of opinions that flatter your self-esteem. Both men and women, nine times out of ten, are firmly convinced of the superior excellence of their own sex. There is abundant evidence on both sides. If you are a man, you can point out that most poets and men of science are male; if you are a woman, you can retort that so are most criminals. The question is inherently insoluble, but self-esteem conceals this from most people. We are all, whatever part of the world we come from, persuaded that our own nation is superior to all others. Seeing that each nation has its characteristic merits, we each believe that those possessed by our nation are the really important ones, while its demerits are comparatively trivial. Here, again, the rational man will admit that the question is one to which there is no demonstrably right answer. It is more difficult to deal with the self-esteem of man as man, because we cannot argue out the matter with some non-human mind. The only way I know of dealing with this general human conceit is to remind ourselves that man is a brief episode in the life of a small planet in a little corner of the universe, and that for aught we know, other parts of the cosmos may contain beings as superior to ourselves as we are to jelly-fish.

Scoring Key for "How to Avoid Foolish Opinions"

1. The article suggests procedures for avoiding foolish opinions.
2. First, observe things for yourself whenever possible.
3. Second, if observation is out, discover any biases you may have about an issue./because belief might go beyond evidence.
4. Rid yourself of prejudice by discovering the opinions held by others—whether through meeting people out of your social group, travel, or through the newspaper.
5. Another means is to have an imaginary argument with an hypothetical opponent.
6. Finally, be wary of taking a position which makes you right at the expense of the opposite sex or another nation since it is a no-win situation. /Be wary of opinions that flatter your self-esteem. Linking: intro that procedures/rules for avoiding foolish opinions/dogmatism.

Modern Constitutions, by K. C. Whears

Most countries make the Constitution superior to the ordinary law.

If we investigate the origins of modern Constitutions, we find that, practically without exception, they were drawn up and adopted because people wished to make a fresh start, so far as the statement of their system of government was concerned. The desire or need for a fresh start arose either because, as in the United States, some neighboring communities wished to unite together under a new government, or because, as in Austria and Hungary or Czechoslovakia after 1918, communities had been released from an Empire as the result of a war and were now free to govern themselves; or because a revolution had made a break with the past and a new form of government on new principles was desired; or because defeat in war had broken the continuity of government and a fresh start was needed after the war. The circumstances in which a break with the past and the need for a fresh start come about vary from country to country, but in almost every case in modern times, countries have a Constitution for the very simple and elementary reason that they wanted, for some reason, to begin again and so they put down in writing the main outline, at least, of their proposed system of government. This has been the practice certainly since 1781 when the American Constitution was drafted, and as the years passed, no doubt imitation and the force of example have led all countries to think it necessary to have a Constitution.

This does not explain, however, why many countries think it necessary to give the Constitution a higher status in law than other rules of law. The short explanation of this phenomenon is that in many countries a Constitution is thought of as an instrument by which government can be controlled. Constitutions spring from a belief in limited government. Countries differ, however, in the extent to which they wish to impose limitations. Sometimes the Constitution limits the legislature also, but only so far as amendment of the Constitution itself is concerned; and sometimes it imposes restrictions upon the legislature which go far beyond this point and forbid it to make laws upon certain subjects or in a certain way or with certain effects. Whatever the nature and the extent of the restrictions, however, they are based on a common belief in limited government and in the use of a constitution to impose these limitations. The nature of the limitations to be imposed on a government, and therefore the degree to which a Constitution will be supreme over a government, depends upon the objects which the framers of the Constitution wish to safeguard. In the first place they may want to do no more than ensure that the Constitution is not altered casually or carelessly or by subterfuge or by implication; they may want to secure that this important document is not lightly tampered with, but solemnly, with due notice and deliberation, consciously amended. In that case it is legitimate to require some special process of constitutional amendment—say, that the legislature may amend the Constitution only by a two-thirds majority or after a general election or perhaps upon three months notice.

The framers of Constitutions have more than this in mind. They may feel that a certain kind of relationship between legislators and the executive is important, or that the judicatures should have a certain guaranteed degree of independence of the legislature and executive. They may feel that there are certain rights which citizens have and which the legislature or the executive must not invade or remove. They may feel that certain laws should not be made at all. The framers of the American Constitution, for example, forbade Congress to pass an ex-post facto law, that is, a law made after the occurrence of the action or the situation which it seeks to regulate—a type of law which may render a man guilty of an offence through an action which, when he committed it, was innocent. The framers of the Irish Constitution of 1937 forbade the legislature to pass any law permitting divorce.

Further safeguards may be called for when distinct and different communities decide to join together under a common government but are anxious to retain certain rights for themselves. If these communities differ in language, race, and religion, safeguards may be needed to guarantee to them a free exercise of these national characteristics. Those who framed the Swiss, the Canadian, and the South African Constitutions, to name a few only, had to consider these questions. Even when communities do not differ in language, race, or religion, they may still be unwilling to unite unless they are guaranteed a measure of independence inside the union. To meet this demand the Constitution must not only divide powers between the government of the Union and the governments of the individual component parts, but it must also be supreme in so far at any rate as it enshrines and safeguards this division of powers.

In some countries only one of the considerations mentioned above may operate;

in others some, and in some, all. Thus, in the Irish Constitution, the framers were anxious that amendment should be a deliberate process, that the rights of citizens should be safeguarded, and that certain types of laws should not be passed at all, and therefore, they made the Constitution supreme and imposed restrictions upon the legislature to achieve these ends. The framers of the American Constitution also had these objects in mind, but on top of that they had to provide for the desire of the thirteen colonies to be united for some purposes only and to remain independent for others. This was an additional reason for giving supremacy to the Constitution and for introducing certain extra safeguards into it.

Scoring Key for "Modern Constitutions"

1. The text first gives the historical reason for constitutions—namely, that people wanted to have a fresh start at their system of government.
2. Usually the constitution was put above other laws that the legislature or executive might wish to instate. /supremacy of Constitution to control government.
3. This power was granted the constitution to guard against efforts to tamper with the constitutional process.
4. Thus, constitutions often include rights (of citizens) which cannot be invaded or removed by the government. /to limit the legislature as to amendment of the Constitution. /to limit the powers of government.
5. There may also be stipulations protecting the rights of special communities governed by the same constitution. [constituent states/colonies in the case of the US]
6. It is noted that countries differ as to the number of special checks and balances stipulated by their constitution. Linking: Opening topic sentence about Constitution serving as fresh start./Degree to which the Constitution limits government depends on. . . .

Specialization, by Ortega y Gasset

Specialization commences precisely at a period which gives civilized man the title "encyclopedic." The intellectual history of the nineteenth century starts on its course under the direction of beings who live "encyclopedically," though their production already has some tinge of specialism. In the following generation, the balance is upset and specialism begins to dislodge culture from the individual scientist. When, by 1890, a third generation assumes intellectual command in Europe we meet with a type of scientist unparalleled in history. He is one who, out of all that has to be known in order to be a man of judgement, is only acquainted with one science—and, even of that one, he only knows the small corner in which he is an active investigator. He even proclaims it as a virtue that he takes no cognizance of what lies outside the narrow territory specially cultivated by himself and gives the name of "dilettantism" to any curiosity for the general scheme of knowledge.

What happens is that, enclosed within the narrow limits of his visual field, he does actually succeed in discovering new facts and in advancing the progress of the science which he hardly knows—and, incidentally, the encyclopedia of thought of which he is conscientiously ignorant. How has such a thing been possible, how is it still possible? For it is necessary to insist upon this extraordinary but undeniable fact: experimental science has progressed thanks in great part to the work of men astoundingly mediocre and even less than mediocre. That is to say, modern science, the root and symbol of our actual civilization, finds a place for the intellectually commonplace man and allows his to work therein with success. The reason for this lies in what is at the same time the great advantage and the gravest peril of the new science, and of the civilization directed and represented by it, namely, mechanization. A fair amount of the things that have to be done in physics or in biology is mechanical work of the mind which can be done by anyone, or almost anyone. For the purpose of innumerable investigations it is possible to divide science into small sections, to enclose oneself in one of these, and to leave out of consideration all the rest. The solidity and exactitude of the methods allow for this temporary but quite real dismemberment of knowledge. The work is done under one of these methods as with a machine and, in order to obtain quite abundant results, it is not even necessary to have rigorous notions of their meaning and foundations. In this way the majority of scientists help the general advance of science while shut up in the narrow cell of their laboratory, like the bee in the cell of the hive.

But this creates an extraordinarily strange type of man. The investigator who has discovered a new fact of nature must necessarily experience a feeling of power and self assurance. With a certain apparent justice, he will look upon himself as "a man who knows." And, in fact, there is in him a portion of something which, added to many other portions not existing in him, does really constitute knowledge. This is the true inner nature of the specialist who, in the first years of this century, has reached the wildest stage of exaggeration. The specialist "knows" very well his own, tiny corner of the universe; he is radically ignorant of all the rest. Here we have a precise example of this strange new man, whom I have attempted to define, from both of these two opposite aspects. I have said that he was a human product unparalleled in history. The specialist serves as a striking, concrete example of the species, making clear to us that radical nature of the novelty. For, previously, a man could be divided simply into the learned and the ignorant—those who fit the former category and those that fit the latter. But our specialist cannot be brought in under either of these two categories. He is not learned, for he is formally ignorant of all that does not enter into his specialty; but neither is he ignorant, because he is "a scientist," and "knows" very well his own tiny portion of the universe. We shall have to say that he is a learned ignoramus—which is a very serious matter, as it implies that he is a person who is ignorant, not in the fashion of the ignorant may, but with all the petulance of one who is learned in his own special line.

Scoring Key for "Specialization"
1. By the end of the nineteenth century the intellectual generalists had given way to specialists, people versed only in one science rather than having a broad knowledge base. (during the 19th C.) [not necessarily contrasting with intellectual generalists]
2. While these scientists have made progress in their fields, they remain ignorant of the rest of the world.
3. Even in their fields, mechanization has allowed them to do successful work on the basis of a minimum of knowledge.
4. The author sees the situation to be producing strange new people: specialists who are not learned, yet are not ignorant in that they are scientists, hence "learned ignoramuses."

Appendix 8B: Test Instructions

Translation of the Elaborated Instructions for Reading the Text and Writing a Summary of the Text

Before you are four texts, two in Hebrew and two in English.

Instructions for Reading
Read each text so as to extract the most important points from it, that is, those points that contain the key sentences (for the given paragraph); or those points that the reader of the summary will be interested in reading.

Instructions for Writing the Summary (in Hebrew)
1. Reduce the information to main points only: avoid the inclusion of redundant information. Including this information will detract from your score. 2. Write briefly: the length of the summary is to be 80 words for the first passage and 120 words for the second. 3. Write the summary as a single passage: use connecting words to link the points together. 4. Do not translate literally: write the summary in your own words. 5. Write a draft first, and then copy it over legibly.

Translation of the Traditional Brief Instructions for Reading the Text and Writing a Summary of the Text

Before you are four texts, two in Hebrew and two in English. You are to read each one so as to write a summary of it.

Instructions for Writing the Summary (in Hebrew)
1. Write briefly: the length of the summary is to be 80 words for the first passage and 120 words for the second. 2. Write a draft first, and then copy it over legibly.

Part II

Developing New Tests of Communicative Language Ability

9

A Comprehensive Criterion-Referenced Language Testing Project

James Dean Brown
University of Hawai'i at Manoa

The English Language Institute (ELI) at the University of Hawai'i at Manoa (UHM) regularly offers seven courses in academic listening, reading, and writing. The curriculum for each course has been extensively revised through complete needs analysis and development of objectives, criterion-referenced tests (CRTs), and materials as well as improvements in teaching practices and regularly conducted formative evaluation procedures. This paper reports on the CRT development portion of the curriculum. The discussion centers on the problems encountered in developing such a comprehensive testing program, then turns to the benefits of CRTs for overall curriculum development.

Two forms of a CRT are designed expressly to measure the objectives of each of the seven ELI courses. The forms are administered at the beginning and end of instruction in a counterbalanced design. Thus the testing project is large in scale, including 14 different tests administered before and after instruction for about 500–600 students per year. Although the objectives and resulting tests differ in organization and form across the seven courses, the processes involved in putting the tests in place are quite similar. In this paper I describe in general terms the initial item development, piloting, and revision processes; provide details about the results of the administrations of the CRTs during fall 1989; present descriptive and item statistics for each test; give dependability estimates; and provide evidence for the content and construct validity of the tests.

Immediately on arrival at UHM, all foreign students who have been admitted are required to report to the ELI for clearance. The purpose of the clearance process is to determine the amount of English as a second language (ESL) training students must undergo, if any. Students may be entirely exempted from ESL courses or be required to take between one and six 3-unit courses during the 1st year or 2 of their stay at UHM. These classes may be taken concurrently with other courses at the university, but, according to university policy, they take precedence over all other coursework.

In addition to the seven academic listening, reading, and writing classes offered at ELI, a new course, Speaking for Foreign Teaching Assistants, was offered in the fall semester 1990. The courses are organized into four skill areas and two levels (which correspond roughly to Test of English as a Foreign Language [TOEFL] ranges of 500–549 for the courses numbered in the 70s and 550–599 for those numbered in the 80s or higher) (see Figure 9-2 below).

Curriculum Context

Since 1986, the curriculum for the courses at the ELI has been extensively revised. The revisions have included (a) a thorough needs analysis, (b) the development of objectives, (c) the design and implementation of tests, (d) materials development, (e) improvements in teaching practices, and (f) regularly conducted formative evaluation procedures. Figure 9-1 illustrates the relationships among these elements in the curriculum. Testing is central in the model, and program evaluation is formative and is constantly involved in all the other elements of the curriculum development process. (For more complete descriptions of the model, see Brown, 1989b, in preparation.)

I report here on the testing facet of the new curriculum, focusing on the development and implementation of CRTs for individual courses. As shown in Figure 9-1, testing comes into play primarily after the establishment of clear

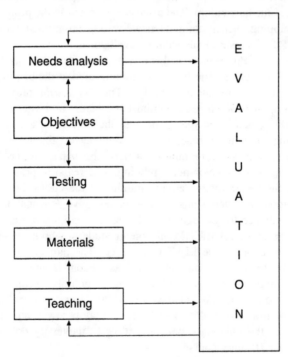

Figure 9-1. Systemative approach to curriculum development in the ELI. Adapted from Brown, 1989a.

program and course objectives. Tests serve a number of purposes in the program, as described below, but it is the development of course-level CRTs that is of primary interest here. As indicated by the arrows in the figure, the development of such tests interacts with objectives, materials development, and teaching, so that each can be used to improve the others (sometimes through the program evaluation processes). We at the ELI consider the interactions among objectives, CRTs, materials, and teaching as essential to the success of the testing program and, indeed, to the growth of the entire curriculum.

Testing Program

As director of the ELI, it is my duty to see that decision-making mechanisms are in place to ensure that students are working at the correct level and progressing satisfactorily through the program. To those ends, we have designed four sets of procedures: (a) initial screening procedures, (b) placement procedures, (c) 1st-week assessment procedures, and (d) achievement procedures. In this section I discuss the decision-making context in which the CRTs operate (see Figure 9-2).

Initial Screening Procedures

Before students are admitted to UHM, the Office of Admissions carefully screens their previous academic records, letters of recommendation, TOEFL scores, and financial situations. From the perspective of the ELI, one of the most important pieces of information is the TOEFL score because only students with total scores of 500 or more are accepted for admission to UHM. Each student's TOEFL subtest and total scores are immediately sent to the ELI. Students with scores above 600 are automatically exempted from any further ELI requirement and are notified of that fact before arriving. Those students who scored between 500 and 599 are informed that they must clear the ELI immediately on arrival at the university. The initial screening procedures clearly serve the beneficial purpose of narrowing the range (see arrows to the left of Figure 9-2) of overall English proficiency with which the ELI must concern itself.

At any stage of this process, any student may request an interview with the director for reconsideration of his or her particular case. This option permits some flexibility and a chance to identify students who may easily be exempted from ELI training without any further testing (e.g., students who were born in foreign countries but attended K–12 in Honolulu, or students from India who completed their education in English-medium schools). In Hawai'i we encounter many interesting situations, particularly with immigrants, which can only be decided case by case.

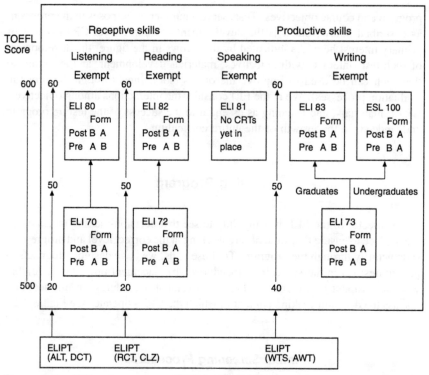

Figure 9-2. ELI testing program. ELIPT = English Language Institute Placement Test; ALT = Academic Listening Test; DCT = Dictation; RCT = Reading Comprehension Test; CLZ = Cloze Procedure; WTS = Writing Sample; AWT = Academic Writing Test.

Placement Procedures

A majority of the students who score between 500 and 599 on the TOEFL are required to take the ELI Placement Test (ELIPT) as soon as they arrive on campus. This test serves three purposes: (a) it gives us more detailed information than TOEFL scores do, (b) it yields information that is more recent than the TOEFL scores (which can be up to 2 years old), and (c) it provides information about how the students will fit into the ELI's particular language program (in terms of their level in each skill area). Placement procedures are particularly important in our program because of its different tracks and levels (as shown in Figure 9-2): four tracks, each focused on one skill, and within the tracks, up to two levels. As a result, the placement tests focus as clearly as possible on the skills and levels of ability found in the ELI.

The ELIPT is a 3-hour test battery made up of six subtests: the Academic Listening Test (ALT), Dictation (DCT), Reading Comprehension Test (RCT), Cloze Procedure (CLZ), Writing Sample (WTS), and Academic Writing Test (AWT). The ALT and DCT are used to place students into listening skill courses (see arrows to the left of ELI 70 and 80 in Figure 9-2); the RCT and CLZ, for the reading skill courses (see arrows to the left of ELI 72 and 82); and the AWT and WTS, for placing students in a writing track (arrows to the left of ELI 83, ESL 100 and ELI 73). Two test scores are available to help place students into each of the three primary skill areas we teach, an arrangement that provides two different views of each student's abilities within a particular skill area.[1]

Placement decisions are based on much more than the students' ELIPT scores. Each student is actually placed during an individual interview conducted by an ELI instructor. The interviewers are given the student's file and test scores and are told to base their placement decisions for each skill area not only on the two ELIPT subtest scores for that skill but also on any other pertinent information in the student's records (e.g., the length of English study, the amount of time since that study, TOEFL subtest scores, spoken production in the interview, academic records, and any other information available at the time). When the instructor cannot decide or when a student disputes the decision, the ELI director (or assistant director) interviews the student and makes a final decision.

First-Week Assessment Procedures

During the 2nd week of classes, teachers administer a CRT designed to test the course objectives. The tests, currently used in two forms (A and B), are administered in a counterbalanced design: half the students in each course take Form A at the beginning and half take Form B; at the end of the course, all students take the opposite form (see Figure 9-2).

The 1st-week test administration has three purposes: (a) it helps teachers to determine which students have been misplaced, (b) it gives teachers an opportunity to diagnose any weak students who may need special help, and (c) it allows the curriculum committee to take a hard look at the degree to which students across sections of a course actually need to learn (i.e., score low on) each objective. Thus pretest administration is an integral part of the ELI's placement, diagnosis, and curriculum development processes.

Achievement Procedures

The same CRT (the opposite form) is administered to each student at the end of the course. Based on this test and the student's classroom performance, the teachers must decide whether to pass or to fail the student, or to suggest exemption from any further study in a particular skill area. Again, when necessary, students are interviewed by the ELI director and advised on what the staff feel is most appropriate for them. The teacher fills out a student performance report for each student. On that form, the teacher grades the student, specifies the level of ELI course the student should take next, rates the student on six different scales (e.g., attendance, participation, content mastery, and so on), and writes a description of the student's content mastery and conduct in class. Copies of these reports are then sent to the students' academic departments so that their advisors will know how they performed. In this way, all students can be treated fairly, and those who have learned more than their peers can be identified and their subsequent placement adjusted.

The system of procedures is enhanced by (but not limited to) information provided by tests. The initial screening procedures rely primarily on the norm-referenced overall proficiency scores provided by the TOEFL. The placement procedures depend, in large part, on the norm-referenced placement results provided by the ELIPT. The 1st-week assessment procedures are based partly on the criterion-referenced diagnostic test given at the beginning of each course, and the achievement procedures are largely based on criterion-referenced posttest scores.

Why Criterion-Referenced Tests?

Richards, Platt, and Weber (1985) provide one definition of a CRT: a test that measures a student's performance according to a particular standard or criterion that has been agreed on. The student must reach that level of performance to pass the test, and a student's score is therefore interpreted with reference to the criterion score, rather than to the scores of other students. This definition differs markedly from that for a norm-referenced test (NRT) taken from the same source: a test designed to measure how the performance of a particular student or group of students compares with the performance of another student or group of students whose scores are given as the norm. A student's score is therefore interpreted with reference to the scores of others rather than to an agreed-on criterion score.

Although these definitions may not be the most comprehensive available, they point to the most important difference between the two types of tests: the performance of each student on a CRT is compared with a particular standard called a criterion level (e.g., if the passing score on a test is set at 60%, a student who answers 66% of the questions correctly passes), whereas on an NRT each student's performance is compared with the performances of other students in the group that has been designated as the norm (e.g., a pupil who scores in the 98th percentile has performed better than 98 of 100 people who took the test, without reference to the actual number, or percentage, of items correctly answered).

The key to understanding the difference between CRTs and NRTs lies in the distinction between the terms percentage and percentile. In administering a CRT, the primary focus is on the amount of material the students know. As a result, it makes sense to report the results in the form of a percentage, i.e., the percent of the questions that the students can answer correctly in relation both to the material taught in the course and to a previously established criterion level for passing. On an NRT, the concerns are entirely different: how each student's score relates to the scores of the other students who took the test. The central issue is the student's position in the distribution of scores. The score can be expressed in terms of a percentile because such scores reveal the proportion of students who scored above and below a given student. In short, CRTs are generally designed to assess the amount of material each student knows whereas NRTs examine the relationship of each student's performance to the scores of all the other students. These definitions cover the primary difference between the two types of tests— that is, that the scores are interpreted differently. As a result of this primary distinction, however, five other differences arise in practice: (a) the kinds of elements the tests are used to measure, (b) the purposes of the tests involved, (c) the resulting distributions of scores, (d) the testing formats, and (e) the degree to which students know what content to expect (see Brown, 1989a, 1990).

The separation of tests by their norm-referenced and criterion-referenced interpretations is becoming increasingly important in the language testing literature (e.g., Cartier, 1968; Cziko, 1982, 1983; Hudson & Lynch, 1984; Delamere, 1985; Henning, 1987; Bachman, 1989, 1990; Brown, 1984b, 1989a, 1989b, 1989c, 1990). The issue has been an important one for years (beginning with Glaser, 1963) in educational testing circles. For example, almost any recent volume of the *Journal of Educational Measurement* or *Applied Psychological Measurement* will contain at least one article on CRT issues. More important to the ELI, the NRT-CRT distinction is becoming increasingly useful for developing and analyzing the various kinds of tests we need for admission, placement, diagnosis, and achievement decisions.

The following research questions frame the description of the results of the CRT side of ELI's testing program:

1. What are the descriptive characteristics of CRTs when used in a variety of courses? How do they differ across skills, levels, and courses?
2. What item statistics are most useful for revising CRTs in such a context? How do the usefulness of NRT, CRT, and IRT (item response theory) approaches compare?
3. To what degree are the CRTs consistent in what they test? How do NRT reliability and CRT dependability approaches compare in usefulness? How do they differ?
4. To what degree are the CRTs valid? Through what strategies can we best investigate the validity of CRTs in a practical situation?

Method

Subjects

The 294 students involved in the study were enrolled in the fall semester 1989 in the ELI at UHM. The group was composed of 29% graduate students, 58% undergraduates, 9% unclassified, and 4% with other classifications. They came mostly from countries in Asia, with 26% from the People's Republic of China, 14% from Hong Kong, 11% from Korea, 9% from Japan, 8% from the Philippines, 6% from Vietnam, 6% from Taiwan, 4% from Indonesia, 3% from Thailand, 2% from Macao, 2% from Malaysia, and the remaining 9% from 18 other countries. Of these students, 85% were new to the ELI and 15% had taken ELI coursework previously. Of the total number of ELI course enrollments, 9% were in ELI 70, 20% in ELI 80, 12% in ELI 72, 25% in ELI 82, 13% in ELI 73, 7% in ELI 83, and 14% in ESL 100.

Materials and Procedures

Although the objectives and resulting tests differed in organization and form across the seven courses, the processes involved in putting the tests in place were quite similar. Teachers in each skill area initially developed items as part of their overall commitment to curriculum development. After a thorough needs analysis for each course and the establishment of tentative sets of objectives, the work of writing items to measure those objectives began. Piloting and revision are ongoing, with various tests at different stages of development at any given time. The tests were administered in the students' classrooms during the 2nd week of class and again during final examination week.

The CRTs created by the ELI teachers differed considerably in organization and form across the skill areas and levels. Because the teachers made all decisions about test content and methods by consensus, the test methods ranged considerably, from multiple-choice format to open-ended writing tasks, depending on the skill being tested. For instance, a typical multiple-choice item might be the following "inference" item, which was used in the directions on the test for the lower-level reading course:

> Out of the darkness of the cold, wintry night came the clatter of a toppled garbage can lid. Startled, Peter dropped his book and ran to the back door.
>
> Ex. 1: What was Peter doing before he heard the noise?
>
> A. singing
>
> C. washing
>
> B. reading
>
> D. sleeping

Naturally, the reading passages in the test itself were considerably longer and more academic in nature.

The writing tasks assigned to the students also tended to have an academic focus. One such task, meant to simulate an in-class essay, required the students to read a five-page selection on genetic engineering and then answer an essay question on the ethics of genetic engineering in 60 minutes (with no notes). They were rated using a scoring grid developed specifically to reflect the ELI objectives (similar to one shown in Brown & Bailey, 1984). The listening teachers in ELI 80 used a similar strategy to score in-class presentations.

Unfortunately, because of the time constraints for scoring (especially during the final examinations), we have tended to favor machine-scorable test formats. However, as we gain experience and confidence in criterion-referenced testing, we are becoming increasingly willing to experiment with more imaginative test types. For instance, we are currently focusing on the development of task-based subtests to be assigned during the last week of classes and scored in conjunction with the students' final examinations. In one such task, students in the upper-level reading course are required to go to the library, retrieve specific information, and report it back to the teacher on open-ended forms. Their answers will then be scored for accuracy and completeness, and the scores will be included in their overall final examination scores.

Analyses

Because we were breaking new ground, we used a variety of testing statistics in our analyses. We borrowed techniques from classical (NRT) theory approaches, from the CRT literature, including generalizability theory, and from IRT. The analyses were performed entirely on an IBM AT desktop computer using the QuattroPro spreadsheet program (Borland International, 1989) and a test analysis program called TESTAT (SYSTAT, 1987). Thus the technology required is well within the resources of many language programs.

Descriptive statistics include the mean, standard deviation, range, number of items, and number of subjects. Item statistics include traditional NRT statistics (item facility and discrimination indexes), CRT estimates (difference index, item phi, B-index, and item agreement index), as well as IRT (item difficulty and discrimination estimates). Consistency estimates include NRT approaches (Cronbach α, split-half adjusted, and Guttman estimates), and CRT methods (ϕ domain score dependability index and $\phi[\lambda]$ squared-error loss agreement coefficient). The NRT standard error of measurement is reported, as well as the analogous CRT confidence intervals. Content validity is discussed, and construct validity is also considered from the perspectives of intervention and differential groups.

Results

Descriptive Statistics

The descriptive statistics for the study, presented in Table 9-1, are given for each form (A and B) when administered at the beginning of the course (Pre) as well as at the end (Post). Where no results are shown, the test was either not

Table 9-1

Descriptive Statistics

Test	N	k	M	SD	Min.	Max.	Range
			Reading classes				
ELI 72							
PreA	35	46	31.11	5.18	15	39	25
PreB	29	46	30.90	5.47	16	41	26
PostA	26	46	34.73	4.86	20	42	23
PostB	35	46	33.57	3.81	28	41	14
ELI 82							
PreA	87	34	21.05	3.95	13	31	19
PreB	65	34	21.26	3.92	10	30	21
PostA	63	34	23.44	3.94	14	31	18
PostB	67	34	23.12	3.90	14	31	18
			Writing classes				
ELI 73							
PreA	41	50	33.71	3.49	25	41	17
PreB	23	50	32.35	5.55	18	41	24
PostA	—	—	—	—	—	—	—
PostB	64	50	33.78	5.81	16	45	30
ELI 83[a]							
PreA	—	—	—	—	—	—	—
PreB	—	—	—	—	—	—	—
PostA	37	9	4.27	2.18	0	8	9
PostB	—	—	—	—	—	—	—
ESL 100[a]							
PreA	47	32	24.89	3.24	16	30	15
PreB	—	—	—	—	—	—	—
PostA	67	32	27.90	3.54	11	32	22
PostB	—	—	—	—	—	—	—
			Listening classes				
ELI 70							
PreA	—	—	—	—	—	—	—
PreB	—	—	—	—	—	—	—
PostA	122	24	16.07	3.07	5	22	18
PostB	122	24	16.30	3.07	9	22	14
ELI 80[b,c]							
PreA	112	24	14.80	4.15	5	24	20
PreB	117	24	14.27	3.41	4	23	20
PostA	95	24	15.71	2.91	7	22	15
PostB	116	24	15.36	3.31	6	23	18

[a]In-class essay not included. [b]In-class presentation not included. [c]Includes 87 students who took the same forms of the same test, but at the beginning and end of ELI 80 in spring 1988.

ready at the time (e.g., ELI 70 PreA and PreB) or inadvertently omitted (e.g., ELI 73 PostA).

Item Statistics

The mean item statistics for the project, shown in Table 9-2, include NRT, IRT, and CRT estimates, all of which we use in thinking about item selection and test revision. Naturally, we are much more interested in the statistics for each individual item, but mean item statistics are the only practical way to provide readers with an overview of the present state of the tests.

The means for the NRT estimates include traditional item facility and item discrimination indexes, which suggest that our tests look statistically very much like NRTs for placement. Indeed, if we were to select items on the basis of these norm-referenced statistics, the tests would probably become increasingly powerful as NRTs. Instead, we have chosen to use the two other types of item analyses to tailor our tests for criterion-referenced purposes.

The means for the IRT item estimates were calculated using a one-parameter model. Our primary purpose in using IRT was to include the item difficulty estimates in our thinking. In all cases the mean difficulty estimates are negative, indicating that the items are on average relatively easy for the students, more so on the posttests than on the pretests. The discrimination estimate reported is the slope (held constant across all items in a one-parameter analysis). Caution must be used in thinking about these IRT results because in a number of cases our sample sizes are too small to be appropriate for even the one-parameter model. We would be much more conmfortable with the IRT results if each sample contained at least 100 students.

Our principal motivation in using IRT analyses was to be able to use the individual student ability estimates for examining appropriate cutpoints for pass-fail decisions. The cutpoints are not given here because the mean ability estimates were zero in all cases. In the long run, we would also like to be able to set up an item bank for each of these courses—a task for which IRT is particularly well suited.

The CRT item statistics include the difference index (DI), item ϕ, the B-index, and the agreement index (A) as described in Shannon and Cliver (1987) and Berk (1984b). The DI is calculated for each item by subtracting its item facility on the pretest from the facility for the same item on the posttest. Item ϕ is an estimate of the degree to which the students' item performances (right or wrong) are related to whether or not they passed the test. The B-index is the difference between proportions of correct answers on each item and the proportions of students passing and failing. The agreement index is defined "as the proportion of consistent item-test outcomes" with regard to those students who correctly answered the item and passed the test, and those who missed the item and failed the test. Thus the agreement statistic is similar at the item level to the

Table 9-2

Mean Item Statistics

Test	NRT		IRT[a]			CRT[b]			
	IF	ID	P	Dif.	Dis.	DI	φ	B	A
Reading classes									
ELI 72									
PreA	.68	.23	.67	−1.46	.38	.08	.07	.18	.34
PreB	.67	.25	.67	−1.31	.44	.06	.09	.23	.36
PostA	.76	.20	.74	−2.01	.42	.08	.18	.33	.76
PostB	.73	.19	.71	−1.96	.38	.06	.00	.00	.73
ELI 82									
PreA	.62	.29	.62	−0.99	.36	.07	.07	.30	.39
PreB	.63	.28	.63	−1.14	.37	.05	.07	.26	.39
PostA	.69	.25	.69	−1.54	.40	.07	.20	.21	.68
PostB	.68	.25	.68	−1.45	.38	.05	.19	.17	.64
Writing classes									
ELI 73									
PreA	.67	.00	.67	−2.47	.24	n.a.	.04	.11	.33
PreB	.65	.24	.65	−1.27	.35	.03	.09	.18	.38
PostA	—	—	—	—	—	—	—	—	—
PostB	.68	.24	.67	−1.46	.41	.03	.21	.22	.68
ELI 83									
PreA	—	—	—	—	—	—	—	—	—
PreB	—	—	—	—	—	—	—	—	—
PostA	.47	.52	.52	−0.03	.85	n.a.	.43	.39	.69
PostB	—	—	—	—	—	—	—	—	—
ESL 100									
PreA	.78	.07	.78	−2.12	.50	.09	.06	.10	.28
PreB	—	—	—	—	—	—	—	—	—
PostA	.87	.19	.87	−2.32	.68	.09	.30	.39	.87
PostB	—	—	—	—	—	—	—	—	—
Listening classes									
ELI 70									
PreA	—	—	—	—	—	—	—	—	—
PreB	—	—	—	—	—	—	—	—	—
PostA	.67	.27	.66	−1.12	.44	n.a.	.23	.23	.66
PostB	.68	.28	.68	−1.38	.44	n.a.	.25	.24	.67
ELI 80									
PreA	.62	.39	.61	−0.64	.56	.03	.17	.35	.43
PreB	.60	.31	.60	−0.67	.47	.05	.07	.37	.41
PostA	.65	.26	.65	−1.24	.37	.03	.23	.22	.65
PostB	.64	.26	.64	−0.98	.48	.05	.24	.23	.64

Note. IF = item facility index; *ID* = item discrimination index; dif. = mean difficulty estimate; dis. = discrimination index; *DI* = difference index; *B* = B-index; *A* = agreement index. [a]Items and subjects with scores of 0% or 100%. [b]Cutpoints were set at .90 for pretest decisions and .60 for posttest decisions.

agreement coefficient used to explore the overall consistency, or dependability, of tests in decision making (see Cohen, 1960; Subkoviak, 1980, 1988).

Recall that we use the CRT statistics not as the averages summarized in Table 9-2 but item by item. Note also that we calculated each of them for .50, .60, .70, .80, and .90 decision levels, which has proven very useful in thinking about item selection in terms of the kinds of decisions we make with the tests, as well as the relative appropriateness of various cutpoints for our decision making. We make two types of decisions on the basis of these tests. The pretest results are used, among other things, to find students who were misplaced and should be moved up to the next level or be exempted; the posttest administrations are used primarily to decide whether or not students should fail the course. We have tentatively set our decision levels at about .90 for pretest exemption from the course and at about .60 for posttest pass-fail determinations. The values reported in Table 9-2 are therefore based on .90 for pretests and .60 for posttests. Ultimately, we want to select the items that are strong for both types of decisions.

Consistency Estimates

Table 9-3 presents both NRT reliability statistics and CRT dependability estimates. The NRT reliability estimates include Cronbach α, the split-half method (adjusted by the Spearman-Brown prophecy formula), and the Guttman coefficient. These NRT coefficients appear to be fairly low, but remember that the ranges of talent in these courses have been severely restricted by previous NRT selection procedures for admissions and placement. As demonstrated in Brown (1984a), Ebel (1979), and elsewhere, even a good test may appear unreliable if the range of talent is depressed. Given that information, the reliability estimates produced by most of these tests are fairly respectable, even from an NRT perspective.

From the CRT viewpoint, the ϕ coefficients are domain score estimates of the dependability of these tests, and the $\phi(\lambda)$ coefficients are decision consistency estimates based on the squared-error loss agreement approach (see Berk, 1980, 1984a). Both ϕ and $\phi(\lambda)$ are based on the shortcut formulas presented in Brown (1989c). Like the CRT item statistics, the $\phi(\lambda)$ estimates are for .90 cutpoints on the pretests and .60 cutpoints on the posttests.

The standard error of measurement (*SEM*) is presented just to the right of the NRT reliability estimates. In this case, the *SEM* is based on the odd-even, or split-half (adjusted), reliability coefficients. The confidence interval (*CI*), in the last column (which ranged from .057 to .215 in these data), is analogous to the *SEM* but is appropriate for use with CRTs. It should be interpreted as the proportion of error that would be accounted for with 68% confidence around an individual's proportion score. For example, the *CI* in the last row of Table 9-3 indicates that a person receiving a proportion score of .80 (or 80%) would score within +/−1 *CI*, or a band from .704 (.80 − .096 = .704) to .896 (.80 + .096

Table 9-3

Reliability and Dependability of Tests

Test	NRT				CRT		
	α	Odd-even	Guttman	SEM	ϕ	$\phi(\lambda)^a$	CI
Reading classes							
ELI 72							
PreA	.704	.814	.819	2.234	.674	.928	.068
PreB	.750	.822	.816	1.879	.713	.932	.068
PostA	.713	.785	.784	2.253	.691	.892	.062
PostB	.573	.661	.660	2.218	.497	.823	.065
ELI 82							
PreA	.575	.651	.651	2.334	.541	.927	.082
PreB	.986	.722	.722	2.068	.546	.925	.082
PostA	.617	.531	.529	2.695	.584	.719	.078
PostB	.587	.650	.649	2.305	.562	.686	.079
Writing classes							
ELI 73							
PreA	.276	.555	.554	2.320	.239	.921	.215
PreB	.703	.687	.674	3.107	.683	.943	.066
PostA	—	—	—	—	—	—	—
PostB	.750	.789	.786	2.669	.714	.784	.065
ELI 83							
PreA	—	—	—	—	—	—	—
PreB	—	—	—	—	—	—	—
PostA	.712	.739	.738	1.112	.650	.688	.154
PostB	—	—	—	—	—	—	—
ESL 100							
PreA	.630	.690	.689	1.802	.609	.811	.072
PreB	—	—	—	—	—	—	—
PostA	.793	.863	.861	1.319	.757	.963	.057
PostB	—	—	—	—	—	—	—
Listening classes							
ELI 70							
PreA	—	—	—	—	—	—	—
PreB	—	—	—	—	—	—	—
PostA	.554	.583	.581	1.984	.509	.582	.094
PostB	.551	.497	.497	2.179	.512	.615	.044
ELI 80							
PreA	.725	.814	.812	1.788	.711	.919	.095
PreB	.600	.734	.730	1.757	.562	.916	.098
PostA	.428	.535	.533	1.981	.411	.483	.095
PostB	.594	.727	.727	1.731	.556	.559	.096

[a]Cutpoints were set at .90 for pretest decisions and .60 for posttest.

= .896) 68% of the time. In percent score terms, this would be a band between 70.4% and 89.6%. The *CI* is derived from a statistic called the absolute error variance component in generalizability theory (see Bolus, Hinofotis, & Bailey, 1982; Brennan, 1980, 1984; Brown, 1984c; Brown & Bailey, 1984).

Validity

Essentially, two strategies are practical and appropriate for investigating the validity of CRTs: the content and construct approaches.

Content validity, which involves the systematic study of the degree to which the items on a test match the content the test was designed to measure, has become an integral part of the item development process at UHM: items are always written to closely match the objectives of the courses. Thus we are constantly considering content validity item by item and subtest by subtest. Because they are written by the teachers of the courses and carefully reviewed by the lead teachers and director of the ELI, the items are expected not only to match the objectives but to match them as they are addressed in the classrooms. When we become reasonably comfortable with the tests' dependability and validity, we will no doubt turn to outside "experts" for independent judgments of the degree to which the items match our objectives and our objectives match the students' needs (see Popham, 1978, 1981, for more on such strategies).

Construct validity involves the demonstration of the degree to which a test is measuring the psychological construct it claims to be measuring. Such demonstrations can take many forms, but for CRTs the intervention and differential groups methods are the most practical and appropriate strategies. A typical intervention study is one in which students are given a test, are taught whatever construct is involved, and are tested again. If the test is actually measuring the construct, the students should score significantly higher on the posttest than they did on the pretest. In this way, one argument can be built for the construct validity of the test.

The differences found in the study reported here between pretest and posttest means indicate that, in every case, instruction had some effect on the scores. Gains ranged from 3% to 9% as indicated by the difference indexes (*DI*) reported in Table 9-2. The actual gains experienced by the students who took our courses are expected to be somewhat higher for two reasons.

First, the results reported here include all students who took the pretest and posttest. Students who scored high on the pretest and were exempted from the courses did not take the posttest, a fact that diminishes the observed differences. In future analyses, the scores of the exempted students will be eliminated from the pretest results so that only those students who actually received instruction will be included in the analysis. In most cases, we have not yet substantially revised the tests to select the items that are most sensitive to instruction. We expect that when we do (i.e., when we select those items with the largest difference indexes and strengthen the tests further using the other item statistics), much larger gains will be reflected in the tests. This does not necessarily mean that the students will be learning more, but that the tests will become more sensitive to what students do learn.

In addition, we cannot attribute the gains solely to the effects of our courses because students were simultaneously being exposed to English from many other angles in their daily lives, and because many of them were also taking other ELI courses that could have affected their English. Nevertheless, we can interpret the differences as reflecting gains due to the total English language experience that students had during that semester at UHM.

For above reasons, we felt it would be premature to perform statistical analyses of the current differences, especially before addressing the issues explained above. Nevertheless, the intervention study approach to CRT construct validity is much on our minds. At the test level, we are considering the mean gains. At the item level, we are choosing the items that will remain on future revised versions of the tests on the basis of the difference index. Thus construct validity is particularly important for ensuring that the CRTs have a fairly strong relationship with the learning that is occurring in the ELI courses.

Another approach to construct validity also figures into our thinking. The *differential groups approach* usually involves administering a test to a group of students who can be said to possess the construct in question (masters), as well as to another group who lack it (nonmasters) (see Brown, 1984c, for an example). We have used the differential groups approach in two ways. First, we have compared the performances of students who passed the courses (masters) with that of students who failed (nonmasters). Naturally, there were large differences between those groups because passing or failing was determined partly by the test itself. Second and more important, we have examined the individual and mean item ϕ, the B-index, and A. They generally indicate a fairly strong relationship between the accuracy of the students' answers on individual items and whether or not the students pass the course. This type of validity is especially important in thinking about the fairness of the ELI's pass-fail decisions.

We have found one aspect of CRT validity particularly satisfying: the fact that content, intervention, and differential groups strategies are built directly into item development and item analysis. Thus item selection and test revision are integrally related to analyzing and improving test validity. As always with issues of validity, the goal is to marshal evidence from a variety of sources so that, collectively, they can be used to investigate (and perhaps support) the validity of the test in question.

Discussion

We have found that the CRTs developed as of fall semester 1989 at ELI are functioning reasonably well. From a norm-referenced point of view, the tests appear to be functioning about the same across skills, levels, and courses. They are reasonably well centered and disperse students adequately. From a criterion-referenced point of view, the tests generally appear too easy at the beginning of the course and too difficult at the end. The item selection processes and the revisions that we make will be aimed at improving this situation so that (a) the tests better reflect any learning that is occurring and (b) the tests help us to make fair decisions with regard to students' passing or failing courses.

In this effort, all the item statistics seem useful. The NRT statistics are helping us to examine our tests in terms with which we have long been familiar. In addition, items that do not turn out to be appropriate in the CRTs may later serve as new items for our NRT placement tests. Thus NRT item statistics may continue to prove valuable in the future. Similarly, the increasing use of IRT approaches to item analysis is expected to help us to set up item banks and make better pass-fail decisions.

The tests also appear to be at least moderately reliable from the NRT perspective on that concept, especially given the restrictions of range in these courses. From a CRT viewpoint, the tests also appear to be moderately consistent in terms of domain score dependability (as indicated by ϕ). However, the dependability of these tests, as estimated by $\phi(\lambda)$, seems to be more uneven. The estimates range from very high to very low depending on the test and cutpoint. Further analysis of these related issues must be considered when we are making the actual pass-fail decisions. In addition, we must pay careful attention to the CI statistics and obtain additional information about students who fall close to our cutpoints—at least for those students who fall within one CI, plus or minus, of the cutpoint. Thus for pass-fail decisions, the CRT dependability approaches and the CIs will be much more useful than the analogous NRT reliability estimates.

Validity will also continue to be an issue. We note with some pride that each item in the study was carefully scrutinized for content validity by the appropriate ELI teachers. In addition, all tests in this study showed some sensitivity to instruction. We should nevertheless exclude from analysis in future studies those students who are exempted on the basis of their pretest scores.

Conclusions

In this section I briefly touch on the problems encountered in developing a comprehensive CRT program like the one described in this paper. I then turn to the benefits of CRTs for curriculum development.

Problems

The process of test development was made relatively efficient, indeed was made possible, by the appointment of a lead teacher, who is given 50% release time to help in administering, scoring, developing, analyzing, and revising ELI tests. During the norm-referenced placement testing, the lead teacher administers the tests, and the director scores them and analyzes the results as each subtest is completed. During the remainder of the semester, when our attention turns to the CRT diagnostic and achievement decisions, the lead teacher is essential in rallying the teachers to write, review, and revise items. The lead teacher is also responsible for giving the tests to the teachers for administration in their classes, for scoring the tests, and for giving the results to the teachers within 24 hours. Such promptness has made the results particularly useful and has helped foster teacher support for the testing program.

At ELI, it is useful that the director is a language testing specialist and that the lead teacher for testing is typically a graduate assistant who has excelled in UHM's language testing course. The sheer number of tests involved in this project, along with the wide variety of statistics that are necessary, make such a project fairly laborious. The central message seems to be that a program must allocate adequate resources in terms of expertise, time, money, and computer equipment before any such project can succeed on this scale. For smaller programs with fewer courses, a modified version of the project, starting with fewer tests and more select statistics, seems feasible. Naturally, a program should consider these issues long before beginning any such testing project.

It is also important to recognize that we do not always learn what we set out to learn. For instance, the first versions of the ELI 72 reading test were developed in 1987. The first administration of these items indicated that the students already knew virtually all of the material, showing us that our objectives (ones that had been used for years) were aimed far too low for the abilities of our students. As a result, we had to throw out much of the test and revise our objectives considerably. In the reading course we were able to do so by using similar objectives but applying them to much more difficult textual material (college-level texts). It initially hurt to realize that all our efforts in developing that early test were for nothing, but in retrospect it is clear that our early attempt at a CRT and the subsequent failure have served to change our views of our students' language needs. This effect has benefited not only the reading curriculum but that for the other skills as well.

Benefits of a Criterion-Referenced Testing Program

CRTs are not easy to develop, implement, analyze, and revise. In truth, such a project requires a prodigious amount of work. A determined group of teachers and administrators did create these tests, however, and in multiple forms. The payoff is that the information we derive from them applies directly to what we are doing in the ESL classroom *and* helps us to improve all of the elements of the curriculum design process (needs, objectives, materials, tests, teaching, and program evaluation).

First, CRTs tests helped us to reexamine closely our perceptions of the students' needs. Objective by objective, we can now consider how the students perform at the beginning and end of each course on each objective and the degree to which we have defined our objectives in clear and observable terms. Sometimes our initial perceptions turn out to have been wrong and, as described, large portions of tests must be revamped. However, we feel that this result is better than blithely continuing to teach material that our students do not need to learn.

Second, knowing which objectives are working (and which are not) allows us to streamline and concentrate on objectives that reflect the students' needs while adding others that are designed to meet other needs. This strategy enables us to avoid wasting time and effort teaching material that the students already know. We can instead focus on what the students need to learn, and much more efficiently. Perhaps we are succumbing to what Tumposky (1984) sarcastically labeled the "cult of efficiency." However, we are defining the objectives in so many different ways (ranging from experiential to instructional objectives) that her complaints no longer seem applicable. Frankly, we see no problem with attempting to be relatively efficient in the delivery of ESL instruction to students who pay good money for it. In our view, we are simply trying to foster as much language learning as we can during the short period of time that we have with our students.

Third, having CRTs in place allows us the luxury of working together as groups of teachers rather than in isolation to build, implement, analyze, and revise classroom tests that are relatively effective. An additional effect is that information gained from the CRTs can help us improve other types of tests. For instance, information from CRT achievement tests can prove useful in revising the placement procedures to overcome the mismatch that sometimes occurs between placement batteries and the courses to which they are supposed to be related (as noted in Brown, 1984a). One such process of modifying placement procedures to align them more closely with courses is described in Brown (1989b); other strategies are currently being explored at UHM.

Fourth, modifying the objectives based on what we learn from our diagnostic and achievement tests naturally leads us to rethink our materials so that they better match the newly perceived needs of the students. Sometimes the changes have proven to be large, but more often they have taken the form of incremental modifications in materials, teaching techniques and practice exercises. In all cases, the tests help us to gauge the correct level and objectives for the textbooks that we adopt, the materials modules that we develop, and the lessons that we teach.

Fifth, the goal of all of our curriculum activities is to support teaching so that the teachers can do what they do best—teach. Hence one perspective on our CRTs is that they are a way to help teachers do rational and well-designed achievement testing (which is mandated in all undergraduate courses at UHM).

The teachers are welcome to add sections of their own devising to the final examination for their individual courses, but the core test is essentially provided for them. In addition, the tests were jointly developed by the teachers in each course over a period of 3 years. The tests must constantly be reviewed and revised to ensure that they match the objectives of the courses as they are currently taught. Because the tests are so important to the students and teachers, the groups of teachers most directly involved review and revise them. As such, they form an important center on which the teachers can concentrate while working constructively together toward a common goal.

The sixth and last benefit derived from our testing program has to do with program evaluation. In the formative sense of program evaluation, the tests clearly help us to modify our curriculum as it continues to develop. However, if ELI is called on to perform program evaluation in the summative sense, the tests will also put us in a very strong position. When we do need to focus on summative program evaluation (for our program reviews), we will have a staggering amount of information ready to present: norm-referenced information about the overall proficiency of our students in terms of their TOEFL scores for admission as well as information about their placement based on the six subtests of the ELIPT. In addition, the CRTs will supply data on the students' knowledge at the beginning (diagnostic) and end (achievement) of each course, as well as about what and how much the students have learned in our courses. At the very least, we will clearly be in a position to fashion a summary report that describes our program in terms of student needs, program goals and objectives, materials, and teaching. We will also be in a strong position to suggest clear-cut changes in the program in an ongoing process of curriculum development.

Naturally, we hope that a majority of the students who are served by the procedures discussed above are correctly admitted, placed, diagnosed, and promoted. However, decisions are made by human beings and, even when based on seemingly scientific test scores, human judgments can go awry. The problem is that an incorrect decision may cost a student a great deal in the form of extra tuition or extra, unnecessary time spent studying ESL. We therefore take the decisions we make about our students' lives very seriously and base them on the best available information from a variety of sources, including CRTs. Certainly, the ELI's decision-making process requires more effort on the part of the administrators and teachers, but the benefits gained from effective and humane testing procedures accrue to all—students, teachers, and administrators alike. It is hoped that the strategies, which we find so useful, can be adapted to other language programs as well.

Note

1. The speaking course is open only to international teaching assistants. The testing is therefore handled separately from that for the mainstream program.

References

Bachman, L. F. (1989). The development and use of criterion-referenced tests of language ability in language program evaluation. In K. D. Johnson (Ed.), *The second language curriculum* (pp. 242–258). London: Cambridge University.

Bachman, L. F. (1990). *Fundamental considerations in language testing.* Oxford: Oxford University Press.

Berk, R. A. (Ed.). (1980). *Criterion-referenced measurement: The state of the art.* Baltimore: Johns Hopkins University Press.

Berk, R. A. (Ed.). (1984a). *A guide to criterion-referenced test construction.* Baltimore: Johns Hopkins University Press.

Berk, R. A. (1984b). Selecting the index of reliability. In R. A. Berk (Ed.), *A guide to criterion-referenced test construction* (pp. 231–266). Baltimore: Johns Hopkins University Press.

Bolus, R. E., Hinofotis, F. B., & Bailey, K. M. (1982). An introduction to generalizability theory in second language research. *Language Learning, 32*, 245–258.

Borland International (1989). *QuattroPro.* Scotts Valley, CA: Author.

Brennan, R. L. (1980). Applications of generalizability theory. In R. A. Berk (Ed.), *Criterion-referenced measurement: The state of the art* (pp. 186–232). Baltimore: Johns Hopkins University Press.

Brennan, R. L. (1984). Estimating the dependability of the scores. In R. A. Berk (Ed.), *A guide to criterion-referenced test construction* (pp. 292–334). Baltimore: Johns Hopkins University Press.

Brown, J. D. (1984a). A cloze is a cloze is a cloze? In J. Handscombe, R. A. Orem, & B. P. Taylor (Eds.), *On TESOL '83: The question of control* (pp. 109–119). Washington, DC: Teachers of English to Speakers of Other Languages.

Brown, J. D. (1984b). Criterion-referenced language tests: What, how and why? *Gulf Area TESOL Bi-annual, 1*, 32–34.

Brown, J. D. (1984c). A norm-referenced engineering reading test. In A. K. Pugh & J. M. Ulijn (Eds.), *Reading for professional purposes: Studies and practices in native and foreign languages* (pp. 55–98). London: Heinemann Educational Books.

Brown, J. D. (1989a). Improving ESL placement tests using two perspectives. *TESOL Quarterly, 23*, 1.

Brown, J. D. (1989b). Language program evaluation: A synthesis of existing possibilities. In K. D. Johnson (Ed.), *The Second Language Curriculum* (pp. 222–241). London: Cambridge University.

Brown, J. D. (1989c). Short-cut estimates of criterion-referenced test consistency. *University of Hawai'i Working Papers in English as a Second Language, 8*, 1.

Brown, J. D. (1990). Where do tests fit into language programs? *JALT Journal, 12*, 1.

Brown, J. D. (In preparation). *The systematic development of language curriculum.* Honolulu, HI: University of Hawai'i at Manoa.

Brown, J. D., & Bailey, K. M. (1984). A categorical instrument for scoring second language writing skills. *Language Learning, 34*, 21–42.

Cartier, F. A. (1968). Criterion-referenced testing of language skills. *TESOL Quarterly, 2*, 27–32.

Cohen, J. (1960). A coefficient of agreement for nominal scales. *Educational and Psychological Measurement, 20*, 37–46.

Cziko, G. A. (1982). Improving the psychometric, criterion-referenced, and practical qualities of integrative language tests. *TESOL Quarterly, 16*, 367–379.

Cziko, G. A. (1983). Psychometric and edumetric approaches to language testing. *Applied Linguistics, 5*, 23–38.

Delamere, T. (1985). Notional-functional syllabi and criterion-referenced tests: The missing link. *System, 13*, 43–47.

Ebel, R. L. (1979). *Essentials of educational measurement* (3rd ed.). Englewood Cliffs, NJ: Prentice-Hall.

Glaser, R. (1963). Instructional technology and the measurement of learning outcomes: Some questions. *American Psychologist, 18*, 519–521.

Henning, G. (1987). *A guide to language testing: Development, evaluation, research.* Cambridge, MA: Newbury House.

Hudson, T., & Lynch, B. (1984). A criterion-referenced approach to ESL achievement testing. *Language Testing, 1*, 171–201.

Popham, W. J. (1978). *Criterion-referenced measurement.* Englewood Cliffs, NJ: Prentice-Hall.

Popham, W.J. (1981). *Modern educational measurement.* Englewood Cliffs, NJ: Prentice-Hall.

Richards, J. C., Platt, J., & Weber, J. (1985). *Longman dictionary of applied linguistics.* London: Longman.

Shannon, G. A., & Cliver, B. A. (1987). An application of item response theory in the comparison of four conventional item discrimination indices for criterion-referenced tests. *Journal of Educational Measurement, 24*, 347–356.

Subkoviak, M. J. (1980). Decision-consistency approaches. In R. A. Berk (Ed.), *Criterion-referenced measurement: The state of the art* (pp. 129–185). Baltimore: Johns Hopkins University Press.

Subkoviak, M. J. (1988). A practitioner's guide to computation and interpretation of reliability indices for mastery tests. *Journal of Educational Measurement, 25*, 47–55.

SYSTAT (1987). *TESTAT.* Evanston, IL: Author.

Tumposky, N. R. (1984). Behavioral objectives, the cult of efficiency and foreign language learning: Are they compatible? *TESOL Quarterly, 18*, 295–310.

A Collaborative/Diagnostic Feedback Model for Testing Foreign Languages

Elana Shohamy
Tel Aviv University

The purpose of this paper is to describe a model of testing in which tests and other assessment procedures become tools for providing meaningful and diagnostic information about foreign language learning. The testing model has been implemented in 10 schools (with approximately 1,000 students) teaching Hebrew as a foreign language in the United States and Canada. A number of features make this model unique and innovative in the language testing field:

1. The process is collaborative, that is, the schools' faculty and a testing team work cooperatively.
2. The tests assess language ranging from achievement to proficiency.
3. The process provides comparative information about each school in relation to other, similar types of schools.
4. The information provided is diagnostic and covers a variety of language dimensions.
5. The results are interpreted by the school itself.
6. The results and their interpretations are translated into specific actions for change.
7. The assessment is continuous.

This paper presents the background and rationale for the model and describes in detail the model and its application.

Background

Language testing occurs in a variety of contexts. The two most important ones are (a) the *school* context, in which tests and other assessment procedures are used as part of the instructional process to improve teaching and learning in the school, and (b) the *external* context, in which tests are used to make important decisions about the future of individuals, as in granting certificates, accepting candidates for programs, placing students in appropriate class levels, and others. Although information obtained from tests in the school context can provide meaningful feedback to teachers and students, such opportunities are rarely shared in the external testing context. Moreover, results from external tests are generally obtained after it is too late for change. Still, it is interesting that external tests have been more influential in testing theory and research than school tests have and that they draw more attention in test development. Classroom testing, in contrast, has been badly neglected in language testing theory, research, and development.

A recent phenomenon in the language testing field is that external language tests now affect and drive foreign language learning in the school context. Thus language tests traditionally used to make decisions and judgments about the future of individuals now influence the educational context of learning. This phenomenon is the result of the strong authority that external testing holds and its great impact on the lives of test takers. After all, external tests can determine whether test takers will obtain certificates or diplomas, be given jobs, be placed in certain language class levels, or be allowed to continue studies in a higher institution, to cite a few examples. Consequently, external tests have become most powerful devices, capable of changing and prescribing the behavior of those affected by their results—administrators, teachers, and students. Central agencies and decision makers, aware of the authoritative power of external tests, have often used them to impose new curricula, textbooks, and teaching methods. Thus external tests are currently used to motivate students to study, teachers to teach, and principals to modify the curriculum. The use of external tests as a device for affecting the educational process is often referred to as the *washback effect* or *measurement-driven instruction.*

One example of the washback effect in the context of foreign language learning in the United States is the introduction of the *ACTFL Proficiency Guidelines* and the Oral Proficiency Interview (OPI) (American Council for the Teaching of Foreign Languages, 1986). The main purpose of introducing these instruments was to pressure teachers and students to upgrade the level of foreign language learning (mostly of the oral skills) in line with the guidelines and tests. Specifically, the rationale was that the introduction of the guidelines and the OPI would lead to the improvement of foreign language proficiency, as teachers would try to meet the goals and criteria they contained. This example demonstrates a reliance on the power of tests to change the behavior of teachers and students and an overemphasis on proficiency, accompanied by an underemphasis on the means by which the learner arrives at proficiency—instructional activities, teaching methods, classroom learning, curricula, and textbooks, which are part of the learning context.

Although the use of tests to prescribe behavior is widespread in many educational circles, researchers have been skeptical about the extent to which the introduction of tests per se can bring meaningful improvement in learning and teaching (Stake, forthcoming; Shohamy, 1990). Recently questions have been raised not only about the ethics of using tests for purposes other than information but also about whether the use of tests can advance and improve learning in a meaningful way.

Stake (forthcoming), for example, studied the effect of introducing tests as a device for upgrading achievement and found that, although the tests did make teachers more focused in their teaching, they also narrowed the scope of the subject matter being taught: teachers were found to be teaching primarily to achieve better test results. Shohamy (1989), in examining the effect of introducing a new English speaking-test battery on the teaching of English as a foreign language, found that the impact was mostly that of teaching *test language*, that is, language skills and tasks that were likely to appear on the tests, although test language represented only a small domain of the language that needed to be learned.

Such findings should not come as a surprise. After all, when tests alone are relied on to create change; when the emphasis is only on proficiency and not on the means that lead to proficiency (i.e., what takes place in the classroom as part of the learning process); when tests are introduced as authoritative tools and are judgmental, prescriptive, and dictated from above; when tests do not involve the people expected to carry out the change—the teachers; and when the information tests provide is neither detailed nor specific nor contains meaningful feedback and diagnosis that can be used for repair, we cannot expect tests to lead to meaningful improvement in learning. Tests are only one component in the educational process.

Still, the fact that creating change through testing is indeed effective is interesting. Schools will usually strive to meet external standards and will change teaching to improve performance on tests. Unfortunately, however, this method of bringing about change emphasizes only the performance of the students on these tests; the larger effect is a narrowing of the curriculum in ways that are inconsistent with real learning and the real needs of the students. Therefore, we need to look for ways external tests can produce a positive washback.

It is the data obtained from external tests and its utilization that makes tests so valuable, mainly because they provide decision makers (students, teachers, and administrators) with valuable information on and insight into teaching and learning. For example, information obtained from tests can provide evidence of students' ability over a whole range of skills and subskills, on achievement and proficiency, and on a continuous basis. Such information can be useful in judging students' language in relation to expectations laid out in the curriculum, to determine whether the school as a whole is performing well in relation to other schools that share the same curricula, to determine whether the teaching methods and textbooks used are effective tools for achieving those goals, and to determine whether the goals are realistic. Once conclusions are reached based on such information, the curriculum can be aligned accordingly by changing teaching methods, textbooks, or expectations. These changes can then be monitored through repeated administration of the tests.

The Requirements of an Effective Testing Model

To use the information provided by external tests to create change in learning and teaching, we need to incorporate additional factors, which are part of the educational process, and to avoid relying on the power of tests themselves to create change. Frederiksen and Collins (1989) introduced the notion of the *systemic validity* of tests to refer to the introduction of tests along with a set of additional variables that are part of the learning and instructional system. Accordingly, the introduction of tests is a dynamic process in which change in the educational system takes place according to feedback obtained from tests. In systemic models, a valid test is one that brings about, or induces, an improvement in the tested skills after a test has been in the educational system for a period of time. Thus high systemic validity results when a whole set of assessment activities foster it, and Frederiksen and Collins identify and describe a number of such activities. They contend that the efficiency of current testing practices is greatly outweighed by the cost of using a system with low systemic validity—one that has a negative impact on learning and teaching—because the goal of testing must be to support the improvement of learning and teaching. Thus tests used to improve learning can be effective only if they are connected to the educational system and not used in isolation.

The assessment model described here attempts to incorporate important elements that are part of the educational process. It is grounded in foreign language learning to define what needs to be tested and in the field of measurement and evaluation to determine how to incorporate testing information for utilization purposes. Below I describe the main elements of the model.

Achievement and Proficiency

To determine what to test, we must define what knowing a language really means. Unlike most other school subjects, in language a distinction exists between achievement and proficiency. Achievement refers to the language learned in given course, based on the school's curriculum, whereas proficiency relates to the language needed in "real life." This distinction originates from the assumption that in learning a language, what is learned in school is not always the same as what is needed in life. The so-called proficiency movement, through the introduction of the OPI and the ACTFL guidelines, emphasized proficiency. Its purpose was to make teachers more aware of the goal of teaching languages, that is, the actual communication and use of language, while leading them to pay less attention to grammar and linguistic accuracy. Although this shift in itself is welcome, proficiency cannot be reached without the series of steps that precede it. Specifically, language tasks in the real world (i.e., proficiency) are not necessarily the same as problems presented in the classroom. Classroom problems are carefully structured to teach a particular skill, more or less in isolation from other skills, but in the real world these skills are not structured predictably. Instead, they are strongly dependent on the situation (Collins, Brown, & Newman, 1989). We therefore need to emphasize both achievement in the schools' curriculum—what takes place in the classroom—and proficiency for real situations—the transfer of curriculum to new life situations, which are often different from those taught and practiced in school.

Innovative Information

To use information effectively, those who use it must realize its potential to lead to improvement. Therefore, the information needs to be innovative and relevant to the students' context and needs. According to Nitko (1989), the only test scores that will be used are those that provide new and meaningful information. It needs to be detailed, descriptive, and diagnostic, able to address a variety of dimensions, and not collapsible into one general score.

Connecting Teaching With Learning

If information obtained from tests is to lead to change, it must also be translated into instructional activities and actual strategies for teaching and learning. This idea relates to the systemic validity notion of Frederiksen and Collins (1989) mentioned earlier, whereby if a test is to affect learning, it must be accompanied by a set of variables that are part of the learning and instructional system so that changes in the instructional system will take place in accordance with the feedback obtained from tests.

Involvement of the Agents of Change

Another requirement for successful use of test results is the involvement of the school's decision makers—the faculty, principals, and teachers—in different phases of the assessment process, because they are the ones who are expected to carry out change (Nevo, 1989). Thus they should not only share the responsibility for testing but also have authority over it.

The Need for Comparative Information

In testing, a difference often exists between criterion-referenced testing and norm-referenced testing. In criterion-referenced testing, the level of knowledge depends on the goals and objectives of the learning, usually in relation to a given curriculum. In norm-referenced testing, the level of knowledge is judged in relation to others taking the same test. Although there has been strong encouragement to use criterion-referenced testing, that is, to judge schools in relation to their own goals and objectives, we now realize that for results to become meaningful to the school, they have to be *both* criterion and norm referenced. Schools want to know how they are doing in relation to other schools with similar goals (Shavelson, 1988).

The Need for Communicative Tests

Tests need to reflect the current theories of language. Because language must be viewed in a communicative context, which involves full discourse functions, registers, and a set of sociocultural rules, the tests need to focus on the use of language in authentic and direct situations and tasks. "It is thus essential that whatever knowledge and skills are sought, they should be measured directly. Any indirectness in the measure will lead to a misdirection of the learning effort by test takers to the degree it matters to them to do well on the test" (Frederiksen & Collins, 1989, p. 30).

Other needs, not explored here, to consider in the development of testing models that incorporate factors from the educational process are the need for highly reliable and valid tests and the need to allow time for the effect to occur, because no assessment should be a one-time episode. Rather, it should be ongoing so changes can be followed and traced.

Main Features of the Testing Model

The testing model, based on the elements described above, includes the following features:

1. It is collaborative, that is, the school's faculty and a testing team work cooperatively throughout the assessment process. The school defines its curriculum, and when the testing team presents the assessment results, the school interprets the results within its specific context. Because different interpretations may be derived from the same results, knowing the school's goals is essential in interpreting how much students have achieved.
2. The tests tap language ranging from achievement (the specific school's curriculum) to proficiency (application of the curriculum to real-life situations). The tests reflect current theories of what it means to know a language; they are communicative, consist of authentic texts and tasks, and represent language that is expected to be produced in discourse. They are tailor-made by the assessment team according to each school's curriculum, as described by the school. The tests have strong psychometric properties, incorporate

items and tasks that have been tried and revised, and thus provide reliable and valid information.

3. The tests provide information on each school compared with schools that share similar goals and curricula.

4. The information is diagnostic, that is, it is ample, detailed, and innovative and involves a variety of language dimensions within all four language skills tested. The tests are analyzed diagnostically, and the school receives a comprehensive report containing information on a variety of subareas in each of the skills.

5. The school interprets the results within its specific context.

6. The results and their interpretations are to be translated into specific actions for *change* and *improvement* in teaching and learning. Thus, once arriving at its conclusions, the school needs to decide what steps to take to improve performance. For example, the test results may reflect the need for new instructional strategies, new curricula, modified textbooks, or teacher training.

7. The assessment is continuous so that changes can be followed over time and is repeated so changes can be observed and measured on an ongoing basis.

Phases of the Assessment Model

Figure 10-1 displays the phases of the assessment: (a) the school writes a description of the curriculum in the form of a table of specification (a blueprint of the curriculum); (b) the assessment team develops the tests (and attitude questionnaires); (c) the school and the assessment team administer the tests; (d) the assessment team analyzes the tests; (e) the assessment team gives the schools the diagnostic results in the areas tested; (f) the school draws conclusions and implications based on the test results; and (g) the school, along with the assessment team, draws up a plan for improvement based on the test results.

Phase 1: Curriculum Description

The activity in Phase 1 is a workshop in which representatives of each participating school meet with the assessment team to discuss the project and to learn about procedures for describing their curriculum via a table of specification. The workshop, which usually takes place at the beginning of the school year, has three main goals: (a) to familiarize the school's faculty with the different phases of the assessment, (b) to expose them to up-to-date approaches to language testing, and (c) to guide the participants in procedures for constructing the tables of specifications. These tables are condensed versions of the language curriculum that will serve as the map for the tests and that each school's faculty is expected

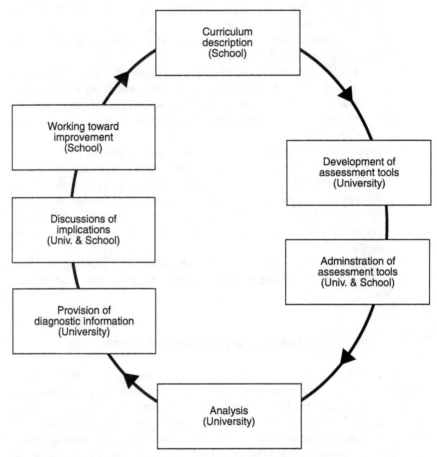

Figure 10-1. Components of the assessment tool.

to construct. The participants obtain a booklet containing step-by-step instructions for constructing such tables, a list of objectives, content areas that they can choose from and that serve as examples for constructing the tables, and examples of tables developed by schools in previous years. The assessment team collects information from each school about the textbooks used, the number of students, teaching methodologies, testing practices, and so on. (This information allows the assessment team to begin preparing the tests while the schools are working on their tables.)

The table of specifications is constructed at the schools, usually during October and November. The meetings involve all the school's faculty and are chaired by the school's principal. The task is for the school to arrive at a number of tables of specifications in each skill tested, which include objectives, contents, and weights. These tables then serve as the blueprint for the construction of the tests.

Table 10-1

Table of Specifications for Reading Comprehension

	Objective (%)				
Type of test	Identify main idea	Identify key words	Arrive at conclusion	Make inference	Total
Narrative	0	10	0	5	15
Plays	10	0	15	0	25
Poems	5	0	10	5	20
Songs	10	0	5	0	15
Exposition	5	3	2	15	25
Total	30	13	32	25	100

The tables are constructed after extensive discussions of the objectives and content and their relative importance within the school's curriculum. The team also determines the weights and proportions for the objectives and content. The process takes, on average, four to five meetings. Once the tables are completed, they are submitted to the assessment team. Table 10-1 is a table of specifications prepared by one of the schools for reading comprehension.

Phase 2: Development of the Assessment Tools

Once the school submits the tables of specifications, the assessment team develops language tests for each school in all language skills taught.

Components of the Tests

Each test consists of three components that tap different types of language along the achievement-proficiency continuum. In Figure 10-2, the extreme left (point S, for school-based) refers to the achievement component, that is, language that directly reflects the school's curriculum; the extreme right (point P, for proficiency) represents language related to the application of the curriculum to new, real-life situations (i.e., proficiency). The middle area (point SP, for school-based proficiency) represents language that is dependent on the curriculum for objectives but is based on similar, content areas not previously learned by the students. Some of the SP and P items are used for comparison because they are based on common language that students in all the schools are expected to know.

Constructing the Tests From the Tables of Specifications

The process of constructing the tests from the tables of specifications is demonstrated below through the example of a reading comprehension test. The same procedure is used in all the other tests.

In the first phase, each school's table of specifications is matched to a general table (GT) that has been prepared for each of the language skills tested. The GT

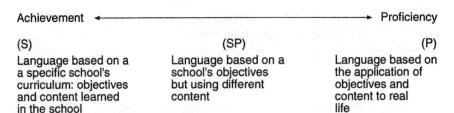

Figure 10-2. The language knowledge continuum.

includes objectives and content based on current theories and understanding of the skill tested. Thus a GT of reading comprehension will include objectives such as understanding the main idea, identifying specific information, predicting, hypothesizing, and so on. In terms of content, it will include areas such as stories, poems, newspaper articles, advertisements, literary texts, and other materials. Table 10-2 shows a filled-in GT for reading comprehension based on a table of specifications submitted by one school. Each letter in the GT represents an item to be included on the test and a certain objective with a certain content area. S, SP, and P indicate whether the item is school-based, school-based proficiency, or proficiency. The GTs in each skill become the maps for constructing tests. Once the general table for each of the language skills is filled in, the items and tasks that match these specifications are written.

Table 10-3 displays a description of a reading comprehension test constructed from a GT. Column 1 represents the item number on the test, columns 2 and 3 relate to the item's objective and content, as given in the table of specifications, and column 4 describes the source of the text. Thus item 1, for example, is a proficiency item that tests comprehension of vocabulary in the context of a form, a request to enroll in a summer camp. The asterisk to the left of the item indicates that it was also selected as an anchor item (i.e., to be used for comparison among schools). Similarly, item 3 tests the objective of identifying the main idea, its content area is a narrative, and it is a school-based (S) item. The table also gives the source and the topic of the item. Other tables present even more detailed descriptions of each item, such as the genre of the texts used, their domain, and the register of the text, as well as information about the test questions themselves (open or closed, in the first or the second language). All this information aids the diagnostic analysis described below.

The Language Tests

The language tests constructed based on the process described above cover reading, listening, writing, and speaking. They are communicative—that is, they use real-life, communicative tasks and authentic materials; have high reliability; and are valid because they are pretested and revised in the pilot phase. A short description of each test follows.

The *reading comprehension* test consists of about 20 texts, each accompanied by one question (or a maximum of two) according to the table of specifications'

Table 10-2

A General Table for Reading Comprehension

Text / Language of text	Content	Comprehend vocabulary in context	Identify grammatical Functions	Indentify logical relations	Follow sequence of events	Discern between relevant and irrelevant	Locate specific information	Identify main idea/ message	Make inferences	Hypothesize
L I T E R A R Y	Story	S	S,S	S,S,S	S,S				SP,S	S
	Poem/song		P					S,S,S	SP,S	
	Tale				S		S			
	Fable							S,S		
	Prayer									
	Biblical text						SP			
	Midrash			SP				SP	SP	
	Proverb/saying							SP		
T E X T B O O K S	Anecdote								P,P	P
	Dialogue						S,S			
	Questions/ instructions									
	Comments									
	Informative text		SP	SP			SP,P,P,P	SP		
I N F O R M A L	Letter/diary						P		P	
	Note									
	Advertisement						P,P	P	P,P	
	Invitation						P			
	Announcement									
	Telegram						P			
	Form	P								
	Sign								P	
JOURNALISTIC	Newspaper item						P	P		
	Headline								P	

Table 10-3

A Map of a Reading Comprehension Test

1 No. of item	2 Objective	3 Content	4 Source of text	5 Topic of text
*1	Comprehend vocabulary in context	Form	P	request to enroll in summer camp
2	Make an inference	Story	SP Newspaper, *Olam Hadash*, 4 (27), 2	Russian Jewry
3	Make an inference	Poem	S *Haderech*, Lea Goldberg, Tal Sela 6, 10	Phases of life
*4	Locate information	Newspaper item	P Newspaper	Shipping fruit from Israel
5	Locate information	Newspaper item	P Children's newspaper, *Kulanu*	Auto accident
6	Identify main idea	Story	S "Haeyi Eliezer ben Yehuda"	Love for books
7	Locate information	Informative text	SP	Instruction on the care of dogs

*Anchor item; used for comparisons among schools.

objectives and content. The texts represent a variety of genres, such as stories, informative texts, talks, textbook stories, advertisements, proverbs, signs, poems, and others, following the S, SP, and P criteria. The items that accompany them are directed toward a variety of reading objectives, such as finding the main idea of a text, locating information, identifying the correct order of events, deriving word meaning from general context, identifying grammatical functions, and arriving at inferences. Different testing methods are used in the reading comprehension test—multiple choice, open ended, true or false, completion, and cloze.

The *writing* test requires the students to write at least a paragraph in response to tasks, such as personal letters with a specific purpose and audience, informal notes, letters, and a narrative based on a sequence of pictures.

The *listening comprehension* test consists of about 10 video situations. All the listening stimuli are based on routine, authentic, spontaneous language as spoken by native speakers. The situations represent a broad sample of stimuli, such as instructions, telephone conversations, narratives, interviews, reports, and discussions. Each situation is accompanied by a number of comprehension questions, focusing on objectives such as identifying the main idea, locating specific information, and guessing the meaning of words from context. The items vary in format, as they do in the reading test—open ended, multiple choice, completion, and others—and are presented in a booklet in which the students respond in the first or second language. The test takers listen to the questions before viewing the video.

The *speaking* tests are conducted individually with a stratified sample of 25% in each school representing low, middle, and high levels of achievement. Students' oral language, elicited from a number of speech interactions, is audio recorded. The tasks include (a) an oral interview, (b) role-playing situations (e.g., coming late to class and apologizing to the teacher, planning a surprise party with classmates), and (c) obtaining information from the tester. In most cases, the school's teachers conduct these tests and send the tapes to the assessment team.

Large schools administer a number of parallel forms of all the tests that use the domain sampling procedure to increase the content validity of the tests. Furthermore, in addition to the language tests just described, attitude and background questionnaires are developed and administered to students, teachers, and parents. Although many of the questions are similar, the questionnaires also include questions of interest to specific schools.

Phase 3: Test Administration

Representatives of the assessment team and the school's faculty administer the tests and questionnaires at the schools. The reading comprehension and writing tests are included in the same packet, and the attitude and background questionnaires appear at the back. It takes students about 50 minutes to complete the two tests. The listening comprehension test takes about 45 minutes to complete, including the viewing time, and the speaking test takes about 15 minutes per student.

Phase 4: Scoring and Analyzing the Tests

All tests are scored and analyzed by a team of raters, who undergo intensive training to ensure high reliability. Reliability is of particular importance for the speaking and writing tests, as well as for the reading and listening tests, because a large number of the questions are open ended. The speaking and writing tests are scored with the aid of rating scales developed specifically for the assessment.

Once the tests are scored and rated, five different types of analyses are performed: general, diagnostic, comparative, qualitative, and itemized. The general analysis consists of means, standard deviations, and frequencies of the scores on each of the language skill tests. The diagnostic analysis includes a variety of language parameters and dimensions within a given skill. For example, in reading comprehension the analysis focuses on dimensions such as identifying the main ideas, locating information, drawing inferences, and making predictions; other dimensions within reading comprehension are the type of genre, the type of domain, the register, and the source of the item (proficiency or achievement). Each dimension is created by combining the test questions that tap these specific dimensions. In the writing section, the diagnostic analysis focuses on dimensions such as communicative versus linguistic. *Communicative* refers to how well the writer transmits the information, and *linguistic* refers to the accuracy of the writing in terms of grammar and vocabulary on a scale ranging from 0 (no writing proficiency) to 5 (high proficiency). The assessment team analyzes these dimensions further by dividing them into subdimensions, such as cohesion, coherence, and sociocultural appropriateness within the communicative dimension, and scoring them on a more narrow scale of 0–5.

The comparative analysis is based on the performance of the test takers on the items identified beforehand as significant for all schools. The qualitative analysis, based on descriptive, impressionistic information that the raters obtain throughout the ratings of each school, relates to the most apparent patterns and also includes examples from the test takers' language samples. For example, the analysis of a school's tests may show that students have problems with syntax, that they do not use communicative strategies (e.g., they use their native language when they do not know a word rather than looking for an approximation of the word in the second language), or that they have problems using appropriate forms in writing letters. This information is summarized and communicated to the schools, providing another perspective on the test results that the quantitative analyses do not address.

The itemized analysis focuses on the performance of the school on each of the items tested. Open-ended questions are analyzed as correct, partially correct, wrong, and missing information; the writing items are reported according to each of the five ratings on the scale in the linguistic and communicative dimensions. Also included are psychometric results, such as difficulty levels and discrimination indices.

Phase 5: Reporting the Results

Results of the above analyses are summarized in a report submitted to the school that consists of a number of sections, depending on the language skill tested. Each section includes the tables of specification submitted by the school, the general table used to prepare the test, the objectives and content that each item is testing, and additional information about the items. The five types of results are presented along with visuals and graphics so that school personnel with no background in statistics can understand them.

The assessment team then meets with the school faculty to deliver the report and discuss the results. Preliminary conclusions and implications are drawn, and the schools often request additional analyses, which the assessment team then supplies.

Phase 6: Conclusions and Interpretation of the Results

This phase usually takes place during the summer months, when the principal and the school staff devote a number of meetings to the study of results and the interpretation within the specific context of the school's goals and objectives. The school's faculty then writes the final report, which details the conclusions, the implications of the results, and the specific areas the school has selected to improve.

At a final summary meeting among representatives of all the schools and the assessment team, each school reports its plans for change. The assessment team also receives feedback from the participating schools.

Phase 7: Working Toward Change and Improvement

In the final phase, an instructional team works closely with the school to determine the change needed and to select areas for improvement as the schools select their priorities. Workshops are conducted, teachers are trained in new teaching methods, books are often replaced (or additional ones selected), and in a few cases the curriculum is revised. The assessment is repeated the following year.

Additional Components of the Model

Two new components added to the model later relate to the model's basic concept of involving the school's faculty in assuming responsibility and authority for the assessment: (a) the training of assessment experts in the schools and in the classroom, and gradually shifting the authority and responsibility for the assessment to the schools; and (b) the construction of an item bank. In addition, the validity of the model is being studied through a examination of its impact and utilization.

A number of teachers in each school are trained to become the school's assessment experts. They will be responsible for conducting the assessment of achievement and will be trained in a variety of language assessment areas, such as test construction, test analysis, utilization of the item bank, assessment of extralinguistic components, classroom assessment, and others. They will also train the other teachers at the school in procedures for classroom assessment so that it can become an integral part of instruction. For example, classroom teachers will assess individual students through a variety of additional procedures, such as portfolios, projects, homework, and observations, which will give classroom teachers continuous information on the performance of their students. External assessment will then supplement or confirm this information. These steps are only initial ones toward the long-range goal of having the school take full responsibility for the whole assessment.

For the item bank, a computerized bank now under preparation, which includes a large number of items and tasks categorized according to a variety of parameters (statistical, linguistic, and educational), will enhance the construction of tests because linguistic and psychometric information about each item and task will be available. The item bank will include items and texts in reading, writing, speaking, and listening, designed in large part by teachers in the participating schools, and will enable the construction of new tests in a more efficient way. The users will have free access to the item bank so they can construct school tests.

As for validation, a study is currently under way to examine empirically the utility of the model and its impact on learning. The study collects qualitative and quantitative data on several dimensions of the testing model, mostly related to the impact of the testing model and the contribution of each phase. Other areas for which data are being collected relate to the type and quality of the feedback, the type of diagnostic information most useful for teachers and administrators, the type of information that best facilitates change, the translation of the results into instructional strategies, and the identification of the types of schools that make the best use of the results, as well as a variety of psychometric issues.

Preliminary findings indicate that in all the schools staff rethought and questioned current programs and practices and intended to implement change. Major differences were found in the impact and utilization of results among different schools and, especially, between the 1st year and the 2nd. Planning the table of specifications seems to contribute to greater utilization of results. The comparative results (among the different schools) were important at the initial phase, but the schools found the other information more valuable as the assessment proceeded.

In some schools, the tests were still used as tools of power, especially by principals who had problems with teachers. This situation was often limited to the 1st year because teacher participation increased in the 2nd year. In general schools felt a strong need for instructional guidance—something they did not recognize before assessment. One unexpected by-product seems to be cooperation among the participating schools (e.g., creating and sharing new materials). Most principals and teachers report that they now view the role of testing differently, that they were not previously aware of the information tests could provide, that testing did affect their teaching, and that it made them question many of their instructional practices. The final analysis of the validation study was completed in the summer of 1991.

Conclusion

The strength of the model described here lies in the principle that a multiple of factors interact in the educational system and that tests alone do not create change. It is the cooperation between the external testers and the school's faculty, the construction of tests that tap a whole range of language knowledge, and the diagnostic and meaningful information provided in the process that are expected to lead to improvement. On the one hand, the tests provide schools with ample information, based on the school's own goals, on the performance of their students in a variety of aspects and dimensions of language; on the other hand, this information is used to make decisions on the modification of teaching and learning strategies at the school.

When test results provide meaningful information, when they involve the school's faculty—the agents of change—when the information is translated into instructional activities, when it is used for actual steps toward change (teaching strategies, textbooks, revised curricula, etc.), and when it is not one effort but a continuous process, then that information can be expected to contribute significantly to the advancement of foreign language learning in schools. To examine the impact of such a testing model requires continuous data collection and experimentation with different aspects of the assessment throughout the implementation process to search for the most effective methods. Some aspects of the model will likely have to be modified for different schools and, especially, for different programs. We need to examine the effectiveness of all the components of the model and the extent to which they need to be modified for different types of language learning programs. It is the continuous feedback system and the principles of involvement, however, that any assessment program needs to consider in order improve foreign language learning.

Acknowledgments

The testing model described in this paper is based on a project directed by the author at the Melton Center for Jewish Education, Hebrew University, Jerusalem, with the collaboration of Jewish Education Services of North America (JESNA), New York. It is sponsored in part by the Shteinshleifer Testing Fund. I acknowledge the contribution of Nava Nevo, the coordinator of the project in Jerusalem, and Dr. Leora Isaacs of JESNA.

References

American Council of Teachers of Foreign Languages. *ACTFL proficiency guidelines.*
    (1986). Hastings-on-Hudson, NY: Author.
Collins, A., Brown J., & Newman, S. (1989). Cognitive apprenticeship: Teaching the
    craft of reading, writing, and mathematics. In L. Resnik (Ed.), *Knowing, learning and
    instruction: Essays in honor of Robert Glaser* (pp. 453–494). Hillsdale, NJ: Lawrence
    Erlbaum Associates.
Frederiksen, J., & Collins, A. (1989). A system approach to educational testing. *Educa-
    tional Researcher, 18*, 27–32.
Nevo, D. (1989). *Useful evaluation.* Tel Aviv: Massada Ltd.
Nitko, A. (1989). Designing tests that are integrated with instruction. In Robert Linn
    (Ed.), *Educational measurement* (pp. 447–474). New York: American Council on
    Education and Macmillan.
Shavelson, R. (1988). Contribution of educational research to policy and Practice. *Educa-
    tional Researcher, 17*, 4–11.
Shohamy, E. (1989). *Assessing the washback effect of introducing a new oral testing
    battery for testing English as a foreign language.* Internal document, Tel Aviv Uni-
    versity.
Shohamy, E. (1990). Language testing, a different perspective. *Foreign Language Annals,
    23*, 385–393.
Stake, R. (Forthcoming). *Effects of changes in assessment policy.* Greenwich, CT: JAI
    Press.

The Relationship Between Grammar and Reading in an English for Academic Purposes Test Battery

J. Charles Alderson
University of Lancaster

This paper reports on the results of one part of the English Language Testing Service (ELTS) Revision Project that I directed on behalf of the British Council, the University of Cambridge Local Examinations Syndicate, and the Australian International Development Programme. The Revision Project was charged with revising the existing ELTS test in the light of operational experience over 10 years, feedback from test users, and the results of the Edinburgh ELTS Validation Project (Criper & Davies, 1988).

An additional task of the Revision Project was to take note of developments in applied linguistic theory in the 10 years since the conception of the original ELTS and, where possible, to incorporate recent thinking into the new test battery. One important aspect of the latter task was to review developments in views of the reading process and the role of a knowledge of the linguistic system— grammar—in that process. The purpose of the research described here was to investigate the role of grammar in reading comprehension. Specifically, this paper focuses on the question of the need for a grammar component in the revised test, now called the International English Language Testing System (IELTS).

Reading and Grammar

Recent research in reading in a foreign language has focused on the role of background knowledge and schemata in text processing and on the relationship between cognitive variables and reading. Another area of interest is the nature of the skills and strategies a reader employs when reading texts in a foreign language. Earlier concerns about a reader's language knowledge, and the linguistic characteristics of text that might affect text processing, have receded somewhat in importance relative to the above interests.

At the same time, however, language testers and applied linguists have been increasingly interested in reexamining the role of *grammar* in language teaching and language testing. In particular, language educators have begun to think that the so-called communicative movement of the 1970s and 1980s may have gone too far in advocating the abandonment of a focus on the form of the language in favor of devising communicative activities modeled on real-life language use. Publications for teachers and students in the 1970s and early 1980s focused much more on *meaning*, *tasks*, and *activities* than on *grammar*. Things seem to have changed recently, however, and the current position seems to be that a language learner needs to learn the *grammar* of the language, that teachers are responsible for helping learners come to grips with the language system, and that testers are responsible for seeing whether the learner has indeed achieved that grip. This shift in attitude does not, of course, necessarily imply that teachers and testers should resurrect pedagogic practice from the early 1970s; rather, they should benefit from the developments of the communicative movement and its focus on meaning and try to devise ways to integrate meaning and form into what is increasingly being called *communicative grammar*.

Thus, whereas research in reading in a foreign language has tended to move away from a focus on the language system, language pedagogy has begun to return to the language system, albeit with enhanced perspectives. Members of the ELTS Revision Project felt that it was important to take some account of these apparently contradictory positions during the development of the revised test battery.

As well as taking account of recent theoretical positions, any new test battery in the 1990s has to reflect and, where possible, to build on the best of current practice in language testing. The common practice in language testing has been to devise tests of *reading comprehension*, or just *reading*, as well as, and wherever possible different from, tests of *grammar*. Clearly a test of grammar has to be administered through some medium, and because most grammar tests are given in writing, candidates will evidently have to read in order to be able to respond to the grammar test items. An often-asked and important question is: to what extent do tests of grammar also test reading, and how much can we reduce the overlap between tests of reading and tests of grammar?

Recent years have seen a strong tendency in so-called communicative language testing to devise separate tests of "the four skills" and to report scores separately for these "macroskills" in so-called profile reports. Examples of this practice in the United Kingdom include the Royal Society of Arts Examination in the Communicative Use of English as a Foreign Language, which includes separate tests at three different levels in reading, writing, listening, and oral interaction; the Associated Examining Board's Test in English for Educational Purposes, which reports a profile score (from subtest components) in reading, writing, and listening; and the British Council-University of Cambridge Local Examinations Syndicate's ELTS test, which consisted of five subtests (Reading, Listening, Study Skills, Writing, and Interview), the results of which are reported in profile form. Note that none of these tests includes a test of grammar, nor is a candidate's grammatical ability reported in a profile score.

Parallel to the perceived changes in attitudes toward grammar within language teaching reported above is some evidence that language testers are beginning to reexamine their attitude toward the testing of grammar (see Rea-Dickins, 1988, for example). Apart from the obvious need for tests to reflect changes in pedagogic practice, there is a detectable tendency among testers to suggest that grammatical competence is part of yet separable from communicative competence, and that therefore designers of language tests—especially proficiency tests—should attempt to measure a learner's ability to process and produce the grammatical system of the language accurately (see Rea-Dickins, 1991, for an argument to this effect).

The ELTS Revision Project

The old version of the ELTS test contained two major sections—a general (G) section and a modular (M) section—and was composed of five subtests: G1 Reading, G2 Listening, M1 Study Skills, M2 Writing, and M3 Interview. Each modular test (M1, M2, and M3) was available in six "subject-specific" versions: Life Sciences, Medicine, Social Studies, Technology, Physical Sciences, and General Academic. In addition, a nonacademic module composed of Reading and Writing was separately available. The revised IELTS test had to be comparable with the old ELTS test, and as a result the structure of the new battery is broadly similar to that of the ELTS, with a general and a modular section, but with some significant differences. The general section consists of a listening test and an oral interview. The modular section consists of two components: Reading and Writing. The modular tests are available in two forms: Modules A, B, and C, for academic audiences, and Module GT, for nonacademic general training purposes.

Before the Revision Project proper began, project members examined the results of the Edinburgh Validation Study. The Edinburgh Report (Criper & Davies, 1988) had found that G1 and G2 (Reading and Listening) formed the most important part of the test, correlating most highly with the overall test total ($r = .83$ and $.80$, respectively, whereas the correlation with M1 [Study Skills] and the total was .72). However, M1 was felt to contribute additional information because its correlation with G1 was only .59. A factor analysis, however, appeared to show that the ELTS test was not multifactorial (Criper & Davies, 1988, pp. 100–102), as only one factor emerged from the analyses.

Correlations between the ELTS test and two other British proficiency tests—the English Proficiency Test Battery (EPTB) and the English Language Battery (ELBA)—revealed a surprising amount of overlap (.81 and .77 respectively). Not surprisingly, a principal components analysis revealed only one dominant factor for ELTS, EPTB, and ELBA (Criper & Davies, 1988, p. 100). However, a factor analysis (varimax rotation) appeared to identify three factors: a general factor on which ELTS G1 Reading and G2 Listening loaded highest, and a reading factor, on which EPTB Grammar and ELBA Reading load highest. (The third factor, labeled listening, is not of interest here.) Criper and Davies claimed that "ELTS does appear to be measuring some aspects of proficiency that are not touched by EPTB or ELBA, though not perhaps as much or the same kind— given the dominance in ELTS of G1 and G2—that was intended by the original construction" (p. 112). Because ELBA and EPTB are both mainly traditional, discrete-point-type tests and because the ELTS test was deliberately constructed to be as different as possible from these two tests, this finding was somewhat surprising. One is tempted to agree with Criper and Davies that the large overlap may well be due to the dominance of G1 and G2, even despite the ELTS test designers' presumed intentions. Both G1 and G2 are mostly discrete-point tests, with a concentration on sentential understanding, that might appear to be little more than tests of grammar in spoken and written modes. The label for G1— Reading—is thus misleading and should perhaps be Grammar, whereas M1— Study Skills—might be more appropriately entitled Reading.

The Edinburgh study also looked at the predictive validity of the ELTS test. The general finding was that the best predictors of academic success were G1 and G2. Surprisingly, perhaps, the specialist modular M1 tests—Study Skills— did not show much predictive value. These findings could be taken as (weak) evidence in favor of using a general test of language proficiency, especially including a grammar section. The findings also clearly have implications for the relationship between so-called tests of grammar and tests of reading.

In summary, then, the Edinburgh Validation Study appeared to show that a general test of grammar was an important component of the old ELTS test, despite the innovations in the modular section that might be said to test reading.

Method

In the initial phases of the Revision Project, project members consulted with a variety of interested parties—British Council officers responsible for administering the test overseas, headquarters staff affected by the ELTS testing service, university admissions officers, presessional language teachers, language test writers, and language testing researchers. This process resulted in a wide variety of responses, of which two competing proposals are relevant to this paper.

One important proposal for the Revision Project was that the revised test should be shorter and simpler to administer than the old test—interpreted to mean less paper, fewer tests or test components, and simpler procedures. At the same time, considerable feedback from the professional informants indicated that the test should incorporate as wide a range of language components as possible. Indeed, the informants recommended that a revised ELTS test should "be a test of reading, writing, listening and speaking, . . . avoiding the overlap of reading/ study skills, and possibly not including any study skills element" (*Report on Questionnaire for Overseas Test Administrators*, 1987, p. 10).

In reporting on this rationale for revising the test, one of the project members wrote:

> Of the 77 test administrators who felt that a subtest should be dropped from the current ELTS, by far the greatest number wanted G1 or M1 to go. 29 wanted G1 to go, chiefly because it duplicates M1, and 15 wanted M1 dropped. Of the pre-sessional teachers too, 6 out of 18 wished to drop G1, mostly because they felt the same skills were tested elsewhere. . . . It was therefore decided . . . to omit Reading from the G component. (Clapham, 1987, p. 18)

However, there was a feeling that the battery should include a test of grammar. At a consultative conference held at the end of the data collection phase of the Revision Project, language testing researchers examined summaries of the results of all the data gathered to date. Participants felt strongly that there should be a test of lexis and structure. In their proposals for the revised ELTS, of the eight language testing researchers who specified the contents of the G component, five wanted a test of vocabulary and grammar. The decision was therefore made to include a test of lexis and structure, later termed Grammar, in the general component of the revised test, and to try to avoid overlap between this test and the test of reading that would be included in the modular section.

Test Specifications

In writing the test specifications during the next phase of the Revision Project, project members made every effort to differentiate between G1 Grammar and M Reading. Test writers were explicitly asked to differentiate the two tests: "Item writers should concentrate on developing tasks which address the academic tasks listed rather than the formal knowledge of grammar" (*Draft Specifications for Module A*, 1989); and "Item writers should not attempt to test those academic skills and functions which are addressed in other parts of the test battery" (*Draft Specifications for the Grammar Test*, 1988). The specifications for the reading test list the functions and skills that the test should sample:

- following instructions
- identifying structure, content, sequence of events and procedures
- finding main ideas which the writer has attempted to make salient
- identifying the underlying theme or concept
- identifying ideas in the text and relationships between them, e.g., probability, solution, cause, effect
- identifying, distinguishing and comparing facts, evidence, opinions, implications, hypotheses and definitions
- evaluating and challenging evidence
- formulating an hypothesis from underlying theme, concept and evidence
- reaching a conclusion by relating supporting evidence to the main idea
- drawing logical inferences.

In addition, although the test items were to be "clerically markable," test writers were instructed not to rely exclusively on multiple-choice test methods; rather, items were to reflect a variety of different types. Suggestions made to item writers in the specifications include the following:

- choosing from a "heading bank" a heading appropriate to identified sections of the text
- copying words, phrases, etc. from the text
- information transfer
- labeling or completing diagrams, tables, charts, graphs or illustrations
- listing items or ideas from text relevant to a given topic of concern
- matching
- multiple choice
- short answer questions, up to three words only
- sorting events into order
- sorting names/objects into sets
- summary completion (gap filling).

Instructions to test writers emphasized that test takers must not be able to complete any item without reading the text and that deletions to be restored should be words that "carry significant meaning, and should not be chosen solely on syntactic grounds."

Item writers for the grammar test were requested to produce items testing syntax, lexis, reference, and cohesion. Within syntax, the specifications listed categories like adjectives, adverbs, modifiers, word order, tenses, and so on, and requested item writers to test the ability to use them within linguistic functions like the following:

- identifying oneself
- leave taking
- giving instructions
- making requests, suggestions
- apologizing.

Candidates' breadth and appropriateness of lexis was to be tested in topic areas relevant to their social needs, for example, health, recreation, the social and physical environment, travel, education, and so on. Reference and cohesion were to be tested both within and between sentences and paragraphs and were to include determiners and demonstratives, substitution, ellipsis, conjunctions of various kinds, and lexical cohesion. The texts on which items were to be based included single sentences, short paragraphs, constructed texts, newspaper articles, short biographies, and extracts from encyclopedias, among others.

Test writers were encouraged to use a variety of test methods, and the item types listed included many of those listed in the reading test specifications, as well as word deletion, word insertion, reorganization of jumbled words, transformation, word formation, and vocabulary sets. In short, the intention of the specifications was not only to provide clear guidance to item writers, but to reduce the possibility of overlap between the two tests and to define what was meant by "grammar" and "reading."

Materials

In 1988, teams of item writers in the United Kingdom and Australia produced the various components of the new test battery for the IELTS. The Revision Project staff then checked the components against the specifications and sample items, revised and edited them, and piloted the test in Australia and the United Kingdom. After test analysis, the tests were again revised, and trial versions were produced.

The grammar test, 30 minutes long, consisted of 38 items divided into six subtests. Section 1 tested four vocabulary items in the context of a short paragraph. The items were multiple choice in format, and the distractors consisted of possible paraphrases of the target word that were inappropriate in the context. Section 2 required the candidate to put the root form of five nouns and verbs into their correct form in a short paragraph. Section 3 tested lexical sets, prepositions, conjunctions, modifiers, and relative pronouns in a contextualized, multiple-choice gap-filling task (15 items). Section 4 tested verb and adverbial forms and a variety of function words in a gap-filling task (8 items). Section 5 tested the ability to identify transformations in multiple-choice format (4 items), and Section 6 focused on the ability to detect reference and cohesion by having students order a series of sentences correctly (2 items). The short passages on which the items were based were thematically linked: the first three sections involved flying saucers, and the last three passages were from a constructed mystery story.

As the reading tests are confidential, it is not possible to give full details, but the following descriptions suffice for the purposes of this paper. Fifty minutes in length, the tests were produced in three different disciplinary areas, labeled Module A, Module B, and Module C, corresponding very broadly to the areas of physical science and technology, life and medical sciences, and arts and social sciences, respectively. In addition, Module GT was constructed for candidates planning to undertake general training or industrial attachments, rather than academic study, in an English-speaking country.

Module A, with 33 items, contained three reading passages from academic magazines. Item types included single-word responses; matching problems, examples, and recommendations; multiple-choice problem-solution matching; four-option multiple-choice; and banked gap-filling.

Module B, with 39 items, contained four reading passages, three from different sections of one academic article and one from a different article. Item types included summary completion, banked gap-filling, four-option multiple-choice, and completion of a diagram outlining text content.

Module C, with 38 items, contained three passages from academic textbooks and articles. Item types included choosing appropriate headings from a heading bank, giving one-word answers, answering true-false questions, and deciding whether statements are supported or rejected by a text.

Module GT (43 items) contained several authentic texts, some very short but one or two several pages in length, on topics related to social survival in the target country and survival in a training context. The item types were intended to reflect the sorts of tasks readers would normally expect to complete with those particular texts, and the formats included four-option multiple-choice, short-answer questions, identification of required information, true-false, and banked gap-filling. The texts and tasks were intended to be considerably easier than the academic reading tests.

The main trials were held in Australia, the United Kingdom, and various locations in countries in Europe, the Middle East, and Asia between January and May 1989.

Results

Because not all students took every test in the battery, and because some took two or more of the modules and sometimes fewer general components, the size of the trialing population varied (see Table 11-1). For technical reasons, the data were analyzed separately according to whether they had been collected in the United Kingdom or Australia.

In the U.K. data the tests are of roughly appropriate difficulty and spread students out satisfactorily. The reliabilities are perfectly acceptable, although that of Module GT is at the lower limit of acceptability. The Australian-based data appear similar to the U.K. data, except that Modules A and B appear to have been somewhat more difficult for the Australian population. Conversely, the latter appear to have found the general tests, both Grammar and Listening, somewhat easier than did the U.K.-based groups.

The correlations of G1 with other subtests and with the total test battery minus G1 itself are shown in Table 11-2. The U.K. data show considerable overlap between G1 and two of the academic reading tests and between G1 and the listening test. Some redundancy apparently occurs between G1 and some of the reading tests. Curiously, there is less overlap with Modules C and GT. Again, in the Australian data G1 and the reading tests overlap, and both Modules C and GT correlate more highly with G1 (in the case of Module GT, showing a high degree of overlap). Conversely, however, Module B now appears to relate less closely to G1 than in the U.K. data. It is impossible to say whether this variation is an artifact of sample size or the nature of the samples. However, G1 and the reading tests indeed show overlap and redundancy. The data for all the subjects show that G1 has a fairly consistently close relationship to the reading tests. The relationship varies somewhat by module, but it is difficult to draw any conclusions on the basis of that variation, which appears neither patterned or principled. What

Table 11-1

Descriptive Statistics for All Tests, by Location

Test	M	Items	SD	KR-20	n
		United Kingdom			
G1	24.62	38	7.99	.91	579
MA	19.79	33	6.91	.89	302
MB	17.85	39	8.36	.91	195
MC	17.72	38	6.98	.85	531
MGT	25.78	43	6.69	.83	232
G2	21.62	42	8.79	.92	706
		Australia			
Gl	26.00	38	6.37	.82	842
MA	14.93	33	7.92	.90	477
MB	15.84	39	9.43	.92	438
MC	17.33	38	8.88	.90	615
MGT	25.18	43	6.72	.79	591
G2	23.72	42	7.49	.83	748
		All subjects			
G1	25.43	38	7.11	.86	1,421
MA	16.82	33	7.90	.90	779
MB	16.46	39	9.16	.91	633
MC	17.51	38	8.05	.88	1,146
MGT	25.35	43	6.71	.79	823
G2	22.70	42	8.21	.87	1,454

Note. G1 = Grammar Test; MA = Science and Technology Reading Test; MB = Life Science Reading Test; MC = Arts and Social Sciences Reading Test; MGT = Nonacademic Reading Test; G2 = Listening Test. KR-20 = Kuder-Richardson reliability formula 20.

is clear is that the attempts by the ELTS Revision Project to reduce or remove the overlap between G1 and M1 on the old ELTS did not successfully translate into clearly distinct grammar and reading tests on the new IELTS.

The data in Table 11-3 enable a further exploration of that conclusion by showing the relationships among the different reading tests compared with their relationships to the grammar test. In the U.K. data, Module C overlaps more with the other reading tests than with the general tests, either Grammar or Listening. However, Module B appears to overlap more with the grammar and listening tests than with the other reading tests. Module A has more in common with Module C than with Grammar, but more in common with Grammar than with Module B. The Australian data show a somewhat different picture: Modules A, C, and GT relate more closely to Grammar than to the other reading tests. Only Module B shows similar relationships with Grammar and with the other reading tests.

The data for all the subjects again show some variation. For Module A, the relationship to Grammar is closer than that to the other reading tests (.76 versus .49, .67, and .74). For Module B, too, the correlation with Grammar is higher

Table 11-2

Correlations Between the Grammar Test (G1) and All Tests, by Location

	G2	MC	MB	MA	MGT	G2-MC	G2-MB	G2-MA	G2-MGT
				United Kingdom					
G1	.79	.61	.76	.74	.62	.58	.86	.82	.45
	(443)	(183)	(80)	(79)	(124)	(120)	(72)	(48)	(60)
				Australia					
G1	.79	.69	.58	.80	.78	.76	.74	.80	.84
	(676)	(198)	(88)	(123)	(272)	(173)	(86)	(93)	(239)
				All subjects					
G1	.78	.64	.74	.76	.68	.69	.85	.77	.80
	(1,119)	(381)	(168)	(202)	(396)	(327)	(163)	(153)	(313)

Note. Numbers in parentheses are sample sizes. For abbreviations, see note to Table 11-1.

Table 11-3

Intercorrelations Among the Reading Tests and Correlations Between the Reading
Tests and the Grammar and Listening Tests, by Location

	MB	MA	MGT	Gl	G2
			United Kingdom		
MC	.66	.81	.42	.61	.62
	(64)	(64)	(28)		
MB	—	.47	n.a.	.76	.71
		(39)			
MA	—	—	n.a.	.74	.71
MGT	—	—	—	.62	.44
			Australia		
MC	.58	.47	.58	.69	.62
	(90)	(100)	(74)	(198)	
MB	—	.65	.59	.58	.66
		(114)	(68)	(88)	
MA	—	—	.49	.80	.79
			(60)	(123)	
MGT	—	—	—	.78	.77
				(272)	
			All subjects		
MC	.59	.74	.64	.64	.61
	(154)	(164)	(102)	(381)	(466)
MB	—	.67	.59	.74	.75
		(153)	(68)	(168)	(177)
MA	—	—	.49	.76	.74
			(60)	(202)	(250)
MGT	—	—	—	.68	.68
				(396)	(327)

Note. Numbers in parentheses are sample sizes. For abbreviations, see note to Table 11-1.

than that with the other reading tests (.74 versus .59, .59, and .67). For Module GT the same is true (.68 versus .49, .59, and .64). Only Module C is not more closely related to Grammar than to the other reading tests. However, even here the relationship to Grammar is higher than that to Module B and equal to that to Module GT. In fact, only one correlation out of the relevant 10 (for all subjects) shows a closer relationship between a reading test and another reading test than between a reading test and the grammar test! This fact does not necessarily mean that the reading tests are testing grammar. The relationship between Reading and Listening is as close as or closer than the relationship between one reading test and other reading tests! Of course, Listening may test grammar (the correlation with G1 is consistently high; see Table 11-2). Equally, all the tests may test something called comprehension or general proficiency.

A factor analysis of the test results would yield further insight into the relationship between grammar and reading. However, the data set does not make such an analysis easy. Candidates did not take all the tests (that would have involved at least 7 hours of test taking and considerable persuasion, if not coercion). It was, however, possible to factor analyze different combinations of tests. For the U.K. data, for example, analyses were conducted separately for each module with G1 and G2 and were repeated including the writing test score. For the Australian data, we performed the same analyses, and additional analyses included students' self-evaluations of their reading, listening, grammatical, and writing abilities. The results are far too detailed to present here. In general, an analysis of reading, grammar, and listening yielded only one common factor. The addition of writing occasionally gave rise to a second factor, and the addition of self-evaluation added a very clear second factor associated only with self-evaluation. Table 11-4A gives the results of a factor analysis of the whole test population on Reading, Grammar, and Listening for Module A. Factor analyses for Modules B, C, and GT yielded similar results. When Writing is added to the analysis (Table 11-4B), a separate writing factor emerges. However, Grammar and Reading continue to load heavily on the strong first factor.

The factor analyses confirm previous findings by failing to identify separate factors for reading and grammar. Whatever these tests measure appears to be common to all the tests.

Parallel Tests?

Evidence of the relationship between parallel forms of IELTS tests provides a context for an interpretation of the correlations in Table 11-2. One of the (many) briefs of the Revision Project was to produce testing materials that prospective test candidates could study in order to prepare themselves to take the test. These tests—the exemplar tests—were developed in the usual way and were tried out alongside the trial tests (which have since, with minor modifications, become the

Table 11-4A

Factor Analysis, Reading, Grammar, and Listening Tests, All Subjects

Test	Factor 1
G1	.925
G2	.917
MA	.909

Note. Factor 1 eigenvalue = 2.523; 84% of variance. For abbreviations, see note to Table 11-1.

Table 11-4B

Factor Analysis of Three Academic Modules, Both Reading and Writing, All Subjects

Test	Factor 1	Factor 2
G1	.842	.319
G2	.826	.339
MC	.742	.291
MB	.856	.169
MA	.887	.195
MC Writing	.123	.935
MB Writing	.354	.647
MA Writing	.268	.694

Note. Factor 1 eigenvalue = 4.692; 59% of variance. Factor 2 eigenvalue = 1.12; 14% of variance. For abbreviations, see note to Table 11-1.

first operational version of the IELTS test). Table 11-5 presents the correlations between the operational tests and the parallel exemplar tests.

A comparison of Tables 11-2 (all subjects) and 11-5 shows that Grammar correlates more highly with Module A than parallel forms of the test correlate with each other! Modules C and GT correlate only slightly more highly with the parallel test than with Grammar, and only Module B correlates with the parallel test notably (.81 versus .74) more highly than with Grammar. In other words, the evidence suggests that grammar and reading are very closely related.

Table 11-6 shows the results of a piggy-backing exercise, in which candidates taking the old ELTS test were asked to take an additional test from the new IELTS battery. The purpose was to enable the calculation of band scores for the new

Table 11-5

Correlations Between Trial Tests and Parallel Specimen Tests

Module	r	n
A	.64	60
B	.81	51
C	.69	61
GT	.73	63

Note. For abbreviations, see note to Table 11-1.

Table 11-6

Correlation of New Reading Tests With Old ELTS Subtests and Battery ("Piggy-Backing Operation")

New reading test	Old ELTS test						
	MA	MC	G1	G2	Writing	Speaking	Total
MA	.39	—	.45	.41	.49	.18	.53
MC	—	.76	.75	.75	.64	.51	.80

Note. For abbreviations, see note to Table 11-1.

test (test scores are not reported raw, but in bands of scores, which are simple transformations of raw scores). Because some parts of the new test are quite different from the old, especially in the modular section, these correlations should be interpreted with caution.

Table 11-6 shows clearly the considerable variation in the relationship between the new and the old reading tests. The new IELTS test was supposed to improve on the old test, and the old test was not directly parallel to the new test in content or topic. Nevertheless, the difference in the interrelationships between Module A and Module C is so great as to preclude sensible interpretation, other than to say that the relationship between the new grammar test and the new reading tests is at least as close as that between the new reading test and the old reading test! Such a result must begin to cast doubt on the separability of reading tests from grammar tests. It is clearly difficult to produce a (reading) test that can be demonstrated to be a replica, or a closely parallel form, of another (reading) test. It is arguably at least no more difficult to produce a grammar test that will overlap to the same extent with a reading test!

Reliability of the Test Battery With and Without Grammar

Despite the evidence of considerable overlap between Grammar and Reading, one technical reason for including a test of grammar in a test like the IELTS might be that it contributes significantly to the reliability of the total test battery. To investigate the contribution of Grammar to test reliability, we compared the reliabilities for the total test battery of listening, grammar, and reading tests with the reliability of the battery without the grammar test (Table 11-7).

Although the reliability of the total test battery does decline somewhat when the grammar test is deleted, this decline is relatively unimportant, with the arguable exception of MGT, the General Training Module. The grammar test does not seem to contribute substantially to the reliability of the test battery, or, to put things another way, dropping the grammar test from the battery would not adversely affect test reliability.

Table 11-7

Reliability of the Test Battery With and Without Grammar (United Kingdom)

Test	r	n	Test	r	n
G1-G2-MC	.897	120	G2-MC	.848	258
G1-G2-MB	.97	72	G2-MB	.964	79
G1-G2-MA	.96	48	G2-MA	.939	142
G1-G2-MGT	.809	60	G2-MGT	.76	69

Note. For abbreviations, see note to Table 11-1.

Discussion and Conclusion

A considerable overlap exists between the grammar test and the modular tests of reading. The grammar test appears to contribute little to the test battery. Remember that one of the major briefs of the Revision Project was to make the test simpler and, where possible, shorter. The assembled evidence suggests the test could be shortened by 30 minutes by dropping the grammar test, without materially affecting test reliability. One could argue the converse and suggest dropping the reading tests, but the reading tests provide important input for the writing test and so are less dispensible. In addition, test users have grown accustomed to interpreting an ELTS test profile that includes a statement about a candidate's reading ability, so it would be difficult to dispense with the reading test. Also, the ELTS test has come to be accepted over the years at least partly because it contains subject-specific tests—the modular tests. Dropping the reading tests would remove a major element of this "specific-purpose" orientation. Moreover, from a face validity point of view, it is hard to justify a test of English for academic purposes that does not contain a test of reading, but many lay people, including admissions officers, might well argue that they do not care about a student's grammar provided that he or she can perform academic tasks (like reading and writing) satisfactorily in English.

Persuasive evidence indicated that we had failed to reduce or remove the overlap between the old Reading and Study Skills tests despite our attempt to design clearly distinguishable tests of grammar, and reasons, both practical and statistical, existed for dropping Grammar from our battery. That, in fact, is what we decided to do. The new IELTS test consists of only four components: Listening, Speaking, Reading, and Writing.

We were obliged to decide whether to retain or drop the grammar test before the new IELTS battery became operational. We therefore have no evidence of the grammar test's effect on predictive validity. However, given the overlap between Grammar and Reading, and the minimal increase in reliability gained by retaining Grammar, it seems reasonable to conclude that dropping Grammar is unlikely to compromise seriously the test's predictive validity.

The decision to drop Grammar may have been justifiable from a practical, testing point of view, but what are the implications for theory? The first conclusion must be a cautionary one. Although we have gathered powerful statistical evidence on the functioning of the tests, we do not have a clear picture of what they are actually testing. We have reasonably explicit test specifications, but they do not guarantee the content validity of the test. Possibly, despite the statistical evidence, when students take the tests they actually engage in different processes. In the grammar test they may consciously process and reflect on grammar, whereas in the reading tests they may focus on meaning and information and process the grammar, if at all, only on a subconscious level. The reading tests may tap an automatized grammatical ability, whereas the Grammar test might call upon a reflective awareness of grammar. Until we have accounts from students of what they actually think about when taking these tests, we are in no position to do more than speculate about this possibility. In the near future, therefore, we need to gather data from students on what is happening "inside their heads" while they take the different tests. Thus the first conclusion is that we need more research of a different kind from that described here.

However, we can draw tentative conclusions while awaiting further evidence. One conclusion must be that the overlap between Reading and Study Skills on the old ELTS cannot be an artifact of test method, specifically the multiple-choice technique. The IELTS tests employed a variety of different methods, almost certainly sufficient to counter any specific method effect, yet there was clear evidence of overlap. To resolve this issue satisfactorily would require a specially designed study, probably of a multitrait, multimethod nature. Our results do not encourage us to believe that such a study would shed much light on the matter.

More important, what do we now know about the relationship between reading and grammar? We believe that we have strong evidence of substantial overlap between the two. The obvious caveat is that our conclusions are based on test results, and taking tests may not be, indeed likely is not, the same as "real reading." Answering somebody else's questions is probably not real reading either, but it is difficult to see how else one might operationalize the trait or externalize the process and its products.

It must be the case that, in some intuitive sense, a reader must process the grammar in a text in order to understand it. Although this statement is not a claim that a knowledge or awareness of syntax is central to text processing, the evidence certainly does not support any claim that one can succesfully understand text without grammatical abilities. Indeed, we believe our evidence supports the former position all the more strongly precisely because the test of grammar was not designed to test candidates' knowledge of the grammar of the particular texts, but rather *grammar in general*. In other words, the test probably measured a fairly generalized, if not general, grammatical ability.

It is difficult to be more precise than that in a definition of grammar in this context (until, that is, we have the results of the qualitative research we suggested above, and even then it is likely to be only tentative). Had we tested the specific lexis, syntax, and cohesion of the particular passages, our findings might be somewhat less surprising. However, we did not; as explained earlier, the two types of test were deliberately designed to be as different from each other as was justified in the testing context.

The results, then, appear to show that a (vaguely defined) generalized grammatical ability is an important component in reading in a foreign language. Indeed, we have no evidence that other components are more important. Again we stress that this conclusion does not imply that background knowledge and the activation of appropriate schemata, for example, might not be important in the understanding of text: we did not set out to investigate this, although Clapham (in a separate study of the same tests in this volume, chap. 14) has gathered persuasive general evidence that background knowledge may not be very important in the processing of *these* texts, at least. But the evidence we do have strongly suggests the importance of grammar in reading in a foreign language.

Arguably, the converse might also apply: a reading ability in a foreign language is an important part of the ability to perform on grammar tests. Clearly a reading ability is involved in the item types we devised. This characteristic was deliberate in the sense that we wished to test a student's ability to process and produce appropriate and accurate forms in meaningful contexts. We fully intended that a student would need to understand the co-text and to pay attention to various aspects of meaning in order to complete the tasks on the grammar test successfully. Presumably, that generally is what is meant by the phrase *communicative grammar*, and we did not feel that in designing a test for the 1990s we were justified in constructing a traditional discrete-point grammar test in which students would not need to process meaning but could perform adequately simply by paying attention to form without reference to meaning. That we have thereby introduced a degree of "contamination" is indisputable, but we assert, as many teachers would, that the ability to manipulate form without attention to meaning is of limited value and probably rather rare. It is, perhaps, not surprising that linguists have considerable difficulty making clear distinctions between syntax and semantics, or meaning more generally.

To take this matter further, tasks and tests intended to allow the exploration of particular hypotheses must be designed. It might be fruitful to attempt to devise tasks that require no processing of meaning and to contrast performance on them with performance on more meaning-oriented tasks, as well as on a series of defined reading tasks. Conducting such research as part of a test development project is difficult if not unethical. However, we believe our results have raised important questions, and we hope they stimulate further study of the relationship between grammar and reading in a foreign language.

References

Clapham, C. M. (1987). *The rationale for the structure of the revised ELTS test*. Unpublished manuscript, ELTS Revision Project, University of Lancaster.

Criper, C., & Davies, A. (1988). ELTS validation project report. *ELTS Research Report*

1(i). London: The British Council and University of Cambridge Local Examinations Syndicate.

Draft specifications for the grammar test. (1988). Unpublished manuscript, ELTS Revision Project, University of Lancaster.

Draft specifications for Module A. (1989). Unpublished manuscript, ELTS Revision Project, University of Lancaster.

Rea-Dickins, P. M. (1988). *The relationship between grammatical abilities and aspects of communicative competence with special reference to the testing of grammar*. Unpublished doctoral thesis, University of Lancaster, United Kingdom.

Rea-Dickins, P. M. (1991). What makes a grammar test communicative? In J. C. Alderson & B. North (Eds.), *Language testing in the 1990s* (pp. 112–131). London: Macmillan.

Report of questionnaire for overseas administrators. (1987). Unpublished manuscript, ELTS Revision Project, University of Lancaster.

12

Assessing Speaking Proficiency in the International English Language Testing System

D. E. Ingram and Elaine Wylie
Griffith University, Australia

The International English Language Testing System (IELTS) aims to assess the general English proficiency and the proficiency in English for specific (especially academic) purposes (ESP) of nonnative speakers who wish to undertake academic studies, follow a training program, or learn English in an English-speaking country. IELTS is the result of a joint project by Britain and Australia, with some formal participation by Canada and assistance in certain areas from testing experts elsewhere. Although the project was called the ELTS Revision Project, the differences between the British Council–University of Cambridge Local Examinations Syndicate's former ELTS and the IELTS are substantial; indeed, the only feature the project team was required to maintain was the notion of reporting via 9-level bandscales or proficiency scales. The four macroskills are tested and reported separately. The listening and speaking tests focus on general proficiency for all candidates; the reading and writing tests focus on proficiency in one of the three broad discipline areas for those aiming to undertake academic studies and on general proficiency for those intending to take a training program or English language course. An overall or average bandscale level is also reported. IELTS is designed to be administered virtually on demand anywhere in the world and by persons who, for practical reasons, may have received only a minimum of training in its administration.

This paper discusses the nature of proficiency and the use of proficiency scales in assessment, and describes the IELTS Speaking test, indicating how it has developed to meet the constraints imposed by the scope and administrative conditions mentioned above.

The Nature of Proficiency and Proficiency Scales

An underlying problem in considering proficiency scales and tests is defining what is meant by proficiency itself. During early data collection phases of the

ELTS Revision Project, the project team consulted a number of applied linguists to gain their views on the nature of language proficiency. Westaway, Alderson, and Clapham (1990) reported on this process: "We are, perhaps not surprisingly, far from consensus and, in this regard, ELTS is likely to have to break new ground in devising and operationalizing a construct" (p. 252).

Since the advent of the "integrative-sociolinguistic trend" in testing in the 1960s (Spolsky, 1978), there has, in fact, been some agreement at a very general level:

> Language proficiency is one of the most poorly defined concepts in the field of language testing. Nevertheless, in spite of differing theoretical views as to its definition, a general issue on which many scholars seem to agree is that the focus of proficiency is on the student's ability to use language. (Farhady, 1982, p. 44)

A number of definitions have focused solely on the use of the language. Clark (1975), for example, has defined proficiency as the "ability to receive or transmit information in the test language for some pragmatically useful purpose within a real-life setting" (p. 10).

As argued in Ingram (1985), which contains a comprehensive discussion of different theoretical views, purely functional descriptions of proficiency are not sufficient for practical assessment purposes. Many functions and even some relatively complex communication tasks can be performed with minimal use of language by a good communicator who exploits the existing knowledge and/or attitudes of an interlocutor. For example, in a recent training interview observed by one of the writers, the trainee interviewer was impressed by the interviewee's ability to give a "detailed" description of a local park; she did not realize that she herself, by dint of her knowledge of the park at that time of the year and of courting customs, had filled in gaps between very general images expressed in fragmentary snatches of language: "In the park . . . er . . . many beautiful trees . . . er . . . (smile) many boyfriends and girlfriends."

Other, nonfunctional criteria have therefore been included in the descriptions of proficiency levels in scales such as the Interagency Language Roundtable (ILR) Language Skill Level Descriptions (ILR, 1985) and the Australian Second Language Proficiency Ratings (ASLPR) (Ingram & Wylie, 1979), which took the forerunner of the ILR scale, the Foreign Service Institute (FSI) Absolute Language Proficiency Ratings (FSI, 1968) as its starting point. Underlying the ASLPR is the view that proficiency entails the ability to mobilize knowledge of the various systems of the target language to carry out communication tasks in particular situational contexts; the focus is both on the sorts of tasks that can be performed and on the ways in which they are performed, that is, the linguistic, paralinguistic, and sociolinguistic features used in carrying out the tasks (Ingram & Wylie, 1983; Ingram, 1979).

Some researchers have criticized the intermingling of criterion types (Clark, 1972; Brindley, 1986; Weir, 1987; Spolsky, 1989). However, if a theory of language can link the sociocultural, semantic, and linguistic systems (Halliday,

1978), if the test tasks require candidates to integrate elements from the various systems (which the tasks must do if they reflect actual language use), and if patterns of coincidence or coemergence of elements from the various systems can be observed in learners' use (which the analysis of the interlanguage of thousands of learners in the development and use of such scales suggests), then it does seem appropriate to combine different types of criteria in scale descriptors. Moreover, the inclusion of nonfunctional criteria may reduce concerns about extrapolation from the candidate's performance on one set of tasks to his or her performance on "the indefinitely large universe of tasks" (Weir, 1981, p. 32) that cannot, for obvious practical reasons, be tested.

The Draft IELTS Bandscale for Speaking (see Appendix 12A) identifies the sorts of tasks learners can perform at various levels and describes very broad parameters of phonological, grammatical, discoursal, and sociolinguistic development. At the upper levels there is some reference to fluency, the smoothness with which the elements of the various systems are mobilized to perform the tasks, and to the development of the strategic use of circumlocution (cf. Canale & Swain, 1980; Canale, 1983).

Many scales differentiate between macroskills, and proficiency is reported in a profile showing the levels assigned in the different macroskills. Bachman and Palmer's (1983) study of the construct validity of the FSI Oral Interview, in which speaking and reading are rated separately, has supported this approach; the findings of the study clearly demonstrate the distinctness of speaking and reading as traits and therefore the invalidity of the strong form of Oller's unitary language ability. In a study during the development of the ASLPR, which has separate scales for speaking, listening, writing, and reading, only 6 of 20 moderately to well-educated learners were rated at the same level in all four macroskills, and individuals' macroskill levels differed by up to 3 steps on the 12-step scale (Ingram, 1984). Anecdotal evidence from teachers and administrators in the Australian Adult Migrant Education Program indicates that, with learners who have less formal education, the differences are even greater.

The ILR Scale is designed to measure general proficiency. Lowe (1986) stated:

> The system rates general rather than job-specific language. Though the tasks which government employees must accomplish using a foreign language range from general, through work-related, to job-specific language, the common requirement for transferability of skills precludes rating solely job-specific performances. On a proficiency test, outstanding performance in job-specific language must be matched in level and consistency with similar performance on general topics at the same level for a specific rating to be assigned. (p. 393)

Present versions of the ASLPR describe the development of general proficiency, defined by Ingram as the ability to use the language "in everyday situations in which we, as human beings living in a physical and social world, are necessarily involved" (1984, p. 10). The American Council on the Teaching of Foreign Languages (ACTFL) Guidelines, which are derived from the ILR Scale, with substantial borrowing from the ASLPR, are intended for academic use, that is, in foreign language learning programs in secondary schools, colleges, and universities, but are not scales for measuring language for academic purposes in the sense of a subset of language for specific purposes. A rating provides the candidate and other consumers with a statement of "how the individual will function abroad linguistically in everyday life" (Liskin-Gasparro, 1982, p. 3).

On the other hand, of the 22 separate "yardsticks" or scales created for the U.K. English Speaking Union "Framework" Project, there are four scales (for listening, speaking, reading, and writing) for business purposes, and another four for study/training purposes (Carroll & West, 1989). Specific purpose versions of the ASLPR (for academic purposes, business purposes, and engineering purposes) are being developed. The Council of Europe is planning to develop a range of specific, work-related scales (G. Egloff, personal communication).

In the former ELTS, the Speaking test for academic candidates was in the Modular (specific purposes) component of the test. In IELTS, it is in the General Proficiency component for all candidates; it aims to assess candidates' ability to function in situations relevant to their everyday lives as students in an English-speaking country, not in the situations relevant to their proposed course of study in a particular discipline. This change reflects practical problems; Westaway et al. (1990) reported that attempts at "authentic academic exchange" in the previous ELTS interview format were largely unsuccessful because the interviewer and candidate were often from different disciplines (p. 251).

The validity of the new approach should be the subject of future research. The Edinburgh ELTS Validation Study (Criper & Davies, 1988) did not demonstrate conclusively the validity of ESP as a construct; Davies (1990) noted that "the S of LSP stands up but not as expected" (p. 193). Certainly the appropriateness of a focus on the register of a chosen discipline area for prospective undergraduate students in particular must be questioned, as even native-speaking matriculands often have very little command of the registers of the disciplines they are about to enter. The issue of ESP testing is explored in the IELTS context by Clapham (this volume, chap. 14).

The descriptions of Bands 6, 7, and 8 in the Draft Bandscale for Speaking (Appendix 12A) refer to candidates' ability to communicate on topics relevant to their own academic, vocational, or leisure interests, and candidates rated at the higher levels will therefore have demonstrated some level of mastery of a specific register or registers. However, it is the candidates' register flexibility, or ability to cope with different register requirements, that is being tested, rather than their ability to cope with any particular specific register (in contrast to the Occupational English Test described by McNamara, 1990). Moreover, the topics, even if they are related to an academic discipline, do not necessarily reflect the register of the proposed course of study (the specific purpose for which the candidate is taking the test) because he or she may be entering a new field. For example, a candidate may demonstrate mastery of the register of international diplomacy acquired during previous studies or through listening to the BBC World Service or Radio

Australia, but this mastery is not directly relevant if the candidate is applying for admission to a faculty of engineering. In terms of topics, the IELTS Speaking test would appear to give candidates "the opportunity to perform at their best" (Bachman & Savignon, 1986, p. 387).

The Nature of the Speaking Test

In their report on a study of test formats and item types for the Test of English as a Foreign Language (TOEFL) Test of Spoken English, Clark and Swinton (1979) observed that, in situations where it is important to have a very accurate indication of the examinee's level of speaking proficiency, "there would appear to be no suitable alternative to testing this language skill on a direct and explicit basis" (pp. 1–2). Clark (1975) has defined direct testing as follows: "In direct proficiency testing, the test format and procedure attempt to duplicate as closely as possible the setting and operation of the real-life situations in which the proficiency is normally demonstrated" (p. 10).

Indirect tests, according to Clark (1972), "cannot have the same psychological value for the student or the same instructional impact" (p. 132). Other writers to point out the positive washback effects of direct testing include Shohamy (1982), Stansfield and Webster (1986), and Westaway et al. (1990). Shohamy (1982) reported that learners have positive attitudes toward direct tests of proficiency, preferring them to indirect measures such as cloze. The most widely known direct test of speaking is the ILR interview. An overview of this technique and of one of its most refined variants, that used by the Central Intelligence Agency, is given in Wilds (1975).

An interview was used to test speaking in the former ELTS and, despite some concerns about reliability, the ELTS Revision Steering Committee felt that this feature of the test should be retained. However, the committee was faced with financial and other operational constraints very similar to those that had ruled out the possibility of any direct assessment of speaking in the TOEFL (Clark & Swinton, 1979). In order to constrain administration costs, it was decided that the interview should last no longer than 15 minutes (and no less than 11 minutes) out of a total length for the IELTS test of 145 minutes. Cost factors also excluded the possibility of involving a second person in the interview, a technique that Mullen (1980) found gave greater reliability and that is used for all interviews for the U.S. government (Lowe, 1987). The other major constraining factor is that the test has to be administrable anywhere in the world, often in circumstances in which relatively little control can be exercised over the selection and skills of interviewers. To maximize reliability, therefore, the interview has been tightly structured to control what the interviewer can do, and a process of monitoring of interview quality and rating accuracy is built into administrative proceedings.

The interview consists of five phases requiring progressively higher proficiency levels. Interviewers are required to lead candidates through all five phases (except with very low level candidates who are manifestly unable to proceed). The timing of each phase may be varied slightly within specified guidelines, so that higher-level candidates may be led more rapidly through the earlier phases and spend a little longer on later phases where their higher proficiency levels are more readily demonstrated; on the other hand, lower-level candidates may take more time on earlier phases. The interview is intended to flow as much as possible like a normal conversation, albeit a guided and structured conversation, and hence interviewers should provide smooth bridges from one phase to the next (except between Phases 2 and 3, as will be seen below).

Though the General component of IELTS focuses around Band 4 of the 9-point bandscales, the Speaking test, with the graduated nature of its activities, is able to assess candidates throughout the proficiency range, or at least from Band 3 up. For the great majority of candidates, the emphasis is on what they can do rather than what they cannot do (cf. Shohamy, 1982).

The interviewer matches the language elicited from the candidate directly against the Bandscale for Speaking, and the candidate is assigned to the band that his or her global proficiency most closely resembles. The global approach to rating acknowledges the complex nature of language and its development, the differences between individual learners' developmental paths (Griffin, Adams, Martin, & Tomlinson, 1986), and the skillful use learners can make of compensating strategies (Ingram, 1979). It does, however, require the rater to use judgment in balancing different aspects of development against each other, which may have a negative effect on reliability. Adams (1978) found that some of the least reliable ratings from FSI interviews involved "difficult decisions of factor weighting, such as near native fluency and pronunciation against serious grammatical errors" (p. 144). On the other hand, during the trialing of the ASLPR, we found that what was considered atypical development (the ASLPR uses only a global approach to rating, and so no factor subscales are recorded) posed less of a problem for raters than the actual level of the learners they were rating, the highest mean standard deviation in ratings being found with learners at Level 3 on the scales of 0 to 5 (Ingram, 1984).

The Structure of the Interview

The five phases of the interview are as follows.

Phase 1, the *Introduction*, focuses at the Band 3 level, though more proficient candidates may well perform at higher levels. The phase lasts from 1 to 2 minutes, and its purpose is to allow interviewers to introduce themselves, to exchange greetings, to check the candidate's identity, and to settle the candidate down in readiness for the main part of the interview. According to the specifications, the main skills and functions to be elicited are *using social formulas, providing personal information,* and *providing general factual information.*

Phase 2, the *Extended Discourse* phase, focuses around Bands 3 and 4 and lasts from 3 to 4 minutes. It is designed to give candidates an opportunity to take the initiative and to speak at length on some topic well known to them, such as an aspect of life in their country. The candidate should do most of the talking, with the interviewer mainly using stimulus questions or comments to prompt candidates should they "dry up." The main skills and functions to be elicited are *providing general factual information, expressing likes and dislikes, giving directions and instructions, describing and comparing, narrating events and sequences of events,* and *explaining how something works.*

Phase 3, the *Elicitation* phase, contains activities geared to the Band 3 to 6 range and lasts from 3 to 4 minutes. In this phase the usual interviewer-led situation is reversed in order to ascertain whether candidates can ask questions and take the initiative in a communication situation. To highlight this, the transition from Phase 2 into Phase 3 is signaled more overtly than is the case between other phases; the interviewer is required to state categorically that the candidate is to ask questions. The main skills and functions are *eliciting general factual information, eliciting information about objects, events and sequences of events, eliciting opinions, attitudes and values,* and *eliciting explanations of how something works or why something is the case.*

Phase 4, the *Speculation and Attitudes* phase, is designed to allow candidates at Band 5 and above to demonstrate their proficiency. It lasts from 3 to 4 minutes. Activities require the candidate to speculate; to express ideas, attitudes, and plans with some precision; to demonstrate the ability to switch register; and to use language relevant to their particular academic, vocational, or other interests. The interviewer is likely to be a layperson with regard to these interest areas, and thus the test situation reflects as closely as possible (cf. Alderson, 1981) everyday, nonspecialist discussions in the target community, which is in keeping with the aim of the Speaking test. The main skills and functions are *providing general, personal, and factual information; expressing opinions, intentions, attitudes and emotions; describing and comparing objects, events, and sequences of events;* and *speculating on future events and their consequences.*

In Phase 5, the *Conclusion,* the interviewer rounds off the interview with activities that allow the candidate to perform at his or her own level. The phase lasts about 1 minute. The main skills and functions are *using social formulas, saying farewell,* and *thanking.*

Test Activities

A considerable number of activities are specified for each phase in each version of the Speaking test. Interviewers are required to select from among these a range of activities that will allow each candidate to demonstrate his or her true ability. In their selection, they must take into account whether a particular activity is appropriate in terms of the proficiency level (some Phase 2 activities, for example, lend themselves to a relatively complex discourse structure or specialized lexis) and the background of the candidate, and also whether the range of topics to be covered in the interview as a whole is suitably wide. Interviewers must be flexible and ready to move to an alternative activity if the one chosen initially does not work or appears to have provoked a rote-memorized response. It is stressed in interviewer training that variety is essential for test security.

The emphasis is on realistic activities that candidates could conceivably be involved in, especially on arrival in the country to which they are going. Role play in which candidates are asked to take on a role other than themselves is specifically ruled out because of the likely interference of factors such as dramatic ability and imagination, which are not part of language proficiency (cf. Jones, 1979).

Because the IELTS is a secure test, we cannot give actual examples of the activities that make up the Speaking test, but we can indicate the sorts of activities that are listed. The examples below have been taken from the exemplar test that is publicly available.

In Phase 1, candidates are required to answer simple questions about their name, their family, their home locality, and their interests.

In Phase 2, candidates are given the opportunity to speak at length on some topic well known to them. They could be asked to talk about how their food is prepared and eaten, about entertainment (theater, dancing, festivals, etc.) or about sports and games in their country. The interviewer is advised to give the candidate the chance to talk about more than one topic if that is necessary to elicit extended speech.

Phase 3 activities give the initiative to the candidates and require them to ask questions in information-gap tasks of a type that students studying or training overseas commonly face. For example, the candidate could be given a sketch map and instructed to ask questions of the interviewer (who has a complete map with full details of street names, etc.) to find the way to a certain building; or the candidate could be given a timetable showing lectures and other study activities and be told to ask the interviewer (who has a language laboratory schedule) questions to find out when some private language laboratory practice sessions could be arranged. In this phase, simple artifacts containing minimal language may be used (e.g., a map, a photograph, a diagram), and the candidate is given a cue card with a very short, simply worded instruction and several one- or two-word cues for questions to ask. At present, the specifications require that all candidates be given the cue card, though some of those who have worked on the development of the test believe that the card should be used only if the candidate "dries up" and needs the prompts. Research is needed into implications for the validity and reliability of the test of the "routine" versus the "optional" use of the card.

In Phase 4, candidates are led to talk about their future plans, their hopes and ambitions, the relevance to their country of what they are planning to do, and so on. To assist the interviewer with this phase, all candidates are asked before the interview to fill out a brief curriculum vitae.

Phase 5 usually flows on directly from Phase 4, requiring a brief reference to something that has already been discussed, and concludes with expressions of farewell and good wishes.

Training

Whereas pencil-and-paper test types depend largely on statistical procedures for determining their validity and reliability, interview-based tests depend heavily on the quality of training of the interviewers and raters. For this reason, the Speaking test is administered only by trained English as a second language (ESL) teachers who have undergone a short IELTS training program. This program includes consideration (either in a training class or through self-access) of the principles of direct proficiency assessment; an introduction to the documentation of the test (see below); discussion of the principles of interviewing and rating; viewing, discussing, and rating videotaped interviews; and conducting live interviews. Finally, trainees are required to conduct interviews, which are recorded, and to rate them successfully before they can be accredited. In addition, the training package contains documentation explaining the Speaking test and its conduct, an administration manual, and a videotaped program prepared under our supervision. The program, intended to be used as a basis for discussing interview techniques and for practicing rating, contains a 32-minute introduction to the Speaking test, 23 full-length (11- to 15-minute) interviews with ESL learners from a range of backgrounds and proficiency levels, and commentaries on each interview by the present writers. All interviewers will be required to work through the training package at regular intervals if their certification is to remain valid.

A monitoring system is being established to ensure that the quality of interviewing and rating is maintained. All interviews are audiotaped, and 1 in 10—randomly chosen—for each interviewer will be returned to a center in Britain or Australia for moderation.

Test Documentation

The Speaking test is accompanied by the following documentation:

1. The *Specifications* provide explicit guidance to item writers on the preparation of future parallel forms of the test. The specifications include statements on the general purpose of the IELTS and the Speaking test in particular, the test focus, cultural appropriateness (a complex issue in an international test developed by two culturally distinct countries), the structure of the test, scoring and interpretation, and the administration of the test. Probably the most important of these sections is that on the

structure of the test, which outlines the various phases and specifies the content of each in terms of its purpose, band focus, tasks and stimuli, and skills and functions.

2. An *Assessment Guide* or training manual provides training for potential interviewers in how to conduct the Speaking test. It is accompanied by videotaped excerpts from interviews and some complete interviews that illustrate points raised in the manual. Another, more formal, training manual is intended for trainers.

3. The *Administration Manual* gives procedural guidance to interviewers and administrators.

4. An *Exemplar* or *Specimen Test* available to candidates provides brief examples of the sorts of activities candidates can expect in each phase of the Speaking test.

5. The *Bandscale for Speaking* (see Appendix 12A) is the scale against which candidates' speaking proficiency is rated. It consists of 9 band levels from zero to nativelike ability to communicate in spoken English, each of which is a short behavioral description of the speaking ability observed at that level.

Future Research and Conclusion

To date, the Speaking test has been completed in its initial form, a specimen test has been written, the other documentation referred to above has been prepared, and the videotaped training material has been completed. The formal trials of the IELTS have included some attention to the Speaking test, though much more research into aspects of the test is expected in the future. Some of the many issues that should be considered include the following:

1. the validity of the test, specifically its relationship with the other subtests of the IELTS and with other tests (such as the TOEFL, and those used with the ILR and ASLPR scales). Though the trials to date have done some of this, earlier drafts of the IELTS were used and interviewer training programs were not entirely satisfactory.

2. the predictive validity of the test for candidates entering academic or other training programs

3. the validity of the bandscale descriptors, including their accuracy in terms of the coincidences of the different developmental strands

4. the usefulness of the descriptors to raters and to test consumers, including candidates

5. the reliability of the scale, specifically the extent to which ratings are influenced in particular countries by the variety of English spoken by the tester and the target variety of the candidate

6. the reliability of the interview, that is, the extent of agreement between ratings when the same candidate is interviewed by different interviewers

7. the reliability of the interviewing and rating of laypersons as opposed to trained ESL teachers
8. the effect on reliability of particular types of training in interviewing and rating
9. the validity and reliability of the structured interview in comparison with the freer interview used with scales such as the ILR or ASLPR
10. the effects of different interview situations (for example, a formal across-the-table interview as opposed to a more relaxed situation) on different candidates
11. the effect of different strategies within the test, for example, giving the cue card at the start of Phase 3 or withholding it until (and if) it becomes necessary
12. interviewer fatigue, its effect on the quality of interviewing and rating, and how to counter any negative effects
13. comparison of ratings made with the present, global scale and those made with more analytic scales such as are used in assessing the IELTS writing scripts
14. comparison of ratings assigned by the interviewer with those assigned by a separate rater
15. comparison of live ratings with ratings of the same interviews recorded on audio- or videotape
16. the monitoring and moderation process, how to manage it, and its effects on the reliability of the test

Research into these and other issues will reveal much more about the effectiveness of the IELTS Speaking test.

References

Adams, M. L. (1978). Measuring foreign language speaking proficiency: A study of agreement among raters. In J. L. D. Clark (Ed.), *Direct testing of speaking proficiency: Theory and application*. Princeton, NJ: Educational Testing Service (ETS).

Alderson, J. C. (1981). Report on the discussion on communicative language testing. In J. C. Alderson & A. Hughes (Eds.), *ELT documents 111—Issues in language testing*. London: British Council.

Bachman, L. F., & Palmer, A. S. (1983). The construct validity of the FSI Oral Interview. In J. W. Oller (Ed.), *Issues in language testing research*. Rowley, MA: Newbury House.

Bachman, L. F., & Savignon, S. J. (1986). The evaluation of communicative language proficiency: A critique of the ACTFL Oral Interview. *Modern Language Journal, 70*, 380–390.

Brindley, G. (1986). *The assessment of second language proficiency: Issues and approaches*. Adelaide: National Curriculum Resource Centre, Adult Migration Education Program.

Canale, M. (1983). From communicative competence to language pedagogy. In J. Richards & R. Schmidt (Eds.), *Language and communication* (pp. 2–27). London: Longman.

Canale, M., & Swain, M. (1980). Theoretical bases of communicative approaches to second language teaching and testing. *Applied Linguistics, 1*, 1–47.

Carroll, B. J., & West, R. (1989). *ESU framework: Performance scales for English language examinations*. Essex: Longman.

Clark, J. L. D. (1972). *Foreign language testing: Theory and practice*. Philadelphia: Center for Curriculum Development.

Clark, J. L. D. (1975). Theoretical and technical considerations in oral proficiency testing. In R. L. Jones & B. Spolsky (Eds.), *Testing language proficiency*. Arlington, VA: Center for Applied Linguistics.

Clark, J. L. D., & Swinton, S. S. (1979). *An exploration of the speaking proficiency measures in the TOEFL context* (TOEFL Research Report 4). Princeton, NJ: ETS.

Criper, C., & Davies, A. (Eds.). (1988). ELTS validation report. *ELTS Research Report, 1*(1). Cambridge: University of Cambridge Local Examinations Syndicate.

Davies, A. (1990). Operationalising uncertainty in language testing: An argument in favour of content validity. In J. H. A. L. de Jong & D. Stevenson (Eds.), *Individualizing the assessment of language abilities* (pp. 179–195). Clevedon, Avon: Multilingual Matters.

Farhady, H. (1982). Measures of language proficiency from the learners's perspective. *TESOL Quarterly, 16*, 43–61.

Foreign Service Institute. (1968). *Absolute Language Proficiency Ratings* [circular]. Washington, DC: Author. Reprinted in Sollenberger, H. E. (1978). Development and current use of the FSI interview test. In J. L. D. Clark (Ed.), *Direct testing of speaking proficiency: Theory and application*. Princeton, NJ: ETS.

Griffin, P. E., Adams, R. J., Martin, L., & Tomlinson, B. (1986). *Proficiency in English as a second language: The development of an interim test for adult migrants*. Victoria, Australia: Ministry of Education.

Halliday, M. A. K. (1978). *Language as social semiotic*. London: Edward Arnold.

Ingram, D. E. (1979). Introduction to the Australian Second Language Proficiency Ratings. In *Adult Migrant Education Program teachers manual*. Canberra: Department of Immigration and Ethnic Affairs. Reprinted in Ingram, D. E., & Wylie, E. (1984). *Australian Second Language Proficiency Ratings*. Canberra: Australian Government Publishing Service.

Ingram, D. E. (1984). *Report on the formal trialling of the Australian Second Language Proficiency Ratings (ASLPR)*. Canberra: Australian Government Publishing Service.

Ingram, D. E. (1985). Assessing proficiency: An overview on some aspects of testing. In K. Hyltenstam & M. Pienemann (Eds.), *Modeling and assessing second language acquisition*. Clevedon, Avon: Multilingual Matters.

Ingram, D. E., & Wylie, E. (1979). Australian Second Language Proficiency Ratings. In *Adult migrant education program teachers manual*. Canberra: Department of Immigration and Ethnic Affairs. Reprinted (1984). Canberra: Australian Government Publishing Service.

Ingram, D. E., & Wylie, E. (1983). Introduction to the ASLPR [videotape]. Canberra: Film Australia.

Interagency Language Roundtable. (1985). *Language Skill Level Descriptions*. Washington, DC: Author. Also available as Appendix E in Duran, R. P., Canale, M., Penfield, M., Stansfield, C. W., & Liskin-Gasparro, J. E. (1985). *TOEFL from a communicative viewpoint on language proficiency: A working paper.* (TOEFL Research Report 17). Princeton, NJ: ETS.

Jones, R. L. (1979). The oral interview of the Foreign Service Institute. In B. Spolsky (Ed.), *Some major tests.* Arlington, VA: Center for Applied Linguistics.

Liskin-Gasparro, J. (1982). *Oral proficiency testing manual.* Princeton, NJ: ETS.

Lowe, P. (1986). Proficiency: Panacea, framework, process? A reply to Kramsch, Schulz, and, particularly, to Bachman and Savignon. *Modern Language Journal, 70,* 391–397.

Lowe, P. (1987). Interagency language roundtable oral proficiency interview. In J. C. Alderson, K. J. Kranke, & C. W. Stansfield (Eds.), *Reviews of English language proficiency tests.* Washington, DC: Teachers of English to Speakers of Other Languages.

McNamara, T. F. (1990). Item response theory and the validation of an ESP test for health professionals. *Language Testing, 7,* 52–75.

Mullen, K. A. (1980). Rater reliability and oral proficiency evaluations. In J. W. Oller & K. Perkins (Eds.), *Research in language testing.* Rowley, MA: Newbury House.

Shohamy, E. (1982). Affective considerations in language testing. *Modern Language Journal, 66,* 13–17.

Spolsky, B. (1978). Introduction: Linguists and language testers. In B. Spolsky (Ed.), *Advances in language testing research: Approaches to language testing, 2* (pp. v–x). Arlington, VA: Center for Applied Linguistics.

Spolsky, B. (1989). Communicative competence, language proficiency and beyond. *Applied Linguistics, 10,* 138–156.

Stansfield, C. W., & Webster, R. (1986). The new TOEFL writing test. *TESOL Newsletter, 20*(5), 7–18.

Weir, C. J. (1981). Reaction to the Morrow paper (1). In *ELT documents 111—Issues in language testing.* London: British Council.

Weir, C. J. (1987). Review of English Language Testing Service. In J. C. Alderson, K. J. Kranke, & C. W. Stansfield, *Reviews of English language proficiency tests* (pp. 28–31). Washington, DC: TESOL.

Westaway, G., Alderson, J. C., & Clapham, C. M. (1990). Directions in testing for specific purposes. In J. H. A. L. de Jong & D. Stevenson (Eds.), *Individualizing the assessment of language abilities* (pp. 239–256). Clevedon, Avon: Multilingual Matters.

Wilds, C. (1975). The oral interview test. In R. L. Jones & B. Spolsky (Eds.), *Testing language proficiency.* Arlington, VA: Center for Applied Linguistics.

Appendix 12A
Draft Bandscale for Speaking

(Drafted by Greg Deakin, Elaine Wylie, and David Ingram in July 1989; revised August 1989.)

9. Speech is fluent, situationally appropriate and fully acceptable in all features though a slight non-intrusive accent may be observed.

8. Communicates effectively on all general, academic, vocational or leisure topics relevant to own interests and experiences. Speech is fluent and readily comprehensible though occasional non-systematic errors in grammar, vocabulary and sometimes a strong accent may occur without impeding communication. Can use speculative, argumentative, descriptive, and narrative language flexibly to convey precise meanings. Extended structuring including cohesive features is accurate and appropriate. Can vary the language to suit situational (i.e. register) requirements with only occasional inappropriacies.

7. Communicates effectively on a wide range of general, academic, vocational or leisure topics. Occasional errors in vocabulary and structures may occur without inhibiting communication. Communicates readily and fairly precisely using complex sentence forms and a wide range of modifiers, connectives and cohesive features. Displays some flexibility in the use of speculative, argumentative, descriptive, and narrative language. Can generally vary the language to suit situational (i.e. register) requirements and can talk on own subject area with ease and fluency.

6. Generally communicates effectively on general topics and on other matters relevant to own immediate academic, vocational or leisure interests. Can use complex sentence forms and a wide range of modifiers, connectives, and cohesive features to convey most meanings fairly precisely though errors in grammar and vocabulary may occur and occasionally interfere with communication. Is generally able to use circumlocution to cover gaps in vocabulary and structure. Can present speculation, extended argument, and long and complex description and narration though errors in structure or coherence may sometimes occur. Shows some skill in varying language to suit situational (i.e. register) requirements.

5. Is broadly able to convey meaning on most general topics though errors in structure and vocabulary may interfere with communication. Can engage in extended conversation on most general topics, generally making use of relevant connectives and other cohesive features. Has some ability to use complex sentence forms and modifiers. However, has difficulty in presenting speculation and extended argument, while long or complex description or narration may lose coherence. Lacks flexibility and is unable to vary language significantly to suit situational (i.e. register) requirements.

4. Can convey basic meaning on familiar topics. Can give uncomplicated directions and use common question forms to elicit information (though not necessarily with correct word order). Has control of basic sentence forms but longer utterances tend to break down. Can link simple sentences using the most frequently occurring connectives. Errors in grammar and vocabulary are frequent and may interfere with communication. Tentative use of modifiers limits ability to describe, give precise information or express attitudes. Pronunciation may often be faulty and impede communication.

3. Can convey only simple meaning on very familiar topics. Can answer simple questions and respond to simple statements. Has only limited ability to take the initiative with original statements and questions. Basic sentence forms appear to be used though grammatical errors are numerous except in memorized utterances. Essentially no ability to link sentences or use modifiers. Pronunciation is likely to be strongly influenced by the first language and to significantly impede communication.

2. Little communication is possible except for the most rudimentary information using very limited vocabulary. Utterances consist of isolated words or short memorized phrases. Frequent pauses may occur as the candidate searches for words. Pronunciation is strongly influenced by the first language and is often unintelligible.

1. Essentially unable to speak English. Limited to at most a very few isolated words, memorized utterances or fragments of virtually no communicative significance.

0. Candidate did not attempt the interview. No assessable information provided.

(A glossary of terms provided for these descriptors is not included here.)

Performance on a General Versus a Field-Specific Test of Speaking Proficiency by International Teaching Assistants

Dan Douglas
Iowa State University
Larry Selinker
University of Michigan

In 1980, the Educational Testing Service (ETS), in response to requests from U.S. institutions of higher education for a standardized measure of English speaking ability, introduced the Test of Spoken English (TSE), a tape-recorded test requiring candidates to perform a series of seven oral tasks that are recorded on another tape and rated by trained evaluators at ETS. The test manual (ETS, 1982) states that "the test is not targeted to a single academic discipline, field of employment, or other specialized language usage . . . " (p. 5). In one application of the test, "academic institutions may use TSE scores to evaluate the spoken English of applicants for teaching assistantships . . . " (p. 5). In 1985, ETS made a retired version of the TSE available commercially to institutions that wanted to give the test locally and score it themselves. This test, designated as the Speaking Proficiency English Assessment Kit (SPEAK), has a number of equivalent forms and is used widely to evaluate the speaking proficiency of prospective teaching assistants whose first language is not English. It is used at Iowa State University as part of the SPEAK/TEACH international teaching assistant (ITA) evaluation and training program.

Users of the TSE/SPEAK have frequently suggested that the test is too general to be used as a valid measure of an ITA's ability to use English for teaching in fields such as mathematics, chemistry, or physics. The test takers, and their supervisors, suggest that the ITAs would do much better if given a test of their ability to talk about their major fields.

In one study (Smith, 1989) conducted to explore differences in performance on the SPEAK and field-specific versions, very little systematic difference was found. However, Douglas (1989) suggested that "contextualization cues" (Gumperz, 1976) present in the two testing situations may not have been sufficiently different to promote differential "domain engagement" (Douglas & Selinker, 1985) and, consequently, differential interlanguage performance. Such contextualization cues, consisting in spoken language of changes in tempo, pitch, stress, intonation, volume, overt rhetorical markers, gesture, and eye contact, signal shifts in the dynamics of the communicative event, promoting, it is assumed, shifts in the planning, execution, and assessment of communicative moves and consequently in the marshaling of interlanguage resources brought to bear. Relating contextual cues to language tests, Bachman (1990) has suggested a framework of "test method facets," including testing environment facets, test rubric facets, facets of the input and the expected response, and facets associated with the interaction between the input and response, "which provide much of the context of language tests, [and] affect performance on language tests" (p. 113).

Research Questions

The project described here was designed to explore variation in test performance in terms of the features of the context as represented by test method facets, particularly in terms of the instructions, and the nature of the language including vocabulary, distribution of information, level of abstraction, topic, and genre. In particular, the study investigated the question of whether a specific-purpose test of English speaking ability will produce a different result than a general test of English speaking ability.

Method

Subjects

Fifteen international graduate students were tested with MATHSPEAK: seven Chinese, three Indian, two Korean, one Polish, one Turkish, and one Iranian. Two were women. Twelve of the subjects were graduate students in mathematics, two were studying statistics, and one was studying economics. The latter three were included in the study as a way of examining the degree of specificity of MATHSPEAK.

All the subjects had taken the SPEAK as part of their evaluation for teaching assistantships within the previous 12 months; six had taken it within 6 weeks. Arguably, it would have been better to find subjects who had all taken the SPEAK quite recently, but there were simply not enough in the subject pool. Alternatively, all the students could have been given both tests in a crossover design, but we thought it better to use the SPEAK results produced under actual test conditions. We comment further on this issue in the discussion of our results.

Materials

Working with a subject specialist informant, a professor in the Mathematics Department at Iowa State University specializing in mathematics education, we produced a field-specific version of the SPEAK, dubbed MATHSPEAK. After piloting a preliminary version on a small number of international graduate students in mathematics, we adjusted a number of items and prepared the final version (see Appendix 13A).

The instructions for MATHSPEAK differ from those for the SPEAK in a number of ways. The general instruction includes the information that the test taker "will be able to demonstrate how well you can talk about mathematics in English." Throughout the test, instructions refer to academic contexts, most often that of student-teacher interaction. For example, in Section One test takers are advised to answer the questions "as if you were talking to another student"; in Section Two, to read a printed paragraph aloud "as if you were a mathematics teacher reading to your students from a textbook"; in Section Three, sentence completion, to "imagine that a mathematics instructor has spoken to you and you heard only the first part of the statement; you have to guess what the speaker is likely to have said"; in Section Four, to refer to three diagrams in explaining the three cases of the roots of a quadratic equation "as if you were a teacher speaking to your class"; in Section Five, to answer questions about a theorem and to "imagine that the questions are from your students"; and in Section Six, to give their opinion on topics of interest to mathematicians: "Remember that this is a test of your ability to talk about mathematics in English. When it is graded, the graders will be interested in the way you express mathematical ideas." The intent behind these instructions was to provide test takers with some reason for performing the required tasks other than that they were taking an English test.

The content of the test was developed in consultation with the mathematics informant: he provided the reading passage, worked with one of the researchers on devising the sentence completion items, produced the graphs and instructions for Section Four, edited the questions for Sections Five and Six, and provided a mathematics class schedule for Section Seven. Our intent was to create a set of test materials that would seem representative to the test takers of the type of mathematical ideas they would need to talk about with their students and instructors.

The reading passage in Section Two is from one of our informant's "favorite books" and is written in a somewhat flowery and convoluted style. It may be intrinsically more difficult than the passages in the SPEAK and may also differ somewhat from the sparse style used in most mathematics texts. However, we included it in the test, perhaps against our better judgment, at the urging of the informant on the grounds that it represented the type of reading with which professional mathematicians ought to be familiar.

The sentence completion items in Section Three were written to mirror as faithfully as possible the grammatical structures used in the SPEAK. Perhaps as a result of this restriction, about half the items do not require much in the way of mathematical knowledge to complete. For example, "When I give this class a test next week . . . " or "If I were teaching differential equations right now . . . " may not really be context embedded in the same way as "In order to graph this function . . . " or "Before learning Calculus. . . . "

The diagrams in Section Four represent a fairly elementary algebra concept, but we thought it would require a high degree of familiarity to discuss the three cases fluently.

Section Five, which asks four questions about a single visual input, is based on the theorem, "If a and b are integers, then $ab = ba$." Question 1, "Why is this called the commutative law?" and question 4, "How could the commutative law be restated in your own words?" could possibly be answered by clever nonmathematicians, but the other two questions, "What is another commutative law?" and "What mathematical objects other than integers could be said to satisfy a commutative law?" require some sophistication in the field.

The three open-ended questions in Section Six are the least "mathematical" of the test items in the sense that nonmathematicians could probably speak comprehensibly about all of them. In this section, the instructions might have the most effect on performance, focusing attention on mathematicians and talk about mathematics so that subjects would feel more constrained to couch their responses in field-specific terms. As noted below, nonmathematicians did in fact experience some difficulty with these questions.

Finally, Section Seven, the description of a mathematics class schedule, is context embedded in a slightly different way. Included in the outline schedule are references to features of campus life familiar to students at Iowa State University: Carver Hall, the VAX computer system, help sessions, and course numbers.

Overall, then, MATHSPEAK contains a fair degree of content and task validity, though in hindsight not as high a degree as we might have wished. Nonmathematicians would without doubt have a difficult time with certain parts of the test. A question that this study was not designed to answer directly is whether any psychometric advantage is obtained in evaluating the English ability of mathematics teaching assistants by presenting them with a field-specific instrument such as MATHSPEAK rather than with a general measure such as the SPEAK. The measure is almost certainly different; whether it is more valid than a general one is a question yet to be explored.

The MATHSPEAK test booklet and tape were produced following the format of the SPEAK as far as possible, including the timing of pauses on the tape. Two male voices were used for the tape (see Appendix 13A).

Procedure

To foster the impression in the subjects that MATHSPEAK was more like mathematics than like English, the chair of the Mathematics Department sent out a letter requiring that international graduate students in mathematics who had taken the SPEAK recently as potential teaching assistants submit to further testing to ascertain how well they could use English to talk specifically about mathematics. Fifteen students were requested to appear for testing on 1 of 2 days;

13 did so. Three other students who were not in the Mathematics Department but who were by their own assessment mathematically sophisticated were invited to take MATHSPEAK. The subjects were tested in two groups in a language laboratory, where they heard the test tape through earphones and responded into microphones attached to individual cassette recorders.

The SPEAK was administered under the auspices of the Graduate College, and the sessions were conducted by members of the College staff. The subjects' taped responses were scored by trained SPEAK raters from the regular pool of raters in the Iowa State University ITA evaluation program. The same two raters scored all the tapes independently, and the same third rater scored those requiring a third rating. The raters were asked to comment on the ease or difficulty of rating the MATHSPEAK tapes compared with rating the SPEAK. Our mathematics informant examined transcripts of six of the tapes and commented on their mathematical accuracy. Finally, we analyzed the same six transcripts, looking for rhetorical-grammatical evidence of differences in performance as indicated by the test scores.

Results

Reliability

The two raters, both experienced SPEAK raters, had some difficulty agreeing on their ratings of the SPEAK, and 6 of the 15 tapes had to be scored by a third rater. As Table 13-1 shows, although the two primary raters tended to give different scores on average, the difference was not statistically significant ($t = 1.95$, $df = 14$, $p > .05$). The correlation between their ratings was .62.

SPEAK and MATHSPEAK Results

Table 13-2 shows the mean scores on overall comprehensibility, pronunciation, grammar, and fluency for the whole group of subjects on both the SPEAK and MATHSPEAK. Results of t-tests on these data suggest that, although the grammar and fluency scores were significantly different (grammar: $t = 2.1$, $df = 14$, $p = .03$; fluency: $t = 2.8$, $df = 14$, $p = .01$), the comprehensibility and

Table 13-1
Mean MATHSPEAK ratings by Two Raters (N = 15

Rater	Mean	SD
1	223.3	35.3
2	192.0	48.5

Table 13-2

SPEAK and MATHSPEAK Means, Standard Deviations, and Difference Scores
(N = 15)

| Skill area | SPEAK | | MATHSPEAK | | |
	M	SD	M	SD	Difference
Comprehensibility	204.0	14.1	207.3	38.0	3.3
Pronunciation	1.8	.24	1.8	.28	0.0
Grammar	2.0	.27	2.3	.46	0.3
Fluency	1.8	.33	2.1	.41	0.3

pronunciation scores were not. Because the data include scores both from those
who took the SPEAK more than two months before taking MATHSPEAK and
from the three subjects who were not mathematics graduate students, we analyzed
the scores of a subset of subjects who had taken the SPEAK within 6 weeks of
taking MATHSPEAK and who were majoring in mathematics (see Table 13-3).
T-tests on these data suggest that grammar and fluency scores are significantly
different (grammar: $t = 2.2$, $df = 5$, $p = .04$; fluency: $t = 3.2$, $df = 5$, $p = .01$)
but that comprehensibility and pronunciation scores are not.

For comparison, Table 13-4 shows the results of the three nonmathematics
subjects. Although the results are not statistically significant because of the
small sample size, the nonmathematics students did score consistently lower on
MATHSPEAK than on the SPEAK, the reverse of the mathematics students'
results.

Qualitative Analysis

The SPEAK and MATHSPEAK tapes of six subjects, three of the most recent
SPEAK group and the three nonmathematics students, were transcribed to allow
for a qualitative analysis of their responses as discourse. We asked our mathematics specialist informant to examine transcripts of the three most recent mathemat-

Table 13-3

Means, Standard Deviations, and Difference Scores for Subgroup With Most Recent
SPEAK and MATHSPEAK Results (n = 6)

| Skill area | SPEAK | | MATHSPEAK | | |
	M	SD	M	SD	Difference
Comprehensibility	193.3	9.4	213.3	37.7	20.0
Pronunciation	1.8	.1	1.8	.3	0.0
Grammar	1.9	.2	2.4	.5	0.5
Fluency	1.6	.3	2.2	.4	0.6

Table 13-4

Means, Standard Deviations, and Difference Scores for on SPEAK and MATHSPEAK
for Nonmathematics Majors (n = 3)

| | *SPEAK* | | *MATHSPEAK* | | |
Skill area	M	SD	M	SD	*Difference*
Comprehensibility	203.3	4.7	173.3	26.3	30.0
Pronunciation	1.8	.24	1.7	.22	0.1
Grammar	1.9	.16	1.7	.29	0.2
Fluency	1.9	.19	1.7	.09	0.2

ics subjects and the three nonmathematicians and to comment on the mathematical accuracy of their responses. He was not told which transcripts were those of the mathematics students and which were those of nonmathematics students. With respect to Section Three, item 9, "Whenever the denominator is zero . . . ," he commented that the mathematics students' responses reflected a "matter of taste": two of them said that the fraction "doesn't exist" whereas the other said it is "undefined." Our informant himself preferred the latter but said it really didn't matter. On Section Four, he said all three gave "good answers," although in one case he said the student might better have said the first case had no "real" solution rather than simply "no solution." He was generally satisfied with their responses to Section Five, and indicated that one student had "generalized—that's good" in his response to question 4 ("restate the theorem in your own words"). On the other hand, another mathematics student, he said, hadn't really restated the theorem but had only repeated it (the raters both gave him scores of 2 for pronunciation, grammar, fluency, and comprehensibility on this question). Finally, the informant had only one comment on Section Six regarding one student's response to the question about the computer revolution. The student had produced a somewhat disfluent response, and our informant commented that the isolated fragments made sense but were not connected (the raters, however, uniformly gave him scores of 2 for pronunciation, fluency, and comprehensibility).

Our informant's commentary on the nonmathematics students' responses to Section Three was characterized by statements such as "I don't know what that means," "not much sense in that," and "doesn't mean anything." He wondered at one point if the student whose transcript he was reading had been uncooperative. He also noted a number of false statements (the raters, however, tended to give scores of 2 or 3 to these responses). Concerning Section Four, the informant was critical of a statistics student's answer, expressing surprise that he didn't understand the quadratic formula. Another nonmathematics student, he said, seemed to have confused the commutative law with the transitive law in her responses to Section Five. Our informant was greatly relieved to learn later that these three subjects were not mathematics graduate students. He explained the statistics students' performance by saying, "Most stat people are pretty good in math, but their background isn't in math."

The raters also provided commentary on the performances, both on the rating sheets as they scored the tapes and afterward on a separate comment sheet. They were critical of Section Three, the oral reading passage: "Can any of these guys pronounce 'Archimedes'? His score should have been higher—he was torpedoed by the reading passage." "Section Two is an unfair evaluation of his ability." "The words chosen in Section Two seemed hard to pronounce and were difficult to read with expression. Fluency seemed lower." One rater was critical of Section Four because it used so many letters in place of words, leading, she felt, to an inflated pronunciation and comprehensibility rating for this section. Section Five was criticized for appearing to require more knowledge of mathematics than of English and for allowing too short a time for responses (our mathematics informant commented here that the 12- to 15-second limit meant that "either they know it or they don't"). Two of the raters commented on one subject, a mathematics student, that he seemed not to control the vocabulary in his own discipline but had a well-developed avoidance strategy, particularly noticeable on Sections Five and Six.

Overall, then, commentary by our informant and raters suggests that MATHSPEAK could be improved. The reading passage should be replaced with one of a slightly less literary style, and the questions in Section Five may need to be reworded. Our informant commented overall that the wording of the items often influenced adversely the way subjects responded; we need to look into this possibility more closely. On the other hand, the responses of the mathematics students were clearly distinguishable in content and form from those of the nonmathematics students, suggesting that MATHSPEAK is indeed a "test of ability to talk about mathematics in English."

Recall that we were seeking evidence to account for the fact that the mathematics students had performed better on MATHSPEAK than on the SPEAK, especially in grammar and fluency, and that the mathematics students had performed better than the nonmathematics students on the SPEAK. We checked these data with a number of types of specialist informants and did not find such evidence.

We looked through the transcripts ourselves, gave them to two students to search through, and to one colleague, Cathy Pettinari. No one found consistent grammatical differences. This is important, for the raters gave the mathematics test takers higher ratings on grammar on the SPEAK. Why? Were the students really better in grammar, but somehow their knowledge didn't show? Or, as is more likely, were the raters responding to something else and *calling* it "grammar"? We have thought for a long time that subjective ratings are simply the result of raters arriving at similar conclusions for possibly different reasons. We conclude that raters are attending to "something else" in the responses, that is, the test response as a weird form of discourse. The raters call it "grammar" because that is the only category they have.

We provide an example of one of these "something elses" in the test responses as discourse: rhetorical complexity. It is clear to us that the mathematicians' MATHSPEAK open-ended texts show more rhetorical complexity—more embedding of content information in larger structures. In one intriguing example, the text begins with the metaphor just described, moves to a purpose statement, then to determining factors, next to a subsumed purpose statement, then to a purpose statement of use, then to a result statement, and finally to a comparison and contrast statement. One sees no such complexity in the nonmathematicians' responses to MATHSPEAK. In an interesting case, a nonmathematics test taker appears to begin to develop a complex rhetorical structure, some form of argument, but it is basically empty of content.

> once everyone know . . . have some ideas about mathematics I think uh um eh it will save lots of trouble during our lifetime . . . for example if you go shopping or you make some business with another person then you have to have some ideas about mathematics

Interestingly, the argument fails, and he goes to nonmathematics talk about shopping. Our conclusion is that the form of the mathematics prompt here appeared to allow him to "get out" of mathematics talk.

Discussion

Interrater reliability for MATHSPEAK was not particularly high. Raters said they had difficulty at times separating content from language ability, which made them more uncertain about how to rate responses. For example, one rater commented, "I had difficulty with Section Four [description of three diagrams] because I could not determine if the speaker was describing a correct sequence or not." This problem has long been a major objection to specific-purpose language testing and teaching—that testers and teachers may not know enough about a field to adequately judge performance in it. At the same time, the issue highlights a question with regard to the nonspecificity of the SPEAK: To what extent should and does content influence ratings? This question has consequences for construct validation and possibly for predictive validity as well: Can test takers receive high ratings for responses that are well-pronounced, grammatical, fluent, and comprehensible but that are at the same time illogical, poorly organized, and just plain wrong? In a test of general language ability, does it matter? The two raters in this study seemed to suggest that they do pay attention to content on the SPEAK and felt hampered by an inability to do so in rating MATHSPEAK.

The overall results on the SPEAK and MATHSPEAK give rise to a number of points. The mathematics students tended to do better on the SPEAK than on MATHSPEAK. On average, among the six who had taken the SPEAK most recently, comprehensibility scores were 20 points higher on MATHSPEAK than on the SPEAK, though the difference was not statistically significant. There was almost no difference in pronunciation scores between the two performances. However, in grammar and fluency, students made significant gains on MATH-SPEAK. We discuss our observations on these two areas below. Briefly, the grammar finding in particular suggests to us that there is more to taking a specific-purpose test than simply background knowledge. At least as perceived by raters, the differences in contextual method (as embodied in method facets) between the SPEAK and MATHSPEAK are related to differences in the way language competence is realized.

There appeared to be much more variance on MATHSPEAK than on the SPEAK. Some of the variance is no doubt due to rater uncertainty (i.e., error), but some is probably also due to the effect of background knowledge on performance. Certainly such studies as those by Alderson and Urquhart (1983, 1985) have demonstrated some of the pitfalls of specific-purpose testing, but this area needs to be explored further, with an emphasis on the psychometric advantages of testing background knowledge with highly context-imbedded instruments.

Of the 12 mathematics subjects, 7 scored higher on MATHSPEAK than on the SPEAK, 4 scored higher on the SPEAK than on MATHSPEAK, and 1 stayed the same. Some of the score differences were dramatic, in both directions: one student scored 90 points higher on MATHSPEAK, another 50 points higher, and the average gain was just over 30 points. On the other hand, two students scored 40 points lower on MATHSPEAK. In both cases the same rater gave both candidates extremely low scores; when averaged with the first and third ratings, the scores produced low MATHSPEAK scores. The rater's comments suggest that she was influenced to some extent by the candidates' content knowledge and rhetorical strategies.

Using the Iowa State University standard of 210 on comprehensibility as an acceptable score on the SPEAK, four of the students who failed the SPEAK would have passed if they had taken MATHSPEAK instead; on the other hand, three who passed the SPEAK would have failed if they had taken MATHSPEAK. The other five, of whom two failed and three passed, would have done the same. These results are somewhat analogous to those of Smith (1989). The question of whether using one test versus the other yields a psychometric advantage is not possible to answer based on this study. The students performed differently on the two tests. How those differences might result in better measures is a question that must be answered through a study designed to explore it (namely, Douglas & Selinker, forthcoming).

Future Research and Conclusions

Our next step in this research is to look at tests in other subject areas to see if they replicate our results. We have created and administered CHEMSPEAK, a chemistry-based version of the SPEAK. In analyzing data from CHEMSPEAK, we hope to determine further the effect of context on test performance. Specifically, we intend to investigate the question of whether there may be a measurement advantage to using a field-specific test to make specific judgments about a candidate's language ability.

Acknowledgments

We thank our colleagues Catherine Pettinari and John Swales for helping us to analyze and check our data. In each case they provided important hints for further analysis. We also thank our mathematics informant, Jerry Mathews, who helped us set up these studies and reviewed our data for mathematical accuracy. We received some help, for which we are most grateful, from the following students: Molly MacKillop and Rie Atagi.

References

Alderson, J. C., & Urquhart, A. H. (1983). The effect of student background discipline on comprehension: A pilot study. In A. Hughes & D. Porter (Eds.), *Current developments in language testing* (pp. 121–127). London: Academic Press.

Alderson, J. C., & Urquhart, A. H. (1985). The effect of students' academic discipline on their performance on ESP reading tests. *Language Testing, 2*, 192–204.

Bachman, L. F. (1990). *Fundamental considerations in language testing*. Oxford: Oxford University Press.

Douglas, D. (1989, August). *Context in SLA theory and language testing*. Paper presented at the Educational Testing Service Invitational Symposium, Princeton, NJ.

Douglas, D., & Selinker, L. (1985). Principles for language tests within the "discourse domains" theory of interlanguage: Research, test construction and interpretation. *Language Testing, 2*, 205–226.

Douglas, D., & Selinker, L. (Forthcoming). Analyzing oral proficiency test performance in general and specific purpose tests. *System*.

Educational Testing Service. (1982). *TSE manual for score users*. Princeton, NJ: Author.

Gumperz, J. J. (1976). Language, communication and public negotiation. In P. Sanday (Ed.), *Anthropology and the public interest: Fieldwork and theory* (pp. 273–292). New York: Academic Press.

Smith, J. (1989). Topic and variation in ITA oral proficiency: SPEAK and field-specific oral tests. *English for Specific Purposes, 8*, 155–168.

Appendix 13A
MATHSPEAK

A TEST OF ABILITY TO TALK ABOUT MATHEMATICS IN ENGLISH

DO NOT OPEN THE BOOKLET UNTIL YOU ARE TOLD TO DO SO.

GENERAL DIRECTIONS

In this test, you will be able to demonstrate how well you can talk about mathematics in English. There are seven sections in the test, and special directions will be given for each section. The entire test will last approximately 20 minutes.

As you speak, your voice will be recorded. Your score for the test will be based on what is on the tape. Be sure to speak loudly enough for the machine to record clearly what you say.

If you have a problem with the tape recorder, notify the test supervisor immediately.

Please turn to Section One in your test booklet.

GO ON TO THE NEXT PAGE.

Section One: Directions
In this section of the test, you will be asked to answer some questions about yourself. After each question, you will have a short time to answer the question. Answer the questions as if you were talking to another student. Be sure to speak clearly after you hear each question.

DO NOT TURN THE PAGE UNTIL YOU ARE TOLD TO DO SO.

Section Two: Directions

In this section, you will be asked to read a printed paragraph aloud as if you were a mathematics teacher reading to your students from a textbook. First, you will be given one minute to read the paragraph silently to yourself. Then, you will have one minute to read the paragraph aloud. Go on to the next page and begin reading the paragraph *silently* to yourself.

GO ON TO THE NEXT PAGE.

Archimedes, Newton, and Gauss, these three, are in a class by themselves among the great mathematicians, and it is not for ordinary mortals to attempt to rank them in order of merit. All three started tidal waves in both pure and applied mathematics: Archimedes esteemed his pure mathematics more highly than its applications; Newton appears to have found the chief justification for his mathematical inventions in the scientific uses to which he put them, while Gauss declared that it was all one to him whether he worked on the pure or the applied side. Nevertheless Gauss crowned the higher arithmetic, in his day the least practical of mathematical studies, the queen of all.

DO NOT TURN THE PAGE UNTIL YOU ARE TOLD TO DO SO.

Section Three: Directions

In this section, you will see partial sentences and will be asked to make complete sentences using these parts. Imagine that a mathematics instructor has spoken to you and you heard only the first part of what the speaker is likely to have said. Look at Example X:

Example X: When the computer lab opens . . .

There are a number of possible completions for this sentence. The speaker could say, for example:

When the computer lab opens, I will return the disk. OR
When the computer lab opens, I will go there to work. OR
When the computer lab opens, I will look for the new program.

These are only sample completions. There are many other possibilities.

You may complete each sentence in any way you wish. Try to make the completed sentence meaningful and mathematically correct.

GO ON TO THE NEXT PAGE.

Now complete the ten partial sentences. You will hear only the number of each sentence. Speak when you hear the number and be sure to say the complete sentence.

1. While we were differentiating the function . . .
2. In order to graph this function . . .
3. When I give this class a test next week . . .
4. Although he did the calculations carefully . . .
5. Before learning calculus . . .
6. Because the student had forgotten . . .
7. By simplifying the fraction . . .
8. There isn't enough time during a mathematics test . . .
9. Whenever the denominator is zero . . .
10. If I were teaching differential equations right now . . .

DO NOT TURN THE PAGE UNTIL YOU ARE TOLD TO DO SO.

Section Four: Directions

In this section, you will see a series of diagrams that illustrate a concept in mathematics. Use the diagrams in explaining the three cases of the roots of a quadratic equation as if you were a teacher speaking to your class. First, please study each of the diagrams and the accompanying equation *silently*.

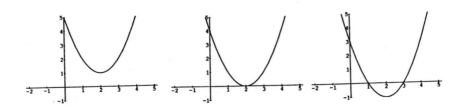

$$ax^2 + bx + c = 0$$

DO NOT GO ON TO THE NEXT PAGE UNTIL YOU ARE TOLD TO DO SO.

Section Five: Directions

In this section, you will be given a theorem and asked four questions about the theorem. Imagine that the questions are from your students. First study the theorem below *silently* before you hear the questions.

Theorem: If a and b are integers, then ab = ba.

DO NOT TURN THE PAGE UNTIL YOU ARE TOLD TO DO SO.

Section Six: Directions

In this section, you will be asked to give your opinion on topics of interest to mathematicians and to describe equipment used by mathematicians. Be sure to say as much as you can in the time allotted for each question. Remember that this is a test of your ability to talk about mathematics in English. When it is graded, the graders will be interested in the way you express mathematical ideas. There will be no sample question for this section.

DO NOT GO ON TO THE NEXT PAGE UNTIL YOU ARE TOLD TO DO SO.

Section Seven: Directions

In this section of the test, you will see a mathematics class schedule and you will be asked to explain this schedule. Imagine that you are a mathematics teacher meeting your class for the first time. You must explain this schedule to your students. Be sure to include all important details in your description. You will have one minute to study the schedule *silently*.

Math 120 "Calculus"

Text: Ellis & Gulick, *Calculus*

Class meetings: M through F, 9–10 a.m.

Calculus lab: Students may take a computer lab, using the interactive VAX computer system. To sign up, add Math 124, 1 credit, and see Dr. Smith in 480 Carver.

Help sessions: Room 449 Carver.
M through Th: 9 a.m.–9 p.m. F: 9 a.m.–5 p.m.

Examinations: Hour exams: September 23, and October 8 and 31. Final: November 15, 1–3 p.m.

STOP. THIS IS THE END OF THE TEST.

14

Is ESP Testing Justified?

Caroline Clapham
University of Lancaster

In recent years there has been increasing agreement among testers that language proficiency tests should, where possible, be related to candidates' future language needs. For example, if doctors are to be tested for their capacity to use English in a hospital where English is spoken, it is considered only sensible to test them on the kinds of English used in the ward and the consulting room. Similarly, future secretaries might be tested on the business English needed in the office. No one is likely to question the good sense of such English for specific purposes (ESP) testing. The issue, however, becomes less clear cut when the proficiency test is aimed at a less sharply defined audience, such as students proposing to embark on tertiary education. Many testers now consider that a language proficiency test for such students should contain samples of the kinds of language tasks required of them in their academic work.

What is not clear is how much, if at all, language tasks differ from discipline to discipline or how much the subject matter of the test should vary according to the discipline of the examinee. The question is whether students in different academic disciplines should take separate tests, or whether all students should take a single test battery. Some evidence shows that the language tasks in different academic disciplines are sufficiently similar for one set of test tasks to be appropriate for all (see Weir, 1983), but it is not clear whether the subject matter of the tests should be different.

Several studies have investigated whether background knowledge affects test scores in university-level language proficiency tests, but none has produced conclusive evidence either for or against the use of ESP tests. In this paper I discuss some of these studies, then describe a pilot study in which performances on two different subject modules were compared, one within the student's own subject area and one outside it.

Background

Three articles by Alderson and Urquhart (1983, 1985a, 1985b) on the effect of background knowledge on test results aroused considerable interest and led to several follow-up studies. They described three studies carried out with students attending English classes in Britain in preparation for going to British universities. In each they compared students' scores on reading tests related to their own field of study with scores on tests in other subject areas. In the third study, three groups of students in different disciplines—business and economics, science and engineering, and liberal arts—took the Social Studies and Technology Modules of the ELTS (English Language Testing Service) test. The students' scores on the modules were somewhat contradictory. On the one hand, for example, science and engineering students taking the Technology Module scored better than business and economics students on it and as well as liberal arts students, although their language proficiency was lower. On the other hand, the business and economics students did no better than the science and engineering group on the Social Studies module. Because the authors used pairwise t-tests to assess the results, they were not able to test for the interaction between students and tests. They concluded, however, that background knowledge had some effect on test scores but that it was not consistent, and that future studies should take account of linguistic proficiency and other factors as well.

Koh (1985) obtained somewhat similar results with three groups of students, two in science and one in business studies at Singapore University. Using analysis of variance to estimate the effect of background knowledge on cloze test results, she found that there was an interaction between student group and test but that students did not always do best in their own subject areas. The business students, for example, had their highest scores on the science text. It turned out that half these students had studied science previously, so that prior knowledge could have affected their scores. The group with the highest language proficiency—one of the science groups—did consistently better than the other two on all the texts, which contained business, history, politics, and science. Koh concluded that prior knowledge did affect test scores but that students could compensate for ignorance of the subject matter with high linguistic proficiency.

Shoham, Peretz, and Vorhaus (1987) rejected the use of cloze in studies of the role of background effect and used comprehension, referent, and vocabulary-in-context questions for their study at Ben Gurion University. They used three-way analysis of variance to analyze their results, but once again the results were inconclusive. Students in the biological and physical sciences did better on the scientific texts, but the humanities and social science students did not do better on the test in their own subject area. The authors' explanation was that the texts were only indirectly related to the students' specialized fields of study, and they suggested that their finding might support Lipson's (1984) suggestion that "a totally unfamiliar text is often easier to comprehend than a text with a partially familiar content." Lipson's contention is indeed radical. If supported by further research, it would be an almost unassailable reason for dropping ESP testing from university proficiency tests, for until the unlikely day when each student has his or her own tailor-made test, ESP tests will have to focus on fairly general subject areas such as law or business studies, which will inevitably be only partly familiar to postgraduates in many highly specialized fields. If Lipson's idea were taken to its logical conclusion, of course, proficiency tests would have to contain material outside any candidate's experience. The Joint Matriculation Board's Test in English Overseas follows just such an approach, with passages in esoteric subjects such as silver markings and heraldic devices. Item writers have difficulty finding suitable texts, and the ensuing materials are often excessively dull.

Hale (1988) commented on the inconclusive results of some of the above studies and on the small sample sizes in some. For his study, he looked at all candidates taking the Test of English as a Foreign Language (TOEFL) over four administrations to see whether larger sample sizes yielded a more consistent interaction between students' major field area and text content. The reading passages were all aimed at the general reader but were based on a wide range of topics in the arts and sciences. The numbers of candidates in the four sessions ranged from approximately 6,000 to 10,000. For the purposes of the main study, subjects were divided into two groups: humanities and social sciences in one, and biological and physical sciences in the other. Using analysis of variance, Hale found that for three of the four test forms the effect of subject area was significant at .001. Students' reading performance was affected by a combination of their major-field area and the nature of the passages, but the effect was not large, possibly, Hale wrote, because the texts were taken from general sources rather than from subject-specific textbooks.

Hale's reason for using such large sample sizes was to provide a greater opportunity to detect any statistically significant effects. Using large sample sizes certainly has this effect, and once the number of subjects becomes very large almost anything can appear significant:

> It is appropriate to repeat the warning that a statistically significant or a statistically non-significant result should not be taken necessarily to imply an educationally significant or non-significant finding, especially in those cases when significance has been "bought" . . . by putting large samples of . . . (students) in various cells. Paradoxical though it might seem at first thought a well designed experiment using small numbers which culminates in significance carries more conviction than a well designed experiment reaching the same level of significance only by the use of large numbers. (Burroughs, 1971, p. 235)

Perversely, therefore, Hale's magnificent sample sizes may militate against his significant results being as informative as he might hope.

A question related to the issue of the effect of prior knowledge on test results is whether tests in students' own subject areas are better predictors than more general ones. Tan (1990) used regression analysis to see whether familiarity with test content or level of language proficiency was the best predictor of ability in reading comprehension. Undergraduates at the University of Malaysia were given "prior knowledge" tests compiled by their own subject teachers, along with discipline-related cloze reading tests and a form of a "general" proficiency test, the English Proficiency Test Battery. In all subject areas under study (medicine, law, and economics), she found that both knowledge of the subject area and language level could predict comprehension of a discipline-related text, but that language level was the better predictor.

What emerges from the above studies is, first, that language proficiency levels seem to play at least as important a role as background knowledge does in the comprehension of reading texts and, second, that background knowledge is not easy to assess. A student of, say, business studies may well have worked previously in another discipline, such as science, or may have scientific interests in his or her spare time. Future studies should take account of students' language proficiency and the finer details of their background knowledge.

It is important to note that the study described here fails to follow either of these recommendations: the numbers involved in the pilot study were too small for separate analyses on students of differing proficiency levels to be worthwhile, and not all the students completed a questionnaire identifying their previous and present areas of study and interest. The questionnaire has now been piloted and will be used in another, more comprehensive study.

Research Question

The research question for this study was: Do students score significantly higher on a reading test within their subject area than on one outside it? This question addresses not the matter of background knowledge per se but whether reading tests in different subject areas should be included in university language proficiency tests.

Subjects

The examinees were nonnative English speakers progressing to undergraduate or postgraduate studies at English-medium universities. Some were already in Australia or Britain taking preparatory English classes; some were still in their home countries. They formed a heterogeneous sample with different linguistic and cultural backgrounds and different levels of language proficiency. Unfortunately, not all the students who took the tests could be included in the study because some had failed to provide details of their fields of study, and the ensuing data set is heavily weighted toward arts and social science students. Table 14-1 lists the first languages of students in the sample.

The students were all taking part in the trials of the revised ELTS, now called the International English Language Testing System (IELTS). They were classified into three groups according to which of three broad discipline areas they would be studying next, rather their past subject areas, as it is a student's future field of study that dictates the choice of IELTS subject module. Universities are interested in information about how students will fare in their future university course, so

Table 14-1

Subjects' Language Backgrounds

Language	n
Chinese	30
French	79
German	24
Indonesian	58
Japanese	14
Javanese	7
Korean	13
Malay	13
Minangkabau	1
Portuguese	1
Spanish	1
Sundanese	1
Thai	10
Turkish	1

it is the student's ability to cope in the future subject area that has to be tested. The classification of students is not always easy, as subjects such as computer studies and architecture border on different subject areas. For consistency's sake I classified the students according to the list supplied in the IELTS Administrators' Manual.

One homogeneous language group, the Indonesians, is sufficiently large for analyses to be carried out (see Table 14-1). All but five of the Indonesians were attending English classes in Indonesia before going on to postgraduate studies in Britain. The other five were attending language classes in Australia. Because the use of a heterogeneous group may well affect findings in unexpected ways, results from the Indonesian group are reported as well as those for the whole sample.

Materials

The tests used in the study were the trial versions of the three academic modules being tested for the revision of the ELTS test. I refer to them here as M(A), M(B), and M(C). Each subject module contains a reading and a writing test. The draft versions of the reading specifications for the three modules initially listed different academic tasks for the three subject areas, but they were altered after comments by university lecturers in a wide range of disciplines (see Clapham & Westaway, forthcoming) and now list almost identical tasks in all three. (For a more detailed description of these tasks, see Alderson, this volume, chap. 11). The specifications differ in the description of the content area of the reading texts. Test writers are required to base their reading passages on magazine articles and learned papers in the appropriate subject areas. For example, in Module A:

There must be at least three reading passages. . . . At least one text should be in the Physical Sciences and one in Technology. . . . The texts used and their topics should be scientific but "neutral"; i.e. they should not be highly discipline-specific nor biased for or against any of the discipline areas covered by the test.

This study therefore employed three reading tests, each of which contained three or four reading passages accompanied by a variety of test types: short answer questions, summary completion, diagrams to label, headings to match to paragraphs, and multiple choice. All tests had been piloted in Australia, Britain, and other countries and had been substantially revised. Table 14-2 gives statistics from the trials of the revised versions.

Table 14-2

Descriptive Statistics and Reliability for Modules A, B, and C

Module	Subjects	Items	M(%)	SD	r[a]
A	779	33	51.0	23.9	.90
B	633	39	42.2	23.5	.91
C	1,146	38	46.1	21.2	.88

[a]Kuder-Richardson Formula 21.

Results

Table 14-3 gives the means and standard deviations for both the whole sample and the Indonesians. Because each group of students took two tests, one in their own subject area and one not, and because an inspection of the distribution statistics showed that the variances of the different groups were homogeneous, I used a repeated measures analysis of variance design, with student-group and test as the two independent variables. Using SPSS-X Repeated Measures Multivariate Analysis of Variance (MANOVA), I analyzed the results to see whether signifi-

Table 14-3

Descriptive Statistics, Whole Sample and Indonesians

Module	N	M(%)	SD
	Whole sample		
A	155	44.2	18.0
B	177	44.1	20.8
C	174	43.7	14.0
	Indonesian subjects		
A	44	44.1	10.7
B	44	40.4	15.3
C	46	37.8	10.8

cant differences existed between the group scores, the test scores, and the interaction of the two.[1] The analyses were carried out in pairs: Groups A and B with tests M(A) and M(B), Groups A and C with M(A) and M(C), and Groups B and C with M(B) and M(C). To show the direction of any differences in mean scores, the results of the three main analyses are shown in the form of tables of means (see Tables 14-4–14-6) giving the mean scores for each group and each test, the overall means, and the means of the diagonals. The diagonals show the interaction of group and test and therefore the effect of subject area on test scores.

Table 14-4 shows the results, for the whole sample and for the Indonesians, of Groups A and B, who took tests M(A) and M(B). Below the means are the F-values and their levels of significance. In the whole sample, Group B (mean 42.5) did better overall than Group A (mean 38.8), though not significantly so. In addition, M(A) was significantly easier for both groups together (mean 43.3) than M(B) was (mean 38.6). From the interaction of group and test effect, we would expect students to perform better at the tests in their own subject areas and would therefore expect the diagonal mean of boxes 1 and 4 together, where Group A

Table 14-4

Comparisons of Mean Scores (%) for Groups A and B, Whole Sample and Indonesians

		Mean scores						
		Whole sample				*Indonesians*		
Group	N	M(A)	M(B)	Overall	N	M(A)	M(B)	Overall
A	17	[1] 43.1	[2] 34.5	38.8	10	[1] 43.3	[2] 31.8	37.7
B	23	[3] 43.3	[4] 41.6	42.5	11	[3] 43.5	[4] 48.7	46.1
Overall		43.3	38.6	41.0		43.4	40.7	42.0
Diagonal mean	39.1			42.3	37.9			46.1

F-values and significance

	M		F	Significance
	Whole sample			
Group	(A)38.8	(B)42.5	.43	NS
Test	M(A)43.3	M(B)38.6	4.20	$p<.05$
Subject area effect	39.1	42.3	1.83	NS
	Indonesians			
Group	(A)37.7	(B)46.1	2.47	NS
Test	M(A)43.4	M(B)40.7	1.13	NS
Subject area effect	37.9	46.1	7.83	$p<.01$

Note. NS = not significant.

students took M(A) and where B students took M(B), to be higher than the diagonal mean of boxes 2 and 3. I will refer to these diagonal means as means of advantage and disadvantage,[2] as students are supposedly being advantaged if they take tests in their own subject area. In this instance the mean of advantage, the diagonal mean of boxes 1 and 4, is the higher (42.3 compared with 39.1), but not significantly so. Subject area, that is, the interaction of group and test effect, therefore did not significantly affect test results. This finding may not be considered surprising in this instance; the two tests are both based on scientific subjects and all the reading passages are inevitably fairly general in content because they have to be appropriate for a wide range of disciplines within the physical and life sciences.

In the Indonesian sample, however, the results were different. There was no significant difference between the two groups nor between the two tests, but the subject area effect was significant at .01, with the effect in the expected direction: the mean of advantage is higher than the mean of disadvantage. The Indonesian students seemed to do better in their own subject module than in the other. It is of course possible to get such a result by chance; the number of students in the Indonesian group is very small, and this investigation was only one of many similar ones. However, it shows that subject area may have had an effect and is clearly worth investigating further.

Table 14-5 gives the results of groups A and C taking M(A) and M(C). For the whole sample the results were similar to those discussed above. The groups were not significantly different, but the tests were: M(A) was easier than M(C). Subject area again had no significant effect, but the mean of disadvantage was slightly higher than the mean of advantage. Students performed marginally better on the tests outside their own subject areas, but not significantly so. This time the Indonesians, too, showed no significant subject effect, although the content was based on what might be considered more disparate subject areas: arts and social sciences, and physical science and technology. This finding surely throws some doubt on the importance of the previous significant result.

The final group to be analyzed is B and C (Table 14-6). The results here were generally similar to those above, though in this case the two groups in the whole sample are significantly different from one another. The subject area effect was once again not significant, but the mean of disadvantage was strikingly higher than the mean of advantage. Once again the whole-group test means were significantly different. For this group of students there seemed to be a consistent effect whereby M(A) was easier than M(B), which was easier than M(C).[3]

One reason for the general lack of a significant subject effect might have been that some students were embarking on new fields of study. As was the case in Koh (1985), some students with science degrees were moving on to business studies. I therefore ran the analyses again with the students reclassified according to their past field of study. There were few changes in the results. For groups A

Table 14-5

Comparisons of Mean Scores (%) for Groups A and C, Whole Sample and Indonesians

		Whole sample				Indonesians		
Group	N	M(A)	M(C)	Overall	N	M(A)	M(C)	Overall
A	10	[1] 43.0	[2] 34.5	38.8	9	[1] 45.5	[2] 35.1	40.3
C	65	[3] 49.0	[4] 44.8	46.9	14	[3] 44.2	[4] 39.5	41.9
Overall		48.2	43.4	45.8		44.7	37.8	41.3
Diagonal mean	47.1			44.6	40.6			41.8

Mean scores

F-values and significance

	M		F	Significance
	Whole sample			
Group	(A)38.8	(C)46.9	2.91	NS
Test	M(A)48.2	M(C)43.4	7.61	$p<.01$
Subject area effect	47.1	44.6	.96	NS
	Indonesians			
Group	(A)40.3	(C)41.9	.16	NS
Test	M(A)44.7	M(C)37.8	7.50	$p<.01$
Subject area effect	40.6	41.8	1.07	NS

Note. NS = not significant.

and B of the whole sample there was no longer a significant difference between the difficulty levels of M(A) and M(B), and for groups B and C there was no longer a significant difference between their scores. In no case was a significant subject area effect found.

Because students' raw scores on the live test were adjusted for test difficulty and reported in the form of a 9-point band scale, and because it is these band levels rather than raw scores that affect students' futures, the analyses were also rerun using band levels rather than percentages. Again there were no marked changes. The only major change was that, as might be expected, there was no longer a significant difference between M(A) and M(B). There was, however, still a significant difference between M(A) and M(C) and between M(B) and M(C): .02 and .000 respectively, the latter implying a difference of half a band. This difference may be of no importance because the study sample was not typical of the trial population. However, the IELTS examiners will need to monitor the comparative difficulty levels of the live academic modules.

Table 14-6

Comparisons of Mean Scores (%) for Groups B and C, Whole Sample and Indonesians

		Mean scores						
		Whole sample				Indonesians		
Group	N	M(B)	M(C)	Overall	N	M(B)	M(C)	Overall
B	11	[1] 38.4	[2] 35.4	37.0	8	[1] 42.3	[2] 36.8	39.5
C	85	[3] 53.0	[4] 45.3	49.2	14	[3] 37.9	[4] 37.8	37.9
Overall		51.4	44.2	47.8		40.0	37.4	38.7
Diagonal mean	51.0			44.5	37.5			39.4

F-values and significance

M		F	Significance
	Whole sample		
Group	(B)37.0 (C)49.2	6.85	$p<.01$
Test	M(B)51.4 M(C)44.2	6.21	$p<.01$
Subject area effect	51.0 44.5	1.15	NS
	Indonesians		
Group	(B)39.5 (C)37.9	.18	NS
Test	M(B)40.0 M(C)37.4	.75	NS
Subject area effect	37.5 39.4	.68	NS

Note. NS = not significant.

Discussion

It is not possible from this study to comment on the effect of background knowledge on test scores, as we know so little about the students' backgrounds. However, it is possible to draw some conclusions of a purely testing nature, though I emphasize that they are necessarily tentative because of the small number of cases involved.

This study yielded almost no evidence that students were disadvantaged if they took an unsuitable subject module. In all but one of the analyses, subject area had no significant effect on scores, and in two of the three whole sample investigations students appeared, if anything, to do slightly better on the tests outside their field of study. The Indonesian sample showed a significant subject effect for the students who took the two science papers: students did better at the test in their own field. However, the result is difficult to credit because there was no apparent subject area effect for the two groups who took an arts and a science paper. What this result does show is the advantage of using a homogeneous group. Having students in the sample who share a first language, culture, and level of previous education greatly reduced the variability of the results. None of the three groups of students were significantly different from each other, and in only one case (M[A] and M[C]) were the tests significantly different.

Because of the small number of cases, the study was not able to take account of the students' varying levels of language proficiency, but there is evidence that the effect of subject area on scores may not be consistent over the whole range of levels. Perhaps elementary language learners depend heavily on background knowledge to tease out the meaning of a passage, whereas higher level students have sufficient language skills to be able to infer meaning from context. This concept is borne out by Koh's (1985) findings (see above).

An exploratory attempt during this study to use covariance to fit regression lines to the present data, with adjustments for language proficiency, showed the two regression lines crossing, conceivably implying that, as students' language proficiency increases, the effect of subject area changes. I did not pursue this line of inquiry for the study, but a future study will use analysis of covariance to take account of language proficiency.

IELTS examiners might cautiously draw two conclusions from this study. First, the evidence from this study does not show the need for three academic subject modules in the test battery, and, second, if students are given academic modules outside their subject areas, they will not be placed at a disadvantage. If the forthcoming study bears out these initial findings, IELTS could, from an empirical point of view, satisfactorily offer just one academic module. However, the performance of the test is not the only criterion; the importance of face validity should never be underestimated. Students who were asked what they thought of the old ELTS test mostly liked it, and one of their reasons was the existence of the subject modules.[4] The danger also exists that under examination conditions students will be upset by unfamiliar material and will not do as well as they might. In addition, many universities and colleges particularly liked the ELTS test because it had subject-specific modules (Alderson & Clapham, 1993).

Future Research

The discussion above shows that the next stage of the research should be wider in scope than the pilot study, and that more information should be gathered about each student's language proficiency and background knowledge.

Language Proficiency

In the next study, it should be possible to have large enough samples of students at different stages of language proficiency to see what effect the interaction of language level and subject area has on test performance. For that study students should ideally be ranked according to some common measure of proficiency. The most satisfactory way of doing so (and it would have the advantage of providing more information about how students perform in subject areas other than their own) would be to give each candidate all three of the reading modules. Unfortunately, however, the examinees will mostly be attending presessional English courses, and not only would few language centers be able to set aside more than half a day for such testing, but students would not have the stamina or the inclination to take three 55-minute tests in one session, especially when two of the three would contain material outside their own subject areas. The length of the tests could be reduced, but test reliability would then drop and the tests would not include a variety of text types, which is one of the strengths of the current modules. The next stage of the research will therefore adopt a compromise: in addition to the two reading modules, all students will take a "general" grammar test, which, though equaling the reading tests in number of items, will be quicker to administer. This test, constructed for the IELTS but never used (see Alderson, this volume, chap. 11), appears to be testing skills similar to those tested in the reading modules.

Background Knowledge

In the pilot study the main question was whether students were disadvantaged if they took reading tests based on subjects outside their own areas of study. No account was taken of the students' background knowledge as distinct from their field of study and, as can be seen from Koh (1985), this omission can bring misleading results. In the next stage, the scope of the research will be broadened to include the question of the effect of background knowledge on test performance. Students will fill out a questionnaire that will ask about their present and future areas of study, about subjects studied at school and afterward, about what they read for work and for pleasure, and about their familiarity with the subject matter of the reading test passages. The short time allowed for the questionnaire makes it impossible to discover all a student's interests and areas of expertise, but it should be possible to get more detailed information about background knowledge than has been acquired in previous studies.

Homogeneous and Heterogeneous Samples

Whether or not to use a culturally and linguistically homogeneous sample is a difficult choice. Although the analysis of the Indonesian sample highlighted the advantages of giving the tests to a group from one country, the disadvantage of using a such a group is that the findings may not be relevant to students in other countries; what applies to one linguistic or cultural group may not apply to another. In the next stage, therefore, where the main focus is on language proficiency tests for students from many countries and where the results may have a practical impact on the contents of future tests of this sort, students in the main sample will come from a wide range of nationalities. However, the related theoretical question of the effect of background knowledge on test performance would be better answered by an analysis of one or preferably several homogeneous groups. The reduction in the sources of variability should make the results more informative, and the research could later be replicated with groups from other nations. If possible, therefore, one or more homogeneous groups will be studied for the effect of background knowledge on test performance.

Analysis of Data

In addition to carrying out the repeated measures analysis of variance and an analysis of covariance, the next study will look more closely at the performance of individual test passages and items to see whether they work similarly for students in the three fields of study. Classical and item response theory item analyses will be used for this purpose and to see whether some or all sections of the tests are biased for or against students in differing disciplines.

Further Research

After the analyses described above, we should have a better idea about the effect of field of study and background knowledge on test performance, but we shall have no idea how examinees use this knowledge. A few students in each of the three main subject areas will therefore be asked to introspect on their thought processes as or after they take the tests. Although there are problems in asking students to make verbal reports in this way (see Cohen, 1984), we should be able to gain some idea of how background knowledge is affecting the student's choice of answer and whether the effect differs according to the test that he or she is taking.

Finally, all the findings from the above studies will depend on the subject specificity of the various reading passages. The texts for the pilot study came from academic or other papers written for the relevant subject areas and were considered appropriate for students in those disciplines.[5] However, although all the texts may be appropriate, some may be more specific to a particular subject area than others are. For example, some, regardless of their discipline, are written so that readers in other disciplines can easily follow them, whereas others seem dependent on specialist concepts and vocabulary that no one outside the subject area could be expected to understand. Presumably the specificity of these texts will affect the results of the study. The forthcoming research, therefore, will include not only a content analysis of the texts and items (using the Communicative Language Ability and Test Method Facets Rating Instruments [Bachman,

1990a, 1990b]) but also a simple classification of each text according to its level of specificity.

Conclusion

There is no evidence from this pilot study that students are disadvantaged if they take a reading module outside their academic discipline. However, the scope of the research was narrow, and the number of cases small. After the next stage of the investigation, during which a greater amount of information will be submitted to a wider variety of analytical methods, we should have a clearer idea of the effect of subject area on test performance and the effect of background knowledge on reading comprehension.

Notes

1. Advice on the appropriate statistical measure was provided by B. J. Francis of the Centre for Applied Statistics, Lancaster University.

2. The terms were coined by J. C. Alderson.

3. This is not the case for the complete trial test population, for whom M(C) was easier than M(B).

4. Those not in favor were those who had been assigned to a module outside their own subject area (Criper & Davies, 1988).

5. See Clapham and Westaway (forthcoming) for an account of university lecturers' comments on the passages.

References

Alderson, J.C., & Clapham, C. M. (Eds.). (1993). *Examining the ELTS test: An account of the first stage of the ELTS Revision Project* (IELTS Research Report 2). London and Canberra: British Council, University of Cambridge Local Examinations Syndicate, and International Development Program.

Alderson, J. C., & & Urquhart, A. H. (1983). Effect of student background discipline on comprehension: A pilot study. In A. Hughes & D. Porter (Eds.), *Current developments in language testing* (pp. 121–127). London: Academic Press.

Alderson, J. C., & Urquhart, A. H. (1985a). The effect of students' academic discipline on their performance on ESP reading tests. *Language Testing, 2*, 192–204.

Alderson, J. C., & Urquhart, A. H. (1985b). This test is unfair: I'm not an economist. In P. C. Hauptman, R. Le Blanc, & M. B. Wesche (Eds.), *Second language performance testing* (pp. 25–43). Ottawa: University of Ottawa Press.

Bachman, L. F. (1990a). *Communicative language ability (CLA) rating instrument.* Los Angeles: Cambridge–University of California, Los Angeles, Language Testing Project.

Bachman, L. F. (1990b). *Test method facets (TMF) rating instrument.* Los Angeles: Cambridge–UCLA Language Testing Project.

Burroughs, G. E. R. (1971). *Design and analysis in educational research* (Educational Monograph 8). Birmingham: School of Education, University of Birmingham.

Clapham, C. M., & Westaway, G. (Forthcoming). ELTSREV: Towards the validation of an international EAP test. In C. M. Clapham and J. C. Alderson (Eds.), *Constructing and trialling the IELTS test* (IELTS Research Report 3). London and Canberra: British Council, University of Cambridge Local Examinations Syndicate, and International Development Program.

Cohen, A. (1984). On taking language tests: What the students report. *Language Testing, 1*, 70–81.

Criper, C., & Davies, A. (1988). *ELTS validation project report* (ELTS Research Report 1[i]). London: British Council and University of Cambridge Local Examinations Syndicate.

Hale, G. A. (1988). Student major field and text content: Interaction effects on reading comprehension in the Test of English as a Foreign Language. *Language Testing, 5*, 49–61.

Koh, M. Y. (1985). The role of prior knowledge in reading comprehension. *Reading in a Foreign Language, 3*, 375–380.

Lipson, M. Y. (1984). Some unexpected issues in prior knowledge and comprehension. *The Reading Teacher*, April, 760–764.

Shoham, M., Peretz, A. S., & Vorhaus, R. (1987). Reading comprehension tests: General or subject specific? *System, 15*, 81–88.

Tan, S. H. (1990). The role of prior knowledge and language proficiency as predictors of reading comprehension among undergraduates. In J. H. A. L. De Jong & D. K. Stevenson (Eds.), *Individualizing the assessment of language abilities* (pp. 214–224). Clevedon and Philadelphia: Multilingual Matters.

Weir, C. (1983). *Identifying the language problems of overseas students in tertiary education in the U.K.* Unpublished doctoral thesis, University of London.

Epilogue

Dedication

Ted Rodgers
University of Hawai'i at Manoa

Over the years, I have had the occasional opportunity to be the chairperson for the Language Testing Research Colloquium (LTRC). I organized the dinner cruise tour of Honolulu Harbor at the TESOL meeting held in Hawaii in 1982 and have had minor social roles at other LTRC gatherings. In 1989 Donna Ilyin asked me to organize a social event to accompany the LTRC meeting to be held at the Metropolitan Club in San Francisco the following year. I had in mind something musically humorous or humorously musical, whichever seemed least appropriate, and sought advice from appropriate consultants. Michael Canale, a friend and a man both humorous and musical, became an early adviser. He liked the idea of a show built around a Don Quixote sort of itinerant test tilter and was the first to volunteer his voice and guitar, if required, as performer.

For all sorts of reasons, I dedicate the show and the script printed here to Michael. I was glad to share the show with Claire Trepanier in San Francisco and to recirculate some of the memories of smiles and songs I had enjoyed with Michael.

In memory of good times shared with Michael . . .

The Tale of the Wandering Mistrial

Ted Rodgers
University of Hawai'i at Manoa

The Plot

A freelance tester, our Wandering Mistrial used to play in a Confidence Interval Band. He has lost his instrument, his lip, and his confidence and is now on a wandering search for a new instrument and a new test-playing faith. He encounters a series of test players along the way, to each of whom he confesses his confusion and from each of whom he solicits advice and guidance. The test players, each a true believer in a particular testing faith, respond to the Wandering Mistrial's questions in statement and song according to their true beliefs. For the sake of brevity I have summarized (and freely adapted) as monologs the performance dialogs between the Wandering Mistrial and the Test-True Believers. Join us as we follow the Wandering Mistrial on his strange and fantastic journey.

The first land into which the Wandering Mistrial wanders is . . .

Bureaucratica

where he meets . . .

Test Player the First (John Clark)

"Now it looks to me like you've gotten yourself in some kind of snafu. If any TESOL TOEFL twit WASP like you is going to make it in Bureaucratica, you're going to have to get yourself personally initialized. Because all of us here are from DLI, NATO, NASA, UNESCO, NOW, CORE, SEATO, and there's even an SOB AWOL from OPEC. We've got other offices, of course, in DC, LA, and NYC, but the COLA's best right here in BURROCRATICA. So no matter if you're a damn DEM or a GOP, get yourself an acro. (You need a new, fluffier hair style, anyway.) Here's a verse from our own ACROHYMN to get you started on the right road."

Acrohymn

(Tune: Can't Help Lovin' that Man of Mine)

Tell me ANOVA, whisper SD,
TESOL, ANCOVA, sigh ESP.
Can't help lovin' that acronym.

FSI Scaling, CIA stealth,
T-Test Two Tailing, ETS wealth.
Love that alpha-numeric hymn.

If it's MLA,
That's a sunny day,
But if it's spelled out,
I'll scream and shout,
That's not OK.

I like KR-20 and love 21,
RAM for computers, BS just for fun.
Can't help lovin' that acronym,
Can't help singin' this acrohymn.

Psycho Metri City

Test Players the Second (John De Jong, John Lett, Elaine Wylie)

"You have arrived in the City of Psychometricians, or what we natives call Psycho Metri City. Our names are Flux, Fracs, and Fidel Figuero, your Facile Faktotums. You need not concern yourself about direction, for from here all roads lead to the HoliCity of Statistical Significance. Our population is small because we all practice the algorithmic method. However, we do believe in numbers—we sing 'em, smoke 'em, play 'em, and poke 'em. Our ruler is hereditary, heretical, and hierarchical, and we, his controlled subjects, are a perfectly randy sample, figuratively speaking. Perhaps a digital ditty can say it better."

Psychometrics

(Tune: "Rubber Ducky, You're the One")

Psychometrics every day
Push-down stores make push-up play,
Psychometrics, I'm awfully fond of you.

Eigenvalues, you're such fun,
You make constructs come out one,
Psychometrics, without you what would I do?

What I see is the IRT in my future,
I can mend anything that I rend,
One-size suture,
Mathematics moocher.

Parametric models know,
Their figures Greek come from crunching Rho,
Psychometrics, you are number one it's true,
Psychometrics, without you what could I do?

Culture Fair Grounds

Test Player the Third (Elana Shohamy)

"Shalom, stranger. I'm Simple Shohamy and I bake the pie diagrams here at the Culture Fair Grounds. See the flags flying over the grounds? All colors, all shapes, all sizes. But all the same value. I'm a Tagger, an African Tagger. (Actually, that's just my little joke. I tag everybody.) 'Tag 'em and box 'em, make the round square. Just you make sure that it's all culture fair.' We've got to make sure our tests discriminate without discriminating, maximize variance without variation, and let loose no bias in the biyous. All roads lead away from the Great White Way and on to the Rainbow Roundabout. So . . . ready for the show? Here's comes the first song. Lights! Camera! Affirmative action!"

Test Culture Fair

(Tune: Scarborough Fair)

Are(n't) you going to Test Culture Fair,
Farsis, Danes, Armenians, Thais.
Nifty nasals, Brillo-shaped hair.
Speak no truth but never tell lies.

Are(n't) you going to Test Culture Fair?
Yellow, Red, Black, all great gals and guys.
Tell the Anglos, I'll meet them there.
In Porteus Maze of one Standard Size.
Tell the Anglos, I'll meet them there.
In Porteus Maze of one Standard Size.

Validation

Test Player the Fourth (Andrew Cohen)

"You are at the crossroads of our nation—built on the Firm Foundation of Validity. Any direction on the compass—Predictive, Concurrent, Content, or Construct—will get you validated. But here at the crossroads, at the capital of Validation, lives our ruler, the King of Validation, King Face. And don't think I'm being Facetious when I say that while he is not a joker he's still quite a card. Our highest Facecard, in fact. Would you rather feel good or look good? Here looks are everything. "For our test of citizenship we say, you don't have to be loyal, just look OK." Deletion, mutilation, EFFACEMENT! That is for CAPITAL crimes. So in Clozing, let's lift our faces in song."

Face

(Tune: You Gotta Have Heart)

It's gotta have FACE,
All you really need is FACE,
Oh, it's fine to have a back end, of course,
But that end of horse won't win the race,
It's just gotta be FACE.

It's gotta have FACE,
Keep those numbers out in space,
Got to be unbiased they rave,
But one thing to save and keep in place,
You just gotta save FACE.
You just gotta save FACE.

Naturalley

Test Player the Fifth (Ted Rodgers)

"YO, BRO! YOU LOOKS LIKE YOU ARE AMONG THE LOST! Well, you have wandered into Naturalley, the main drag here in the Nation of Natural Notions. They call me Nature Goy, and I am the student counselor here at Natural High. Our motto is, if it feels good, do it. I mean, makin' a tot or makin' a test. Just do it! Just do it! What nature does best. Now as to where you might be goin' . . . off to the left is the road to Rack and off to the right is the road to Ruin. I got no idea where you're comin' from, but straight ahead, the way I'm headed, is along the Path of Least Resistance. Let me give you a tip. If you're lookin' for the Perfect Instrument, you don't have to squeeze, it's gonna well up from inside you, just like a breath or a yawn or a sneeze. That's the testicket, like a sneeze! Comes to you when you're least expectin' and just bursts out. Lemme sneeze you a test sample."

Tickle

(Tune: Green Fields)

I feel a tickle of test, like a sneeze,
It twitches my toes and it knocks on my knees,
A test for a sentence, a test for a song,
I feel a tickle of test a-comin' on.
I feel a tickle of test comin' on.

I feel a tickle right here in my core,
It could be Kurtosis, perhaps something more,
A Rasch on my ratio, a split-half that's gone,
But I feel that tickle of test a-comin' on.
I feel that tickle of test comin' on.

I'll never know what makes it come and go,
I'll never find what makes a Cloze my mind,
I only know I start to gasp and groan,
And the only cure I know,
Is to shoot testosterone,
When I feel that tickle of test comin' on.
I feel that test tickle sneeze comin' on.

Moneyland

Test Player the Sixth (Don Porter)

"You find yourself in the land of milk and money, and we are all part of a huge now-profit organization. I, myself, am a worker for the public good. I faithfully field the tills and put my trust in economy, efficiency, and Big Bucks. (Major credit cards also accepted.) As Max Mammon, our mayor, has put it, 'The Goodness of any product is measured by how much it costs. And we want our test products to be as Goodly as possible.' Moneyland has beautiful lawns, and guest houses, and golf courses, and a most amazing mailroom. From here the road leads to all the centres of power and learning in the land. Let me sing you a bar or two of our national anthem."

Money

(Tune: Music, Music, Music)

Put another nickel in,
Don't let the dough just trickle in,
Dollars are my data bank,
Of money, money, money.

I'll do anything for you,
Give you straight or give you skew,
Just pay me, even checks will do,
That money, money, money.

Speed tests or what you need tests,
Just tell me what your numbers need to show,
And I will make those numbers grow.

I will give you Chi's or Phi's,
Mean scores of whatever size,
As long as I can realize,
More money, money, money.

Hi-Tech U

Test Player the Seventh (J. D. Brown)

"Got a slipped disc? Is your unharnessed horsepower going haywire? Is there lumpage in your linkage? Well, you've come to the right place. This is the re-pairing centre at the campus of Hi Tech U. We re-pair by trading what you've-got-tech for what's-really-hot-tech. (Upgrading takes buck-trading, too, of course.) We traded sound cylinders for records for reel to reel for cartridges for cassettes for compacts for laser lollys for audiyodels—the latest thing. Our staff are scabs from the language labs, and our motto is 'If it works, it's obsolete.' So get a carload of C's from the CIA to put some AI in your CAI, and we'll talk tech. 'Telecom to me my Multmedia, Baby.' Or here's another techtune you may know better."

Hi Tech

(Tune: So Long, It's Been Good to Know You)

Hi Tech, it's real good to know you,
Hi Tech, one look, it'll snow you,
Hi Tech, the last step to heaven,

What a great upload with my CRT,
Just turn on and you'll make it like me.

Micropolis

Test Player the Eighth (Adrian Palmer)

"Well, my good sir, you have arrived in Micropolis. 'You ain't so cute if you don't micro-compute.' That's our motto, and you're likely to find a boot up your system if it doesn't become your motto, too. We're not really all that vicious, though. Our bit's bigger than our byte. Here we have no capital punishment for people, we only execute programs. Black and white, on and off, binary's our bag. Our doctors perform only logical operations and our lawyers have to follow suit. The road? The Microad leads to the Macroad. So keep your eyes on the screen and your hands on the keys, and I'll sing you a favorite little ditty to speed you on your way."

Micro

(Tune: Michael, Row the Boat Ashore)

Micro, tow my test to shore,
Halo, Lulia.
Micro softwares always score,
Halo, Lulia.

Micro, tells me what to do,
Halo, Lulia.
Micro errors all come true,
Halo, Luulia.
Hides the dirt we all doodoo,
Halo, Lulia,
Factors feet to fit my shoe.
Halo, Luuuulia.

Co-efficiency Apartments

Test Player the Ninth (Kathi Bailey)

"Hi there, you've come to Bell Curve Island, the island with one peak, and where most of the people are normal, except for a few deviants. I'm Betty Coef! I'm a diagnostic feedback model. I have a schema for the direct testing of competence. It's based on response theory, using a few indiscrete items for the development of statistically significant relationships. From here the road leads up the slope, through the open range. You'll see many forms of TWEs and lots of little lambdas playing in the field dependent domains. My advice to you is to be prompt. See you rater!"

Betty Co-ef

(Tune: Betty Co-ed has Lips of Red)

Betty Co-ef has parts of such Precision,
Betty Co-ef has Alienation skew,
Betty Co-ef has her Determination,
Betty Co-ef Equivalence for you.
Betty Co-ef will vary in her values,
Betty Co-ef has parallel-shaped forms,
Betty Co-ef goes minus squares to dances,
Betty Co-ef has many nubile forms.

(Repeat closing melody for last two lines.)
Betty best-fits your-egress,
Betty Co-ef has many latent norms.

If you've got the product,
Betty's got the moment.

The Wandering Mistrial, at last, finds himself alone . . .

Wandering Mistrial (Lyle Bachman)

Our Wandering Mistrial, having heard all the contradictory and self-seeking advice of each of the Test Players, tries to imagine what a world without tests might be like. A world testless . . .

Testless

(Tune: "Somewhere" from West Side Story)

There's a place for us,
No testing trace for us.
Time to ponder and time to love,
No more push, no more shove.
Testless, not restless,
We'll build a world quaint and questless.
Testless,

Westless,
Ommmmmmmm . . .

THIS IS THE END.
PLEASE PUT DOWN YOUR PENCILS AND CLOSE YOUR
SONG SHEETS.

Works by Michael Canale After 1981

Byrnes, H., & Canale, M. (Eds.). (1987). *Defining and developing proficiency: Guidelines, implementations and concepts.* Skokie, IL: National Textbook Company.

Canale, M. (1982). Communication: How to evaluate it? *Bulletin de l'association canadienne de linguistique appliquée 3*, 2.

Canale, M. (1983). Communicative approaches to second language teaching and testing. *Colloquium on French as a second language: Proceedings* (Review and Evaluation Bulletin 4.4). Toronto: Ontario Ministry of Education.

Canale, M. (1983). From communicative competence to communicative language pedagogy. In J. C. Richards & R. Schmidt (Eds.), *Language and communication.* London: Longman.

Canale, M. (1983). *OAIP/FSL screening trials: Item analysis report* (Final project report on contract 82-5641). Toronto: Ontario Ministry of Education.

Canale, M. (1983). On some dimensions of language proficiency. In J. W. Oller, Jr. (Ed.), *Issues in language testing research.* Rowley, MA: Newbury House.

Canale, M. (1984). A communicative approach to language proficiency assessment in a minority setting. In C. Rivera (Ed.), *The measurement of communicative proficiency: Models and application.* Clevedon, England: Multilingual Matters.

Canale, M. (1984). Considerations in the testing of reading and listening proficiency. *Foreign Language Annals, 17*, 349–360.

Canale, M. (1984). On some theoretical frameworks for language proficiency. In C. Rivera (Ed.), *Language proficiency and academic achievement.* Clevedon, England: Multilingual Matters.

Canale, M. (1984). Some reactions to curriculum dialogue. *Curriculum Inquiry, 14*, 123–124.

Canale, M. (1984). Testing in a communicative approach. In G. A. Jarvis (Ed.), *The challenge for excellence in foreign language education.* Middlebury, VT: Northeast Conference Organization.

Canale, M. (1985). *Evaluation of the Pennsylvania State University and Educational Testing Service oral interview training workshop.* Princeton, NJ: Educational Testing Service (ETS).

Canale, M. (1985). Proficiency-oriented achievement testing. In *ACTFL Master Lecture Series 1985.* Monterey, CA: Defense Language Institute.

Canale, M. (1985). Systèmes educatifs et systèmes d'apprentissage. In G. Milburn & R. Enns (Eds.), *Curriculum Canada VI.* Vancouver: University of British Columbia.

Canale, M. (1985). A theory of strategy-oriented language development. In S. Jaeger (Ed.), *Issues in English language development.* Washington, DC: National Clearinghouse on Bilingual Education.

Canale, M. (1986). Language assessment: The method is the message. In D. Tannen

(Ed.), *Georgetown University Roundtable on Languages and Linguistics 1985*. Washington, DC: Georgetown University Press.

Canale, M. (1986). The promise and threat of computerized adaptive assessment of reading comprehension. In C. Stansfield (Ed.), *Technology and language testing*. Washington, DC: Teachers of English to Speakers of Other Languages and ETS.

Canale, M. (1987). *Review of the MIT Athena Project on computer assisted language learning* (Interim report to the School of Humanities, Massachusetts Institute of Technology). Toronto: Ontario Institute for Studies in Education (OISE), Centre for Franco-Ontarian Studies.

Canale, M. (1987). *Self-directed language learning and computer supported learning environments* (Final report on SSHRC project 451-86-0908). Toronto: OISE, Centre for Franco-Ontarian Studies.

Canale, M. (1988). Language assessment at the university: Practices, problems, promises. In C. Besnard & C. Elkbas (Eds.), *L' Université de demain: courants actuels et apports de la didactique des langues à l'enseignement du français langue seconde*. Toronto: Scholar's Press.

Canale, M. (1988). The measurement of communicative competence. In C. J. Brumfit (Ed.), *Annual Review of Applied Linguistics, 8*. Cambridge: Cambridge University Press.

Canale, M., & Barker, G. (1986). How creative language teachers are using microcomputers. In I. Dutra (Ed.), *TESOL Newsletter* (1) [special supplement].

Canale, M., Barker, G., Belanger, M., MacRury, K., McLean, R. S., & Ragsdale, R. G. (1985). *Microcomputer software for language arts: Survey & analysis*. Toronto: OISE Press.

Canale, M., & Bascunan, L. (1986). *Development of rating scales for assessing sequential interpreters at Immigration Canada* (Final report). Toronto: OISE.

Canale, M., Belanger, M., & Frenette, N. (1982). Analyse préliminaire de l'interaction L1-L2 à l'écrit. In D. Huot & G. Alvarez (Eds.), *Interaction L1-L2 et strategies d'apprentissage*. Quebec: Centre international de recherche sur le bilinguisme.

Canale, M., Belanger, M., & Frenette, N. (1988). Evaluation of minority student writing in first and second languages. In J. Fine (Ed.), *Second language discourse: A textbook of current research*. Norwood, NJ: Ablex.

Canale, M., Esquillo, M., Bascunan, L., Geva, E., & Cummins, J. (1985). *Development of an assessment instrument for assessing the interpretation skills of CEIC Interpreters in Spanish-English* (Final report). Toronto: OISE.

Canale, M., Frenette, N., & Skitri, R. (1983). *Rapport sur le projet de loi 82: Problèmes linguistiques en milieu minoritaire franco-ontarien* (Final project report). Toronto: OISE, CREFO.

Canale, M., Mougeon, R., Belanger, M., & Heller, M. (1986). *Programmes dans les écoles élémentaires de langue française pour les élèves de compétence inégale en français* (Final report on contract MA512-02-478/ASN32854). Toronto: Ontario Ministry of Education.

Canale, M., Mougeon, R., et al. (1983). *Test de compétence en communication: français, cycle intermédiaire* (Final project report). Toronto: OISE, CREFO.

Canale, M., Mougeon, R., & Klokeid, T. (1982). Forensic linguistics? *Canadian Journal of Linguistics, 27*, 150–155.

Canale, M., & Swain, M. (1988). Some theories of communicative competence. In W. Rutherford & M. Sharwood-Smith (Eds.), *Grammar and second language teaching*. New York: Newbury House/Harper & Row.

Carlson, S., Ward, W., Canale, M., Frase, L., & Hull, G. (1988). *A new look at formulating hypotheses items* (GRE Research Report 88-12). Princeton, NJ: ETS.

De Landsheere, G., Canale, M., Furstenberg, J., Lundberg, I., Purvis, A., & Rubin, A. (1986). *Les nouvelles technologies et l'enseignement de la lecture* (Final report in information technologies and basic learning). Paris: Organization for Economic Cooperation and Development.

Duran, R., Canale, M., Penfield, J., Stansfield, C., & Liskin Gasparro, J. E. (1988). The TOEFL from a communicative viewpoint on language proficiency. In R. Freedle & R. Duran (Eds.), *Cognitive and linguistic analyses of test performance*. Norwood, NJ: Ablex. Originally published as Duran, R., Canale, M., Penfield, J., Stansfield, C., & Liskin-Gasparro, J. (1985). *The TOEFL from a communicative viewpoint on language proficiency* (TOEFL Research Report 19). Princeton, NJ: Educational Testing Service.

Frenette, N., Canale, M., Evans, P., & Belanger, M. (1983). *L'évaluation de l'écrit en français et en anglais. 9e and 10e années, cycle intermédiaire* (Rapport final). Toronto: OISE, CREFO.

Mougeon, R., Beniak, F., & Canale, M. (1984). Acquisition et enseignement du français en milieu franco-ontarien. *Le français dans le monde, 185*, 69–76.

Mougeon, R., Beniak, E., & Canale, M. (1984). Le problème des élèves anglo-dominants dans les écoles ontariennes de langue française: Acquisition, emploi et enseignement du français. *Revue canadienne des langues vivantes, 41*, 336–353.

Mougeon, R., Canale, M., Heller, M., & Belanger, M. (1984). *Evaluation of programmes for non-francophones in French-language elementary schools* (Final project report on contract 82-3978). Toronto: OISE, CREFO.

Mougeon, R., Heller, M., Beniak, E., & Canale, M. (1984). Acquisition et enseignement du français en situation minoritaire: Le cas des Franco-ontariens. *Revue canadienne des langues vivantes, 41*, 315–336.

Swain, M., & Canale, M. (1982). The role of grammar in a communicative approach to second language teaching and testing. In S. Seidner (Ed.), *Issues of language assessment*. Springfield, IL: State Board of Education.

Wesche, M., Canale, M., Jones, S., Mendelsohn, D., Tumpane, M., Tyacke, M., & Tyacke, E. (1987). *The Ontario Test of English as a Second Language: A report of the research* (Final report on contract MA512-02-577/ASN30692). Queen's Park, Ontario: Ministry of Colleges and Universities and Ministry of Education.

Also available from TESOL

All Things to All People:
A Primer for K–12 ESL Teachers in Small Programs
Donald N. Flemming, Lucie C. Germer, and Christiane Kelley

A World of Books:
An Annotated Reading List for ESL/EFL Students
Dorothy S. Brown

Children and ESL: Integrating Perspectives
Pat Rigg and D. Scott Enright, Editors

Coherence in Writing: Research and Pedagogical Perspectives
Ulla Connor and Ann Johns, Editors

Current Perspectives on Pronunciation:
Practices Anchored in Theory
Joan Morley, Editor

Dialogue Journal Writing with Nonnative English Speakers:
A Handbook for Teachers
Joy Kreeft Peyton and Leslee Reed

Dialogue Journal Writing with Nonnative English Speakers:
An Instructional Packet for Teachers and Workshop Leaders
Joy Kreeft Peyton and Jana Staton

Directory of Professional Preparation Programs
in TESOL in the United States, 1992–1994

Diversity as Resource:
Redefining Cultural Literacy
Denise E. Murray, Editor

Ending Remediation: Linking ESL
and Content in Higher Education
Sarah Benesch, Editor

Research in Reading in English as a Second Language
Joanne Devine, Patricia L. Carrell, and David E. Eskey, Editors

Selected Articles from the TESOL Newsletter: 1966–1983
John F. Haskell, Editor

Students and Teachers Writing Together:
Perspectives on Journal Writing
Joy Kreeft Peyton, Editor

Video in Second Language Teaching:
Using, Selecting, and Producing Video for the Classroom
Susan Stempleski and Paul Arcario, Editors

For more information, contact
Teachers of English to Speakers of Other Languages, Inc.
1600 Cameron Street, Suite 300
Alexandria, Virginia 22314 USA
Tel 703-836-0774 • Fax 703-836-7864